BEYOND THE MIRACLE OF THE MARKET

New edition

As capitalism defeated socialism in Eastern Europe, the market displaced the state in the developing world. In *Beyond the Miracle of the Market*, Robert Bates focuses on Kenya, a country that continued to grow while others declined in Africa, and mounts a prescient critique of the neo-classical turn in development economics.

Attributing Kenya's exceptionalism to its economic institutions, this book pioneers the use of "new institutionalism" in the field of development. In doing so, however, the author accuses the approach of being apolitical. Institutions introduce power into economic life. To account for their impact, economic analysis must therefore be complemented by political analysis; microeconomics must be embedded in political science. In making this argument, Bates relates Kenya's subsequent economic decline to the change from the Kenyatta to the Moi regime and the subsequent use of the power of economic institutions to redistribute rather than to create wealth.

Robert H. Bates received his Ph.D. from MIT in 1969. Joining the Division of Humanities and Social Sciences at the California Institute of Technology, he rose to full professor before leaving for the Luce Professorship at Duke University in the early 1980s. He joined the faculty at Harvard in 1993, where he still teaches as a professor of government. Bates has conducted fieldwork in Zambia, Kenya, Ghana, and the Sudan and has traveled throughout much of West Africa. He has also conducted fieldwork in Colombia and Brazil, where he conduced research on the politics and economics of the international coffee industry. A consultant for the World Bank and USAID, Bates is also a member of the State Failure Task Force. He also serves as a resource person for the Africa Economic Research Consortium and has for several years held a visiting professorship on the faculty of the economics department at Toulouse University.

POLITICAL ECONOMY OF INSTITUTIONS AND DECISIONS

Series editors

Randall Calvert, Washington University, St. Louis
Thrainn Eggertsson, Max Planck Institute, Germany, and University of Iceland

Founding editors

James E. Alt, Harvard University
Douglass C. North, Washington University, St. Louis

Other books in the series

Alberto Alesina and Howard Rosenthal, *Partisan Politics, Divided Government, and the Economy*
Lee J. Alston, Thrainn Eggertsson, and Douglass C. North, eds., *Empirical Studies in Institutional Change*
Lee J. Alston and Joseph P. Ferrie, *Southern Paternalism and the Rise of the American Welfare State: Economics, Politics, and Institutions, 1865–1965*
James E. Alt and Kenneth Shepsle, eds., *Perspectives on Positive Political Economy*
Josephine T. Andrews, *When Majorities Fail: The Russian Parliament, 1990–1993*
Jeffrey S. Banks and Eric A. Hanushek, eds., *Modern Political Economy: Old Topics, New Directions*
Yoram Barzel, *Economic Analysis of Property Rights*, 2nd edition
Yoram Barzel, *A Theory of the State: Economic Rights, Legal Rights, and the Scope of the State*
Charles M. Cameron, *Veto Bargaining: Presidents and the Politics of Negative Power*
Kelly H. Chang, *Appointing Central Bankers: The Politics of Monetary Policy in the United States and the European Monetary Union*
Peter Cowhey and Mathew McCubbins, eds., *Structure and Policy in Japan and the United States: An Institutionalist Approach*
Gary W. Cox, *The Efficient Secret: The Cabinet and the Development of Political Parties in Victorian England*
Gary W. Cox, *Making Votes Count: Strategic Coordination in the World's Electoral Systems*
Gary W. Cox and Jonathan N. Katz, *Elbridge Gerry's Salamander: The Electoral Consequences of the Reapportionment Revolution*

Continued on page following index

BEYOND THE MIRACLE OF THE MARKET

The political economy of agrarian development in Kenya

New edition

ROBERT H. BATES
Harvard University

CAMBRIDGE
UNIVERSITY PRESS

CAMBRIDGE UNIVERSITY PRESS
Cambridge, New York, Melbourne, Madrid, Cape Town, Singapore, São Paulo

Cambridge University Press
40 West 20th Street, New York, NY 10011-4211, USA

www.cambridge.org
Information on this title: www.cambridge.org/9780521852692

© Robert H. Bates 1989, 2005

First published 1989
First paperback edition 1992
New edition 2005

Printed in the United States of America

A catalog record for this publication is available from the British Library.

Library of Congress Cataloging in Publication Data

ISBN-13   978-0-521-85269-2 hardback
ISBN-10   0-521-85269-2 hardback

ISBN-13   978-0-521-61795-6 paperback
ISBN-10   0-521-61795-2 paperback

To My Mother and Father

Contents

Tables, figures, and maps

TABLES

FIGURES

Tables, figures, and maps

Series editors' preface

The Cambridge Series in the Political Economy of Institutions and Decisions is built around attempts to answer two central questions: How
do institutions evolve in response to individual incentives, strategies, and
choices; and how do institutions affect the performance of political and
economic systems? The scope of the series is comparative and historical
rather than international or specifically American, and the focus is positive rather than normative.

In studying the political economy of agriculture in postwar Kenya,
Robert Bates analyzes how institutions have been formed and the role
they play in Kenya's economy. He examines both their political and their
economic origins, and he explores not only the way in which they compensate for the failure of markets but also the way in which they are
used to vest particular interests.

Bates uses the study of institutions to examine the relationship between
the economics and politics of development. He traces the origins of political demands to the changing structure of Kenya's agrarian economy.
But he also argues that institutions help to determine which economic
demands become effective demands. Institutions, he argues, create incentives for politicians; and the strategies adopted by politicians help to
determine which interests become organized, receive ideological justifi-
cation, and ultimately gain political rewards.

Bates focuses on rural Kenya. He concentrates on the public regulation
of agriculture, including the politics and economics of land distribution,
resettlement, rural property rights, and pricing policies. He studies the
politics of rural radicalism, and its origins in the interaction of colonial
rule and changes in relative values of land and labor. He weaves factors
as disparate as the need for capital, characteristics of agricultural products, and the nature of party and bureaucratic organization into a con-
sistently rich and insightful analysis.

Above all, Bates attempts to develop an institutionally focused form of political economy. This allows him to create a unique understanding of Kenyan "exceptionalism": to explain why Kenya, unlike so many of its neighbors, has nurtured its rural economy, instead of undermining it.

Acknowledgments

Prior to conducting the research for this study, I had been too long absent from Africa. The Division of Humanities and Social Sciences of the California Institute of Technology; the late William Senga, Director of the Institute for Development Studies, University of Nairobi; the Committee on African Studies of the Social Science Research Council; and the National Science Foundation (Grant No. SE 582-16870) helped make possible my return. Peter Hopcraft, Joel Barkan, Michael Lofchie, and especially David and Leslie Leonard graciously eased the transition from university life in the United States to fieldwork in Kenya.

Many persons assisted my work in Kenya. Peter Kinyanjui, Acting Director of the Institute for Development Studies, provided gracious hospitality and institutional support; and my colleagues at the Institute, particularly Shem Migot-Adolla and George Ruigu, offered intellectual guidance and practical counsel. I only wish that the urgency imparted to my work by the famine had not drawn me away from Nairobi and thus from the opportunity for more frequent and probing interchanges with these and other scholars. I owe as well a major debt to David Leonard, John Cohen, Richard Goldman, Michael Westlake, Cathy Jabara, Judith Geist, John Lewis, and Lester Gordon. I could not have done this work without the assistance of the officers of the National Cereals and Produce Board, the Ministry of Agriculture, the Ministry of Cooperatives, and the Provincial and District Administration. At key points, I received assistance from members of the staff of the World Bank, and especially Kevin Cleaver and Uma Lele; the United States Agency for International Development; and the United States Department of Agriculture, particularly Cheryl Christensen. Perhaps my greatest debt is owed to my able research assistants: Philip Omamo, J. Muthengi Musunza, and Felipe Jaramillo.

I began writing while at the Institute of Development Studies at the University of Sussex. I wish to acknowledge the stimulation given my

Acknowledgments

work by Mick Moore, Michael Lipton, Raphael Kaplinsky, and Teddy Brett, and the assistance given me by the staff of the Institute. I later benefited from the hospitality of the Center for Advanced Study in the Behavioral Sciences, where my work was supported by Duke University, the Guggenheim Foundation, the Exxon Foundation, and the National Science Foundation (Grant No. BNS – 801 1495). Special thanks go to the able staff of the Center, particularly Carol Trainer and Leslie Lindzay, and to the librarians at the California Institute of Technology, the Institute of Development Studies, and the Center for Advanced Studies in the Behavioral Sciences. I wish to thank as well Elizabeth Bates; Paulette Higgins, my skilled research assistant at Duke University; and especially Doris C. Cross, my able secretary.

In preparing this manuscript, I incurred numerous intellectual debts. They are particularly owed to my former colleagues at Cal Tech – Thayer Scudder, Philip Hoffman, Donald Lien, and Eleanor Searle; to the members of the reading group on institutions at Duke University, especially Michael Meurer, Peter Lange, George Tsebelis, William Keech, Herbert Kitschelt, Timothy McKeown, John Aldrich, William Ascher, and William Bianco; and to my editors, Douglass North, Barry Weingast, and James Alt.

Many persons have read and commented upon this work: John Lonsdale, Greet Kershaw, Michael Redley, Stanley Engerman, Joel Silbey, Allan Bogue, Anne O. Krueger, David Glover, Terry Sicular, William O. Jones, Barbara Grosh, and participants in seminars at Harvard University, Duke University, Stanford University, the University of Chicago, the University of California at Los Angeles, and Washington University, St. Louis. Douglass North, Jennifer Widner, James Alt, George Tsebelis, Barry Weingast, David Leonard, Michael Lofchie, David Throup, Peter Lange, and two anonymous referees read and criticized the manuscript in its entirety. Elisabeth Case judiciously commented upon its style and organization. To these critics go much of the credit for the merits of this volume. Their persistent, forthright, and often pointed comments have strengthened it. Only my inability or reluctance to adopt their suggestions accounts for the deficiencies that remain.

Portions of the first chapter appeared as "The Agrarian Origins of Mau Mau: A Structural Account" in *Agricultural History*, vol. 61 (Winter 1987):1–28. Other parts of the manuscript appear as chapters in *The Political Economy of Kenya*, ed. Michael Schatzberg (New York: Praeger, 1987) and in *African Agricultural Development*, ed. Ronald Cohen (Gainesville, Florida: University of Florida Press, forthcoming). The materials are used in this volume with the permission of the publishers.

I dedicate this book to my mother and father, with love and gratitude.

A note on weights, measures, and currency

Abbreviation	Definition	Equivalence
mm	millimeter	0.0394 inch
km	kilometer	0.6241 mile
ha	hectare	2.4711 acres
mt	metric ton	1.1023 tons
Ksh	Kenya shilling	approx. 16 to one United States dollar in the mid-1980s
K£	Kenya pound	twenty Kenya shillings
£	Pound sterling	approx. $1.20 in the mid-1980s

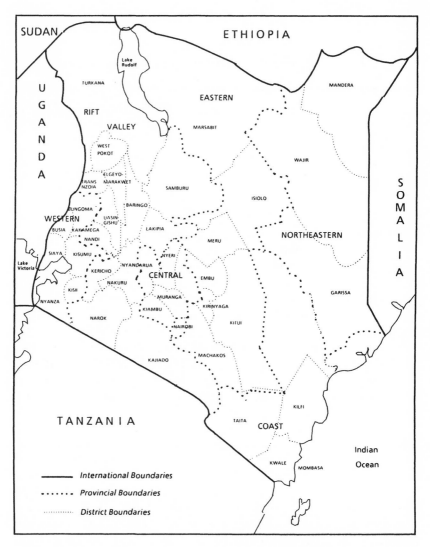

Administrative map of Kenya. *Source*: International Labour Office, *Employment, Incomes, and Equality: A Strategy for Increasing Productive Employment in Kenya* (Geneva: Imprimeries Populaires, 1972).

Preface to the new edition

While *Beyond the Miracle of the Market* was being written, the economies of the world were changing radically, but the radicalism was that of Adam Smith rather than Karl Marx. Ideologically, the impulse came from the right. The sponsors of Reaganism and Thatcherism reigned supreme at home and projected their program abroad through the international institutions that they financed and dominated: the World Bank and the International Monetary Institution. As the developing world underwent structural adjustment, socialist economies became capitalist. One message of *Beyond the Miracle of the Market* was "watch out"; the deeper message was that in the economic realm, the state and the market were complements rather than the substitutes that the prevailing rhetoric assumed.

The reformers were right: markets provide high-powered incentives and "getting the prices right" is therefore essential, if resources and investment are to be mobilized efficiently to ignite growth. But the very arguments that underlie this contention underpin a critique of the reformist's agenda: for prices in markets to be a sufficient source of economic welfare, a series of highly specific conditions must prevail.[1] So demanding are these requirements that their occurrence is unlikely. The implication is clear: the introduction of markets may be necessary for prosperity but no one could plausibly argue that their introduction would be sufficient.

At the time of economic reform, few pointed this out even though the argument derived from the very sources to which the reformers themselves appealed, the so-called fundamental theorems of welfare economics.[2] The silence underscores that the roots of economic reform

[1] K. Arrow and G. Debreu, "Existence of an Equilibrium for a Competitive Economy," *Econometrica* 27 (1954): 82–109.
[2] See the discussion in J. Quirk and R. Saposnik, *Introduction to General Equilibrium Theory and Welfare Economics* (New York: McGraw Hill, 1978).

at the time were political: they derived not from theory but from ideology.

To argue that price signals may be necessary but not sufficient to render the market a source of welfare is not merely to score a debating point, however. It is to introduce into the field of development a new agenda for both scholars and policymakers. This agenda is based on the corpus of economic research that followed the proof of the fundamental theorems of welfare economics and that, at the time of the writing of *Beyond the Miracle of the Market,* had become known as the "new institutionalism."[3] The goal of this book was to explore, to promote, and to critique this agenda.

THE NEW INSTITUTIONALISM

The new institutionalists do not question the significance of prices: they acknowledge the power of economic incentives. But efforts to maximize, they recognize, will in many circumstances lead to choices that lower rather than enhance the social welfare. The incentives for such behavior arise in situations that violate the necessary and sufficient conditions of the fundamental theorems, i.e., those that constitute market "imperfections." Research into those imperfections generates insights into the economic significance of such nonmarket institutions as the law, the state, the family, and the firm.[4]

The basic insight of the new institutionalism is that coercion can be productive. Through the imposition of sanctions, institutions render unattractive economic choices that may offer short-term private gains but that, because of imperfections in markets, may in the longer term impose collective losses. Those who may in the short run benefit from pollution may find it more profitable to refrain from polluting, given the sanctions imposed by law, for example. Or those who may seek to reap the benefits of roads or schools or public health without contributing to their costs – i.e., to free ride – may recalculate the benefits and share the costs in the face of threats by the state. By altering incentives, institutions, such as the law or the state, thus constrain opportunism and strengthen the incentives for socially productive behavior.

In the debates over economic reform in the developing world and the former socialist economies, the lessons of this research were largely

---

[3] Foundational works would include R. Coase, *The Firm, The Market and the Law* (Chicago, University of Chicago Press, 1988) and D. C. North, *Institutions, Institutional Change, and Economic Performance* (Cambridge, Cambridge University Press, 1990).

[4] For a useful review, see D. Mueller, *Public Choice III* (Cambridge, Cambridge University Press, 2003).

ignored. A major goal of *Beyond the Miracle of the Market* was to correct that deficiency by applying this approach to the study of development.

Another goal shaped the book: to compel the new institutionalists to recognize the implications of their intellectual position, in terms of both how they thought and the role they would play in debates over policy. Through the creation of institutions, power enters economic life. By following the path from markets to institutions, economists had entered the realm of political economy. Many were loath to recognize this. And in part for that reason, I would conjecture, many failed to yell "foul" when Reaganism and Thatcherism unleashed market forces throughout the world while also attacking the state, thus failing to introduce the institutions necessary to align greed with the social welfare.

To write *Beyond the Miracle of the Market,* I turned to what many regarded as the most market-friendly of Africa's states, Kenya, and studied the role of institutions in the dominant sector of Kenya's economy: agriculture, the source of more than 50% of Kenya's economic product, more than 80% of its jobs, and more than 90% of its exports. Where many might expect to find markets, I instead found governance structures that enabled managers to supervise, monitor, and enforce – and thereby to organize productive relationships and enhance the efficiency with which resources were employed in agriculture. The nature and orientation of these institutions, I argued, helped to explain Kenya's exceptionalism: its attainment of positive rates of economic growth when other economies in Africa were in decline.

Several additional implications emerged from this research. One was that policymakers should shift their attention from the macro to the micro level. The sources of Kenya's economic performance lay at the level of industry and the firm, whose productive activities inhered in governance structures; with access to laws and sources of authority, these entities were capable of curtailing opportunism and possessed the power to align individual self-interest with collective objectives.

Ironically, the implication for scholars was precisely the opposite: to shift their attention from the micro to the macro level. Institutions introduce power into economic life, and those who possess it can employ their positions of power to extract resources from the economy. Given that this is true, economic agents may not in fact behave more productively when institutions replace markets. For institutions to strengthen incentives, private agents must recognize and believe that it is in the interests of those with power to employ that power in ways that safeguard, rather than despoil, the creation of wealth. The impact of economic institutions thus depends on the incentives generated by the larger political game and whether predation or protection offers the winning political strategy at that level.

Thus the importance to this book of its historical structure of argument. Its treatment of settler institutions highlights the Janus-faced nature of power: the institutions enhanced the profitability of settler agriculture but also enhanced the capacity of settlers to collude against Africans. The book's treatment of the Kenyatta era reveals how a government motivated to maximize payoffs to its core constituency oversaw the panoply of economic institutions – marketing boards, development authorities, credit institutions, and so on – so that these services enhanced the profitability of agriculture. And its treatment of the Moi era – necessarily at less length, given the time of publication – demonstrates how the political incentives led President Moi to use the power of those institutions to redistribute wealth from the relatively prosperous Central Province – the base of the Kenyatta regime – to the less prosperous provinces of the West that provided Moi's core constitutuency.

To a great degree, those concerned with development concur on the importance of macroeconomic stability. In that sense, those who celebrate "the miracle of the market" have prevailed. To a great degree, those concerned with development concur on the importance of institutions. To a growing degree, they recognize that institutions introduce power into economic life; that political incentives shape the manner in which that power will be employed; and that in development studies, at least, research into the "new institutionalism" must therefore become a branch of political economy. Insofar as *Beyond the Miracle of the Market* helped to register those points in the minds of both scholars and policymakers, it has served its intended purpose.

Introduction

This book is about the political economy of development. It is about the politics and economics of agriculture. And it is about Kenya. To elaborate on these concerns, it is best to proceed from the specific case of Kenya to more general themes.

An East African country of roughly twenty million people, Kenya exhibits the hallmarks of any developing society. Its people are poor, earning on average $310 per annum in 1984; and their numbers are rapidly growing.[1] Kenya is agrarian. Ninety percent of its population dwells in the rural areas and over 30 percent of its gross domestic product originates from agriculture. The country is repeatedly visited by food shortages and famines, though to a lesser degree than many of its African neighbors. And it has fallen into debt, with repayments on foreign loans consuming over 20 percent of its export earnings in 1984.[2]

Kenya possesses attributes that distinguish it from other developing countries, however, and that differentiate it in particular from its neighbors in Sub-Saharan Africa. By comparison with its African counterparts, Kenya is rapidly growing; over the period 1965–1973, its gross domestic product grew at 7.9 percent per year, compared with the rate of 3.7 percent achieved by Sub-Saharan Africa as a whole. And while Africa's growth rate fell to 2.0 percent for the period 1973–1984, Kenya sustained a 4.4 percent rate of growth. Nowhere, however, does Kenya differ more clearly than in agriculture, where its rate of growth stands at over twice that of its African counterparts: 6.2 percent for Kenya versus 2.6 percent for Sub-Saharan Africa as a whole over the period 1965–1973, and 3.5 percent versus 1.4 percent for the period 1973–1984.[3]

This book explores Kenya's development experience. It focuses in particular on the economics and politics of agricultural development in that nation. And it attempts to locate the sources of Kenyan exceptionalism.

Introduction

AGRARIAN POLITICS

While focusing on Kenya, this book also explores more general themes. Central among them stands the politics and economics of agriculture.

Almost by definition, developing societies are agrarian. Whether by reviving the Germanic tradition of peasant studies,[4] clinging to variants of modernization theory,[5] or enlisting dependency theory or class analytic forms of Marxism,[6] contemporary scholars have sought better to understand the politics of the developing areas by better comprehending the politics of agriculture. The theme of agrarian politics runs through Kenya's political history. Several events so vividly mark this history that they demand exploration. Their analysis forms much of the content of this book.

Kenya became independent as a consequence of a rural rebellion. Commonly referred to as "Mau Mau," this rebellion attracted widespread notoriety and lurid popularization.[7] A book that focuses on the politics of agriculture in Kenya must account for the forces that impelled Kenya to independence; it therefore must address Mau Mau. Chapter 1 takes up this task.

In the period of the transition to independence, Kenya was torn by deep conflicts. One issue was constitutional and revolved around whether Kenya should possess a unitary or federal form of government. Another was economic and focused upon whether markets or political processes should determine the allocation of basic resources. Central to both issues were debates over the manner in which independent Kenya was to apportion the lands formerly held by the colonial settlers. Chapter 2 focuses on these issues and the way in which their resolution shaped the subsequent structure of political and economic life in that nation.

Not all political issues are grand issues, however; not all involve differences over the constitutional order or over whether "capitalism" or "socialism" is to provide the blueprint for economic development. More often, political conflict focuses on mundane matters that are of immediate concern to but particular segments of the general population. Controversies regarding pricing, licensing, transportation, or the regulation of markets animate much of the politics of rural life in any developing country. What issues dominate "normal" politics in Kenya? Chapter 3 addresses this question.

Behind the normal life of any agrarian society there lurks a pervasive uncertainty, one that results from agriculture's necessary dependence upon the forces of nature. Droughts can inflict crises of subsistence upon rural populations; and when droughts produce famines they can cause political crises as well. These facts of life prevail throughout much of the developing world, particularly in Africa; and they prevailed as well in the past histories of nations that were once agrarian but are now indus-trialized.[8] So fundamental is the impact of subsistence crises that they too must be analyzed. They form the subjects of Chapters 4 and 5.

Focusing on agriculture, this book thus addresses the subjects that it must address, given their prominence in Kenya's political history. The book pursues an even broader agenda, however. It seeks to open up new territory in the political economy of development.

BEYOND THE NEOCLASSICAL REVIVAL

As heralded in a rash of recent publications, neoclassical reasoning has recaptured the field of development economics.[9] Those who subscribe to the neoclassical revival are united by their critique of conventional de-velopment economics, with its emphasis on planning, public investment, and government regulation. They are also united by their faith in the market. Debunking the "myths" of market imperfection that legitimized the broad role for governments propounded by their predecessors, the new development economists instead stress the imperfections of govern-ments. As stated in the preface to Lal's *The Poverty of "Development Economics"*, one of the key texts in this movement:

If there is one piece of policy advice that can be drawn unambiguously from the development experience of the past few decades, it is: "Get the prices right!" Nearly all the disasters have stemmed from widespread resort to "political pric-ing" – most commonly in artificially maintaining exchange rates too high and prices (especially agricultural prices) too low, rationing credit at negative real interest rates, and subjecting luxury imports to prohibitively high tariffs.[10]

At the core of the neoclassical position is a conviction that markets work. Also central is a conviction that government intervention is best kept to a minimum. Thus Harberger, reflecting on the experience of the developing countries in the period since the Second World War, draws a dozen or so basic lessons for policymakers, over two-thirds of which caution against an activist role for governments.[11] It is as if contemporary development economists had converted wholesale to the position of the young Adam Smith, who wrote:

Little else is requisite to carry a state to the highest degree of opulence from the lowest barbarianism, but peace, easy taxes, and a tolerable administration of justice; all the rest being brought about by the natural course of things.[12]

This book focuses on two major deficiencies in the neoclassical posi-tion. The first is the failure adequately to deal with institutions. The second is the failure to analyze politics.

Introduction

Institutions

In a thoughtful recent essay, Hla Myint reflects upon his ambivalence about the neoclassical position.[13] While concurring with the new development economists concerning the merits of free trade, he dissents from their advocacy of a minimalist role for governments. For, he argues, the capacity of developing societies to reap the benefits made possible by trade is limited by their lack of suitable institutions. As Myint states:

[Normally] a developing country will not be on the production possibility curve theoretically attainable with its given resources and technology. Even in the absence of any distortion, it will be on a lower curve – its production feasibility curve – that is feasible with the incomplete state of its domestic organizational framework.[14]

Both experience and theory underscore the significance of appropriate institutions. Studies of some of the most successful of the world's open economies reveal that they are more likely to resemble contemporary socialist systems than the market economy of Smith's liberal republic. Amsden, for example, documents the forms of governmental intervention that promoted economic growth in Taiwan,[15] while Katzenstein and others analyze the forms of state management that have promoted outward oriented trade in the open economies of Europe.[16] In addition, recent theoretical work emphasizes that markets can operate effectively only if underpinned by appropriate institutions. This is as true of competitive markets, involving private goods and perfect information, as it is of imperfect markets, for which public intervention has traditionally been prescribed.

In recent years, economic historians – Douglass North, Lance Davis, and others[17] – have joined with a small number of development economists – Vernon Ruttan, David Feeny, and others[18] – to explore the role of institutions in promoting economic growth. This book seeks to advance the agenda pioneered by these scholars. It does so by exploring the origin of institutions and by examining their impact upon economic behavior.

This book focuses on the role of institutions in development. It attempts as well to expand the field's conception of their significance. It does so by attempting to demonstrate that the study of institutions provides foundations not only for the study of markets but also for the study of political economy.

Governments

Traditionally, development economists located the sources of underdevelopment in the failure of markets. They favored activist governments, liberally prescribing[19] government intervention as a corrective for market failure. By contrast, neoclassical development economists favor minimalist governments. They argue that underdevelopment results as much from the "political failure" of governments as it does from the failure of markets.

While their evaluations of governments are very different, the "traditional" and "new" development economists share a common trait: failure to provide a theory of politics. Traditional development economists suggested why private individuals might make socially incorrect choices in market settings, but offered no theory as to why public intervention would lead to better allocations. And their neoclassical counterparts merely substitute a socially pernicious state for one that was held to be socially benevolent.[20] Normatively, the two schools are at odds; as positive theories, they are alike.

A major objective of this book is to advance the analysis of governmental behavior, and in particular of the ways in which governments make choices that affect the development of their economies. We try to make governmental behavior endogenous. We pursue the economic roots of political behavior and trace the actions of the public sector to their origins in Kenya's agrarian economy. But we also examine the relationships between politics and economics that run in the opposite direction, as it were, by analyzing the political origins of economic interventions by governments. Toward that end, we introduce political institutions into the analysis.[21] These institutions play the same role in politics that markets play in economics: for rational actors, they create incentives that lead to characteristic choices. By creating a system of incentives, they help to account for the decisions taken by governments.

In this book, then, public policies are not explained as the choices made by some reified single actor, called a government. Rather, they are treated as the choices resulting from a struggle among competing interests that takes place within a setting of political institutions, rather than markets. And while we agree with development economists who view politics as a distributional struggle, we incorporate the analysis of this struggle into our explanation of public policy. Public policy is not formed as the result of some optimization process, which is subsequently distorted by private interests. Rather, policy is the product of the interested actions of private parties who bring their resources to bear upon politically ambitious politicians and the political process.

Bringing the state back in

Much of this book thus stands as a dialogue with development economics, particularly the market-oriented variety that has recently risen to prominence. The book also stands as a commentary upon – and extension of – recent work in political science. Indeed, a primary objective is to integrate the two fields of scholarship.

As proclaimed in the title of a recent prominent publication, contemporary scholars have challenged those who work in political economy to "bring the state back in."[22] Criticizing those who work in the tradition of world systems theory, they argue for the significance of domestic policy choice as a determinant of development. They also criticize those who subscribe to historical materialism for economic reductionism and for failing to appreciate the independent significance of politics. The state, they argue, stands relatively autonomous. It can therefore promote development even in the periphery; and nations that have been similarly endowed economically can pursue different growth paths, as a consequence of different policy choices.

Rather than critiquing these arguments, this book seeks to deepen them. It demonstrates the ways in which institutions – such as public agencies, political institutions, bureaucracies, and electoral systems – have an impact upon markets. It shows how political forces transform economic interests, promote their differential mobilization, and thus shape the way in which governments intervene in the economy. It also seeks to explain why Kenya appears to have harbored its agrarian endowment, rather than squandering it as have so many of its African neighbors.

The book thus elaborates central themes from the literature on "the state." But in so doing, it makes two major extensions to its arguments. By focusing on institutions, it integrates the study of "the state" with the study of "the economy." And by stressing the microeconomics of institutions and their impact upon political incentives, it provides the microfoundations for the macrothemes dominating the statist literature. The book thereby moves the study of developmental politics out of the realm of macrosociology and into the realm of political economy.

A unifying perspective

The book is thus motivated by a concern with economic forces on the one hand and with politics on the other. In clarifying the manner in which it seeks to blend the two, it is useful to dwell on one of the canonical texts in contemporary social science: the Coase Theorem.[23]

Coase bases his argument on an example in which a railway runs through a valley populated by farmers. The allocational issue is the number of trains that should operate each day. Transportation is valuable and operating trains produces profits for the railway; but transportation is also costly, for soot and sparks from the passing trains damage the crops of farmers. Acting purely out of a regard for corporate profits, the railway is likely to run too many trains. The costs inflicted upon the farmers by the last several trains may exceed the profits earned by the railway, and society could be made better off by running fewer trains.

Coase argues that a system of property rights could yield the socially efficient outcome: the number of trains that maximizes the sum of the returns to the railway and to the farmers. He also demonstrates that from the point of view of economic efficiency, the precise form of property rights is irrelevant. Equally important, he stresses that this conclusion holds only if there are no transaction costs. It is this last argument that renders Coase's article a contribution to the political economy. For in a world of positive transaction costs, institutions matter. They determine what bargains can be made, what agreements enforced, and therefore what outcomes are attainable through voluntary exchange. They also determine who pays, and who receives payment, when resources are consumed.

One system of property rights would hold that corporations possess an inherent right to make profits. Under this system the farmers would have to compensate the railway for the loss of profits incurred by scheduling fewer trains; and because the value to the farmers, in terms of the reduction in damages to their crops, exceeds the value of the profits that would be forgone by the railway, the farmers could, in effect, bribe the railway to operate fewer trains. The flow of payments would continue, assuming normal production functions, until the number of trains that pass through the valley is reduced to the socially optimal level, i.e., until the damages inflicted by the next train fail to equal the profits it generates, making further bribes inadequate to reduce rail traffic.

Another possible system of property rights would favor the farmers; it would hold that farmers possess an inherent right to clean air and a safe environment. Under this system, the railway would have to compensate the farmers for damage to their crops. And because the magnitude of the payments necessary to compensate for the damages to the farmers' crops exceeds the magnitude of the profits earned when too many trains are run, this system of property rights would provide an incentive for the railway to run fewer trains. Once again, the payment of compensation would continue until the profits earned from the last train run equaled the losses to the farmers, or until the socially optimal number of trains passed through the valley.

Either system of property rights, then, would work. Either system would lead the two parties, as a matter of self-interest, to act in ways that maximize the total value of output in the valley. Seen in this light, the Coase Theorem provides an intellectual foundation for the new neoclassical school of development economics. The government's role should be to establish property rights and it matters not which kind is established.

Once established, market forces will then induce choices that yield the efficient allocation of resources in the developing society. Economic decisions could thus be left to the market.

The Coase Theorem has thus been appropriated by those who seek a minimalist role for governments. But in significant respects the appropriation represents a misuse of Coase's argument. The theorem will be used in this book, rather, to demonstrate the central role of politics.

Politics matters in two major ways. One is by determining the degree to which efficient outcomes are attainable. The costs of reaching enforceable agreements, for example, could be so great that the parties cannot afford to bargain around their conflicts of interests; transaction costs, to use Coase's language, could thereby undermine their capacity to secure mutually beneficial agreements. As we shall see, in many areas in Kenya's economy, mutually beneficial agreements could not be made; the conditions that would have made them advantageous could not be guaranteed. But in others, political institutions made the attainment of agreements possible. By lowering the cost of organizing, they enabled economic interests to reap rewards from the commercialization of agriculture.

Politics also matter in Coase's argument because they influence the distribution of economic benefits. Under the system of corporate rights, efficiency requires a flow of payments from the multitude of farmers to the owners of the railway. Historically, the ownership of railways has been tightly held, and the result of this system would therefore be the creation of a wealthy minority. Under the system of farmers' rights, efficiency requires the flow of payments from the railway to the farmer. As assumed in Coase's argument and as commonly seen in the developing areas, farming tends to be a broad-based industry, with a multitude of small-scale practitioners. This system of property rights is therefore likely to yield a more egalitarian income distribution. The distribution of income is therefore significantly shaped by whether it is the railways or the farmers who dominate the political system and who thereby achieve the power legally to privilege their interests.

Political organization is costly; cooperative agreements are difficult to achieve. In a world of positive transaction costs, political institutions therefore matter. For, as we shall see, they supply the incentives that lead to the organization of interests. They thereby help to determine which economic interests become effective interests, politically, and they thus determine whose fortunes receive institutionalized positions within the economic order.

The significance of this argument is magnified when viewed from a developmental perspective. For in response to the contrasting distributions of income, it is reasonable to anticipate that investors will behave differently. In response to a concentrated distribution of income, they would be likely to create firms producing a small number of very expensive items: luxury cars, opulent furnishings, and costly services, as desired by the small minority with large incomes.[24] By contrast, the result of the more egalitarian distribution would be likely to be investment in firms capable of producing goods in a large volume but of low unit value: clothing, food, and household goods that are affordable by the masses.

Not only would the industrial composition of the two societies diverge. So too would the occupational structure. The pattern of development that supports a demand for luxury goods is likely to lead to the creation of a smaller number of manufacturing jobs, a greater number of service occupations, and a smaller cadre of skilled artisans. By contrast, broad-based industrial development that caters to the mass consumer is likely to produce a larger number of manufacturing jobs, fewer service occupations, and a broad stratum of less skilled craftsmen: tailors, bicycle repairmen, etc.

The two systems of property rights may thus both produce efficient outcomes. But they will yield different distributions of income, and ones that would result in major differences in the structure of demand, the composition of industries, and the kinds of jobs and skills that are socially rewarded.[25] While equivalent in terms of the degrees of economic efficiency, the two institutional bases thus yield radically different developmental outcomes. Which group organizes politically and thereby seizes the power to define the system of property rights thus matters.

This book seeks to bring to the study of development insights generated by the work of Coase, Williamson, Alchian, Demsetz, Klein, Crawford, and others who have explored the significance of institutions.[26] It explores their political as well as economic features. It thereby attempts to create a way of integrating the political with the economic in the study of development.

GEDANKEN: A NOTE ON METHOD

Much of this book thus stands as a dialogue with present-day approaches to the study of development. In the course of this dialogue, we explore the contemporary history of Kenya. And we examine as well the politics and economics of agriculture. In elaborating upon these themes, the book repeatedly engages in "thought experiments" (*gedanken*).

In these *gedanken*, there are two time periods. In the first, the society possesses an economy, the most relevant portion of which is a structure of production in which inputs of land, capital, and labor yield outputs of food and cattle. The society possesses a highly complex natural endowment; the complexity is a consequence of Kenya's topography, which encompasses a wide variety of soils, temperatures, and moisture regimes within a relatively small geographic area (see Figure 2.1 in Chapter 2). The society also possesses an historical legacy of social and political institutions; these can be thought of as "traditional."

The thought experiments perturb this society with a series of exogenous shocks. In the early portions of this work, the shock is the colonial incursion. In the later portions, it is a failure of the rains. In intermediate periods, the shocks include variations in access to land, cash crops, or productive ecological zones.[27] In each case, they lead to changes in the variables whose values are fundamental to economic behavior.

After the external manipulation of key economic variables, the *gedanken* move to a second time period. They then observe the impact of changes in the value of these economic variables upon politics. The *gedanken* thus constitute analytic games that relate changes in the economic foundations of an agrarian society to variations in its politics. The games are thus a species of political economy.

By playing these games, we learn. And what we learn most clearly is the importance of institutions. Rarely do we find a direct and obvious relation between economic changes and political outcomes. Rather, we find the effects refracted, as it were, through the society's institutional endowment.

It is time now to employ this method.

I

The demand for revolution:
the agrarian origins of Mau Mau

Kenya came to independence as a result of armed conflict. A rebellion, which was known as Mau Mau, engulfed the city of Nairobi and major portions of two agricultural provinces: Rift Valley and Central. This chapter focuses on the origins of the demand for revolution in the rural areas of colonial Kenya.

The chapter explores the economic and political impact of the colonial era and the way in which changes precipitated by the colonial occupation unleashed the power of African nationalism. In so doing, it sets the stage for understanding Kenya's postindependence political history.

The chapter also addresses deeper analytic issues. The study of Mau Mau sheds light on a compelling problem in the study of agrarian politics: the origins of rural militancy. Contrasting theoretical frameworks have been brought to bear upon this subject, ranging from dependency theory to class analysis. Exploring the Kenyan case enables us to choose among them. More central to this volume is the analysis of institutions. This chapter advances the study of institutions by exploring their origins and their transformation. The basis for institutional change, it asserts, is economic; but economic institutions are themselves profoundly political. Institutions, and those in control of them, we argue, help to determine who are the winners and who the losers in economic life; and who therefore become defenders of the prevailing order and who the militants, dedicated to its overthrow.

THE CASE STUDY

If a date is to be placed on the beginning of Mau Mau, it should probably be 1944, when political leaders in the Central Province began to organize a clandestine movement. The organizational device was an oath that bound those who pledged it to the support of the movement. If a date is to be placed on the outbreak of violence, it should probably be October

7, 1952. On that day, members of the movement assassinated Senior Chief Waruhiu as he returned from an official visit to the central offices of the government in Nairobi. In response, the governor of Kenya declared a state of emergency, banned the major African political organizations, and detained their leaders. Calling in British military from the Middle East, the government rapidly occupied the territories controlled by the Mau Mau rebellion and began to hunt down their armed units. The campaign lasted four years; the state of emergency several years longer. By 1956, over 80,000 Africans had been detained and over 14,000 killed or wounded.[1]

As noted by Spencer, the Mau Mau rebellion spread geographically in a "V."[2] The apex lay in Nairobi. The left arm extended northward into the White Settler farming areas of the Rift Valley Province; the right arm into Kiambu, Fort Hall, and Nyeri Districts – the districts that together formed the Kikuyu reserves (see Map 1.1). Dividing the two arms were the Aberdare (or more properly the Nyandarua) mountains, in which the armed forces of Mau Mau took refuge and from which they launched many of their attacks on the settlements below.

This configuration of the revolt, with its Rift Valley and Central Province wings and Nairobi apogee, suggests what other sources tend to confirm: that the Mau Mau rebellion was overwhelmingly a Kikuyu rebellion. The rebellion originated among two rural groups: the Kikuyu who worked in the commercial farms of the White Highlands and the Kikuyu who remained behind in the reserves. A central thesis of this chapter is that both the "squatter wing" and the wing in the reserves responded to dynamics whose origins lay in Kikuyu agrarian society.

Mau Mau has generated an enormous literature; one bibliography alone notes over two hundred secondary sources.[3] The volume of this literature suggests the magnitude of the passions spawning the rebellion. This chapter seeks to cut through the emotion and the turmoil of the events surrounding Mau Mau and to highlight the sparse underlying structure that generated the grievances fueling the revolt.

We therefore begin with a model of Kikuyu society. We employ it to account for the subsequent peopling of the White Highlands with cattle-owning squatters.[4] We then shock the model by altering the technology of farming in the White Highlands and one of the fundamental parameters of the economy of the Kikuyu reserves: the relative value of land. By so doing, we derive the conditions that led to the massive political and legal struggles generating the demand for revolution.

This chapter thus ignores the urban wing of the Mau Mau revolt and the cultural conflicts that alienated rural Kenyans from the colonial order. By focusing on the demand for rebellion, it ignores the supply of political organization. It also ignores the dynamics that led elite-level politicians

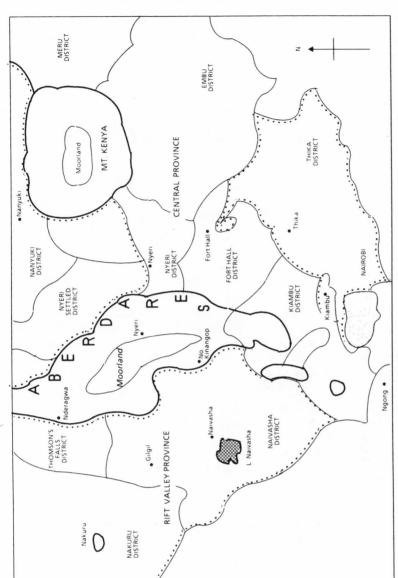

Map 1.1. The regions of revolt. *Source:* Donald L. Barnett and Karari Njama, *Mau Mau from Within* (New York and London: Monthly Revue Press, 1966). Copyright © 1966 by Donald L. Barnett and Karari Njama. Reprinted by permission of Monthly Review Foundation.

to seek to organize a rural political base and the manner in which they did so. Those concerned with the urban, cultural, or organizational dynamics that led the revolt are referred to sources listed below.[5]

THE TRIBAL MODE

The most parsimonious model of Kikuyu society that serves our purposes would include social values, institutional rules, and economic endowments.[6]

The key cultural values relevant to this analysis are the desire to accumulate resources that were highly valued but scarce and the tendency to evaluate personal happiness in terms of future, long-distant states. The critical institutions include the *mbari*, or kin-based units for the acquisition, development, and holding of land; bridewealth, by which cattle and livestock were exchanged for marriage partners; polygamy; and a system of age grade councils, which led to the control of property and authority by those who were genealogically senior. The economic features include that the economic environment of the Kikuyu was agrarian; that it contained two major economic activities – crop and livestock production; and that these activities required different proportions of land and labor. Initially, and this is critical, labor was relatively scarce and land abundant.

Taken together, these features formed a system of tribal life, one that helps to explain the peopling of the White Highlands with Kikuyu squatters and one that, when subject to fundamental changes, provoked feelings of grievance and outrage and generated demands for political action.

Endowments, values, and institutions

Initially, land was abundant and people scarce. Given the values of the Kikuyu, then, a major social aspiration was to accumulate dependents by forming a large family with many children. As stated by one of the most articulate students of Kikuyu, and their most prominent leader, Jomo Kenyatta:

It is a common ambition of every Kikuyu young man to own a hut or huts, which means implicitly to have a wife or wives. The establishment of a homestead gives a man special status in the community; he is referred to as *muthuri* (an elder). . . . Thus, it is the desire of every Kikuyu man to work hard and accumulate property which will enable him to build a homestead of his own. There is a proverb in Kikuyu which says: . . . the quality of a man is judged by his homestead.[7]

So too for the women:

14

When a woman reaches the stage of motherhood she is highly respected, not only by her children, but by all members of the community. Her name becomes sacred and she is addressed by her neighbors and their children as "mother of so-and-so."[8]

Adding to the desire for many dependents was a deep, indeed religious, conviction. The Kikuyu, like many people, believed that the soul outlived the body; descendants were necessary to ensure that the soul found care, welcome, and rest from ceaseless wanderings:

There is no doubt that perpetuation of family or kinship group is the main principle of every Kikuyu marriage. For the extinction of a kinship group means cutting off the ancestral spirits from visiting the earth, because there is no one left to communicate with them. And so when a man has more than one wife and many children, his soul rests in peace with the feeling that, after death, it will not be wandering in the wilderness or lose contact with the earth, for there will always be someone to hold communion with....[9]

For purposes of this analysis, the most critical social unit of the Kikuyu was the *mbari*. A *mbari* was a collection of households who traced their relationship through a single prominent individual, the founder. The greater the size of the *mbari*, the larger the number of dependents and, because the *mbari* bore the name of the founder, the surer the prospects for a peaceful afterlife, as descendants maintain an earthly communion with the soul of the founder.[10]

The establishment of a *mbari* required entrepreneurship and wealth. A founder had first to secede from an existing lineage and claim land whereon to establish his own kin group. Such acts were costly, for in some cases adjacent land was owned by a neighboring tribe and had to be acquired. And even where Kikuyu were the first to colonize, their settlements tended to lie at high elevations and to receive abundant rainfall; as a consequence, the land often had to be cleared of dense forest. Because the settlements lay at the periphery of the established regions of the tribe, they also had to be protected, be it against animals, cattle raiders, or hostile neighbors. The creation of new settlements therefore required large amounts of labor. But labor was scarce.

There were several ways of acquiring this resource. One was by offering the use of land. This option was most attractive to those who possessed livestock, for herding was a relatively land-intensive activity. Entrepreneurs therefore struck bargains with the owners of livestock, offering them access to new lands. Labor was also acquired through the manipulation of family relationships, and in particular through marriage. Once again, this time because of the institution of bridewealth, the keepers of livestock played a central role in entrepreneurial expansion. Entrepreneurs could exchange daughters for cattle, and these cattle could then subsequently be exchanged for marriage partners for sons.[11] In this way,

Table 1.1. *Kikuyu social and political councils*

Ethnic Group			
Metume of Murgang'a	Karura of Kiambu	Gaki of Nyeri	Genealogical stages
Kagwithia	Kagwithia	Kagwithia	Warrior councils
Ita	Ita	Ita	Transition to manhood
Kivindi	Kivindi	Kivindi	Transition from warrior to family head
Mauranja	Kamatimu	Kamatimu	Adult lodge, First Grade (first child approaching initiation)
Nburi Imwe	Muthigi	Metalthi	Second Grade (first child initiated)
Njomo	Bururi	Kinene	Third Grade

Source: B.E. Kipkorir, "The Traditional Background to the Modern Kenyan African Elite: Kenya c. 1890–1930." Paper presented at the Third International Congress of Africanists, Addis Ababa, Ethiopia (December 9–19, 1973).

an entrepreneur could amass a group of sufficient size successfully to secede from an established community and to build a settlement in a new land, to be known by the name of its founder.

Tribal councils formed a second critical institution of Kikuyu society. There were a series of councils. Some governed grazing; others, marriage relations; others, the affairs of particular shrines or locations. The councils were loosely ranked, the higher the council the greater the significance of its jurisdiction. Offenses against ritual and capital cases that crossed family lines, for example, were heard by the highest councils.

A necessary – though not sufficient – condition for the accumulation of influence was genealogical maturity: the establishment of a family and the raising of children. For, as illustrated in Table 1.1, a condition for promotion from one council to the next was the progression of one's children through the stages of life. A person aspiring to influence in tribal affairs therefore needed to have children. But, more to the point, the amount of influence a person possessed depended upon the number and age distribution of his children. Having a large number of dependents of varying ages increased that person's chances of possessing, quite literally, friends in court, for the children would be seeded, as it were, throughout the various councils.

It is here that polygamy, the last of the key social institutions, plays its role. For by marrying a succession of wives and by rearing a large family, a man could amass a following of sufficient size and age structure to dominate the councils of his tribal segment. The accumulation of wealth, preferably in the form of livestock, thus formed a prelude to the accumulation of dependents, and, as a consequence, social standing and political power.

Before making use of this tribal model, it is useful to place it in a broader perspective. Many students of agrarian change have argued that traditional societies were egalitarian; they therefore explain contemporary rural conflict in terms of the resistance of rural populations to the spread of markets, the rise of capitalist forces of production, and the resultant formation of social classes. With their lack of a monarch, chiefs, or an aristocracy, and with their system of government by citizen councils, the Kikuyu exhibit the political hallmarks of an egalitarian society, a fact noted and stressed by many students of the tribe. Our analysis, however, has exposed an underlying pattern of inequality.[12] As noted in the concluding section to this chapter, the implications compel us to advance an explanation of Mau Mau that dissents from theories of rural rebellion that locate the origins of inequality in modern economic forces.

While distinguished from both the anthropological accounts of highly stratified societies, such as those of the intralacustrian areas, and the sociological legends of egalitarian rural democracies, our schematic outline nonetheless bears a striking resemblance to another analytic model: that of the predatory lineage system, as portrayed by Marshall Sahlins.[13] As noted by Sahlins, in some societies the perpetuation and stability of social relations and the attainment of personal objectives require the succession of tribal segments, expansion out of settled lands, and the peopling of new territories. As will be seen, Sahlins's account of the dynamics of lineage segmentation conveys insight into the transformation undergone by the Kikuyu when confronted by the constraints imposed by colonialism. And it therefore helps to account for the subsequent rebellion.

In the early twentieth century the tribal system of Kikuyu was subject to a major exogenous shock. The British alienated the lands to the north – Nyeri, Nanyuki, and Laikipia becoming part of the White Highlands – and the lands to the south – Thika, Nairobi, and parts of Kiambu (see Map 1.1). Establishing ranches, plantations, and mixed farms, the colonists alienated lands over which Kikuyu settlers had established rights; at least as important, they also extinguished the possibility of acquiring new land rights. As laborers and tenants, Kikuyu gained access to these lands; but they were forbidden ownership of them. Reproduction continued; families expanded; the search continued for reputation, power, and prominence in the councils of the tribe. In effect, people became relatively abundant and land rights relatively scarce. This shift in relative values, we argue, gave rise to fundamental changes in the nature of rural institutions and to tensions that sparked the demand for political revolt.

Table 1.2. *Early land holdings*

East African Estates	350,000 acres
East African Syndicate	310,000 acres
E.S. Grogan & F.R. Lingham	132,000 acres
London & South African Agency	128,000 acres
Lord Delamere	109,562 acres
Scottish Mission	64,000 acres

Source: Paul Mosley, *The Settler Economies: Studies in the Economic History of Kenya and Southern Rhodesia, 1900–1963* (Cambridge: Cambridge University Press, 1983), p. 15.

THE SQUATTER WING

To the north of the Kikuyu reserves and to the west in the Rift Valley the colonial incursion led to the alienation of land from native tenure and to the establishment of what became known as the White Highlands.

The process of settlement

To facilitate military access to the interior, and thereby to establish control over the upper reaches of the Nile, the British constructed a railway from Mombasa. The railway was completed in 1901. As with many military investments, the railway proved expensive. The charge laid upon the governors of Kenya by their superiors in Whitehall was to make the railway pay.[14]

Local officials therefore alienated land rights along the railway to concessionaires, who would then develop the properties, sell them to settlers, and thereby generate revenues, in part from the land sales themselves and in part from the increase in rail traffic. Mosley presents data underscoring the magnitude of some of these concessions (Table 1.2). As any student of Kenya will recognize, his list contains the names of the most active "boosters" and "developers" in the colony, including Grogan, Delamere, and others.

The early concessionaires dominated the politics of the colony and their objective was clear: to bully the government into adopting policies that would enhance the value of their lands. They therefore demanded the creation of infrastructure that would attract further settlement, preferably by prosperous and high-class immigrants. As their program promised to generate rail traffic, it was favored by the colonial office in London and its appointees in the government offices of Nairobi.[15]

In their efforts to recruit immigrants, the concessionaires also pressured the government into a policy of zoning. Africans were to be confined to "reserves" and not allowed to own land in the European areas. The adoption of a policy of exclusion mandated the extinction of African property rights in what became known as the White Highlands.

In the early twentieth century, then, there came to exist virtually side by side two farming systems: that of the new European settlers and that of the indigenous community. The most striking difference between them was the factor proportions that characterized their use of farm inputs. The average size of the settler farm in 1905 was 5,488 acres.[16] The best data available suggest that the average farm size of the Kikuyu could not conceivably have exceeded 40 acres.[17]

One consequence of the vesting of land rights in the Highlands was the formation of a market for labor. The settlers possessed abundant land and little labor; the Africans possessed abundant labor but lacked land. The settlers bid for labor and promoted the movement of Africans into the White Highlands – but in the status not of landowners but of workers. And as one would expect from our model of tribal society, those whom they attracted were the keepers of livestock: that segment of the Kikuyu who most needed a low ratio of people to land and who in quest of it ever moved to the spatial periphery of the Kikuyu's agrarian society.

As noted by Wambaa, the settlers actively engaged in the recruitment of labor:

[The recruiter] was often the headman of a particular Rift [Valley] estate, and he would come to the Reserve to meet the local chief and his elders. He would then narrate the advantages of . . . going to the Rift Valley, mentioning that in his area [they] could have as many sheep, cattle and goats as they liked; that there was water nearby and that *posho* [ground maize meal] would be free for the first three months. In addition, he would tell them that they could get transport and sleeping kit, and be given barrels . . . to carry their things in; they could even bring their beehives along if they wanted.[18]

The Africans in the reserves behaved as one might expect. Some initially responded. When they did so, they minimized the costs of entering the market by going to the farms most proximate to their initial locations.[19] Others then followed; they minimized the costs of entering the market by going to areas where friends and relatives had preceded them, receiving from them food, shelter, and information about jobs. As narrated by Wambaa:

When the Kikuyu went up on their own initiative, they would usually get off the train at Elementaita, and there other people would tell them where things were best at the moment . . . [The rich men looking for additional grazing] would usually go to the area called Ndimu, where Delamere's squatters were, or . . . up near Egerton College or the area called Buane, somewhat towards Nakuru from

Njoro. The poorer squatters...would go more towards Londiani, Molo and around Rongai where they could get cultivation.[20]

As noted in these quotations, a primary attraction of moving to the White Highlands was the availability of land on which to graze cattle and livestock. As we have seen, in the densely settled Kikuyu homelands, the locus of herding perpetually drifted toward the extensive land-use margin. Given their abundant land and scarce labor endowments, the estate managers not surprisingly targeted their bids on the cattle herders.

There arose on the White Highlands a characteristic form of farm organization. Commonly, the farm contained a central area of production, managed by an estate foreman (often an African; often highly educated and prosperous, by prevailing standards) and occupying no more than 20 percent of the total acreage of the farm. About the central estate lay the farming and grazing areas occupied by Africans. There was also a characteristic form of farm labor contract. The contracts specified the number of days on which laborers had to work on the central estate. They also specified the number of cattle and livestock which, in exchange, the African laborers could graze, and the areas which they could use for houses and gardens. In many cases the contracts specified as well that any surplus production from the laborers' farms was to be sold through the estate management.

Numerous sources testify that the production of the Kikuyu squatters in the White Highlands represented a major portion of the output of the colonists' farms in the 1920s and 1930s. The settlers insisted that they monopolize the sale of the produce; they successfully pressured the government into banning sales through Indian commercial traders. In this period, then, they secured a major portion of their incomes from the sale rather than the production of produce, production being left in large part in the hands of the African cultivators.

Thus far the image conveyed is one in which the colonial settlers employed political power to seize property rights and then let market forces determine the subsequent allocation of resources. The narrative of Wambaa and the interviews by Furedi reveal that the early African squatters energetically exploited market alternatives, shifting from farm to farm and region to region to secure the best terms available within the existing framework of property rights.[21] Subsequently, as we shall see, all this changed.

Before turning to the restructuring of Highland agriculture, however, it is useful to note that many have interpreted the configuration of land rights on the Highlands in terms of racial segregation, but that our account exposes the weakness of such an interpretation. The restriction of land rights on the Highlands did *not* affect its racial composition; indeed, it supported the formation of a labor market in which the white settlers actively imported black labor. But the system of property rights, while supporting a labor market, profoundly affected the structure of economic relations. During the colonial period, the Kikuyu gained access to land on the Highlands, but in the capacity of workers, not landowners.

The creation of new institutions

The military imperatives of World War II precipitated changes in Kikuyu agriculture.[22] Political directives from London and Cairo instructed the government of Kenya to provision the military in North Africa and the Middle East, to replace the raw materials (in particular, hard fibers) lost to the Japanese in South East Asia, and to feed the cities in the war zones in the Middle East and North Africa.

The government's need for agricultural products was great; its ability to produce them was small. Not only did the bureaucrats lack the skills, information, and techniques to manage agricultural production; but also the war effort led to a reduction in the size of the administrative bureaucracy, as public servants were redeployed to military assignments. The farm settlers, in effect, were deputized to devise mechanisms for securing production targets.[23] The colonial state conferred economic power upon the settlers in exchange for war service.

The result was the creation of new institutions, ones that were to enhance the capacity for collective action on the part of the settlers. Acquisition of the ability to act collectively transformed the significance of the structure of property rights. For in addition to promoting the creation of a market for labor, the unambiguous vesting of land rights in the hands of the settlers, when combined with the capacity to organize, created a capacity to expropriate the wealth of those who supplied labor power.

The settlers took advantage of the government's need for agricultural production by transferring to the state a portion of the risk of commercial farming;[24] they produced commodities that they then sold to the state at controlled prices. This exchange required the formation of new institutions, as the settlers formed agencies to monitor, police, and control their own economic conduct.

The terms of the new economic order were embedded in the provisions of the Increased Production of Crops Ordinance and the Defense (Control of Maize) Regulations of 1942: the provisions for "guaranteed minimum return" and "maize control." By the former, the farmers submitted to the state inspectorate a farm production plan with target acreages of specific ("controlled," in the language of the ordinance) crops and an outline of intended production practices. When approved by an oversight committee, the production plan became a contract: the government promised to purchase the pledged quantity of production at fixed prices, thereby locking in a specified level of revenues for the farmer. In the event of natural disaster, the government guaranteed the farmer a rate of return commensurate with his production program. With the government guarantee, the approved production program also became the basis for farm credit. On the basis of this guarantee, a farmer could secure from other state agencies advances of farm inputs, again at controlled prices; he could also employ the guarantee as collateral for private loans.[25]

The contract between the farmers and the state was vulnerable to two major risks. One arose at the level of produce marketing. The state advanced credit for the purchase of farm inputs in exchange for a promise to provide specified quantities of output. In exchange for lower risk, the state offered controlled prices. The danger was that individual farmers would take the credit but then dispose of the crop to agents who offered prices higher than the state was willing to pay. To secure the benefits of risk reduction, the farmers and the government therefore agreed to the second major provision of the Increased Production of Crops Ordinance: controlled marketing. The farmers' organization, the Kenya Farmers' Association (KFA), became a registered agent of the state, which conferred upon it the power to act as the sole legal buyer of maize. Independent agents were banned from the market in favor of a single buying organization. The KFA became a monopoly.

Not only was there the risk of opportunism at the level of marketing; there was also danger at the level of production. A farmer might submit farm plans that, when approved, would entitle him to draw farm inputs on credit from the state bureaucracy or to secure private loans, and then not perform. He might dispose of the inputs on black markets. Or he might follow careless production practices and attribute his poor harvest to drought, hail storms, or the depredations of pests or wild animals. To implement an institutional framework that would lead to a mutually beneficial transfer of risks, the farmers and the government needed to prevent this form of opportunism.

A major problem was that it was very costly to acquire the information necessary to safeguard against these risks. It was difficult to determine the willingness of individual farmers to cheat. State bureaucrats could not acquire information about the intentions of farmers; less costly to acquire was information concerning reputations. Reputations for probity were built within the community of settler farmers. And the bureaucracy therefore delegated to the community the power to approve, or to deny approval of, the farm production plans that formed the basic element of the contract between the farmers and the state.

Two thousand settler farmers was too great a number to place on one committee. Rather, the farmers in each administrative district formed their own agricultural committees. They vetted each other's farm plans. They inspected each other's farms. And should a farmer claim that his loss of crop was due to an act of God and ask for a payout despite his nonperformance, a committee of "friends and neighbors" would make detailed investigations of his claim. The committees were intensely political, precisely in that they sought to curtail the incentives for individual farmers to act in ways that would undermine the benefits available to settler farmers as a whole: the ability to do business in an uncertain environment, but one where the risks were shared with the state.

The state sought increased output at lower prices; the farmers sought lower risks and steady prices. To secure a mutually advantageous settlement, they therefore devised new institutions. The risks of opportunism led to the formation of collectively binding, restrictive agreements and to the virtual creation of a farmers' cartel.[26]

One result of the creation of these new institutions was economic. Even during the hardships of the war, the colonial farmers invested heavily in grain production and the quantity of production rose. The institutional innovation thus enhanced the productive potential of farming. Another result was political. Through these new institutions, the settlers achieved the power to organize about their collective interests.[27] They secured from the state the authority to regulate their private affairs. They thereby gained the political power to defend their common economic interests, something which led to a significant transformation of the relationship between landholders and laborers in agricultural labor markets.

Economic transformation

The squatters' position in Highland agriculture was inherently precarious.[28] From the very early twentieth century, efforts had been made to limit their rights; and pressures mounted to limit their numbers. For the settlers and the colonial government feared that were squatters to achieve the legal standing of tenants, as opposed to workers, they would then be able successfully to claim under British law permanent land rights in the White Highlands.[29] The tensions marking relations between the squatters and settlers varied in intensity, however. And in the postwar period, Highland agriculture underwent a series of transformations that exacerbated the tensions to the point of armed conflict.

The settlers had always sought public policies that would increase land prices. Toward the end of World War II, they found a government concerned to promote the peaceful demobilization of its armed forces. They were able to convince the government to assist demobilized officers to purchase Kenyan land.

The political leader of the settlers, Cavendish-Bentinck, served as

Chairman of the Agricultural Production and Settlement Board. When postwar development plans were being considered by the government, his Board submitted a detailed and fully costed project for the "closer settlement" of the Highlands. The government was to aid in the purchase of lands for ex-servicemen, lend them funds for developing their farms, and contribute to their training at the newly opened Egerton School of Agriculture in the Rift Valley.[30] The government adopted the plan and placed it high among its priority projects for the postwar period. One result was an intensification of land use in the Highlands. Another was the growth of pressures for the clearance of the squatter population. Subdivisions, when sold, were to be sold unencumbered with tenants; and the new farmers often sought to grow crops on lands that otherwise would have been used by the squatters for the herding of livestock.

Not only were the squatters threatened by subdivision and the reduction of farm sizes; they were also threatened by a transformation of production practices. In particular, they found themselves victimized by efforts on the part of the farm owners to raise the reliability and level of farm profits by introducing "mixed farming."

Mixed farming involved the introduction of a new production activity – dairying. The depression had spurred a demand for diversification as farmers confronted a paucity of economic options following the collapse of grain prices. The pressures for diversification had been abetted during the Second World War, particularly given the government's guarantee of suitable returns to grain production. But the growth of Nairobi and Mombasa during World War II had created a market for milk and dairy products. And the prolonged monocropping of grains during the war had led to a growing concern with soil depletion. Mixed farming was seen as an appropriate response. Egerton, Kenya's new agricultural college, strongly stressed the virtues of mixed farming, making its adoption a hallmark of professionalization in the postwar farming community.

The conversion to mixed farming proved expensive. Land had to be withdrawn from arable production and placed under pasture. Given the tendency of indigenous grasses of low nutritional value to invade new pastures, the pasture lands required extensive preparation and costly care. In support of the new dairy activity, investments had also to be made in fencing, water supplies, and cooling equipment. Off the farm, investments were made in creameries, refrigerated transport for road and rail, and distributional networks for retailing highly perishable dairy products within the urban markets.[31]

The introduction of mixed farming required, in short, the creation of a dairy industry – a set of interdependent investments in the production, processing, and marketing of dairy products. Those who had invested their capital in the industry sought to protect it. And a principal source of vulnerability was at the farm site.

Production externalities

Kenya had long had cattle; pastoral production formed a major component of all local farming systems. The milk yields from local cattle were low, however. And given the expenses of commercial dairying, high yields were required to render the investments profitable. To upgrade production levels, commercial farmers therefore imported high-yielding cattle from Europe.

Although the milk yields from local cattle were too low to generate revenues sufficient to cover the costs of commercial dairying, the local cattle were hardy. In particular, they were resistant to local diseases. This was not true of the more productive varieties imported from abroad. The result was the creation of a production externality between the herders of local cattle and the commercial dairy farmers.

Ticks constitute the major vector for many of the most serious cattle diseases in East Africa. Local livestock had evolved a significant degree of resistance to tick-borne diseases. Exotic cattle had not. Should a tick feed off local livestock and so contract the disease, and then subsequently feast off an exotic, the exotic, perfected in an alien environment, would be defenseless against infection. The implication was clear: Where farmers were investing heavily in dairying, local livestock had to be cleared from the land.

It would not suffice, however, for an individual farmer to implement such a clearance. For cattle are mobile and can cross farm boundaries. And while investing in fencing could reduce such incursions, the fences placed no barriers on the movement of smaller animals that acted as hosts for the ticks: goats, sheep, or wildlife. An individual farmer was therefore unable to protect his dairy investment. He had, perforce, to coordinate his conduct with that of his neighbors.

Political struggle

The right to herd cattle was, of course, a major element in the squatter's labor contract. The transformation of farming in the Highlands and the rise of the dairy industry therefore gave rise to a political struggle within the settler community aimed at altering the nature of the contract that bound labor to land.

Under the powers of the Resident Labour Ordinance of 1937, local district councils could limit the number of squatter stock and the size of their gardens and prescribe the number of days squatters must work on the owner's farm. The district councils were representative bodies and in the Rift Valley were dominated by farmers. It was difficult for the councils to develop a uniform policy toward labor contracts, however, for preferences among the farm owners were not uniform. Many farmers still monocropped grain; this was particularly true among the poorer farmers who could not afford the heavy investments required to transform their farm operations. Such farmers had little interest in clearing the lands of squatters. Other farmers produced labor-intensive crops, sisal in the lower elevations and pyrethrum at higher altitudes. The producers of such crops feared the loss of labor power that might result were they constrained in the contracts they could offer. The result was intense political controversy among the settlers.[32]

From 1946 to 1954, dairy farming appears to have spread. The cultivation of grass leys rose from 860 to 9,480 hectares. The conversion of land to leys spread first in the areas closest to the Nairobi market: Nakuru, Molo, Elburgon, Njoro, Rongai, and Kinagop.[33] It is therefore unsurprising that district councils in the southern Highlands began to form majorities in favor of restricting native livestock; or that the Kikuyu squatters, who were as we have seen concentrated in these regions, were among the first to be faced with the alternative of disposing of their livestock and signing on as hired hands or of quitting the Highlands and returning to the reserves. Adding to the intensity of the postwar struggle was the rise to power in Great Britain of the Labour Party. For Labour favored the conversion of use rights to ownership rights in a variety of economic settings. And many settlers therefore sought to abrogate labor contracts that the colonial government might interpret as offering claims to landownership in the White Highlands.[34]

In some cases the squatters petitioned against the rulings of the local councils. Thus the telegram from Nahasham Njorge, 16 June 1946, beginning:

We Kikuyu squatters numbering 63 men and our families request your kind intervening in our troubles . . . [at] Springfield farm, Nakuyu.[35]

Thus too the letter written on behalf of squatters in Naivasha to the "Honorable Chief Native Commissioner," 1 November 1945: "We squatters with honor and hope write you and kindly beg you to listen to our troubles here."[36]

In other cases, the squatters resisted. Thus the minute by the District Commissioner, Naivasha, who noted that:

The . . . District Council during 1946 enforced a new order [which] meant a drastic reduction in the . . . livestock which had been enjoyed by many Resident Labourers in the Naivasha area for years past. Although the matter had been very thoroughly discussed for several years beforehand, although every effort was made to explain the new rules to the local Kikuyu, the fact was that when steps were taken to enforce the rules, large numbers of Kikuyu . . . laborers refused to accept the reduction or to sign contracts. A complete deadlock continued for some months . . . [37]

In the last instance, the squatters organized. Thus the District Commissioner in Nakuru in 1949 noted the spread of squatter "unrest" and the "numerous meetings . . . due to resentment against the local regulations applying to the . . . numbers of stock which might be held by squatters."[38] The government commented that soon the "novelty [would wear] off,"[39] but was forced the next year to reevaluate the complacency of its position. "In the political sphere," the Provincial Commissioner for the Rift Valley wrote in 1950, "one of the most disturbing events was the discovery at Naivasha of a secret society known as Mau Mau."[40] Among the places it had spread were the areas where the new farming system had been introduced into the White Highlands: Naivasha, Njoro, and Elburgon.[41]

Conclusion

The squatters were thus victimized by an economic transformation taking place in Highlands agriculture. Not only did the intensification of land use limit pastoral production in the Highlands; but also a transformation in production processes generated the potential for production externalities between the pastoral production of squatters and the herds of the colonial settlers. The structure of economic institutions in Highlands agriculture conferred upon the settlers political power; it endowed them with the capacity to coordinate their actions. The settlers used this power to assign to themselves the right to run cattle in the Highlands and to impose the costs created by the production externality upon the owners of indigenous cattle. Some squatters bore these costs in the form of the loss of their herds; they were forced to liquidate their cattle holdings.[42] Others bore them in the forms of a loss of livelihood; they lost their jobs and were physically expelled from the Highlands. The colonial government transported them back to the reserves. There, however, they confronted another structure of institutional power: that of their own tribe. And as we shall see, those who dominated the structure of the tribe refused to share with the squatters the burden of their economic fate.

THE EASTERN WING

Economic change was not confined to the White Highlands. It also took place in the native reserves. With the appropriation of land on every border and the prodigious natality of the Kikuyu, no longer were people relatively scarce and land rights relatively abundant in the reserves. Rather, the opposite proportionality prevailed.[43] As a consequence, land rights rapidly rose in value.

Adding to the rise in land values was the rapid growth of commercial opportunities in agriculture. The Kikuyu reserves lay near Nairobi. Profits could therefore be made by growing fruit and vegetables, raising chickens and small livestock, or producing milk, eggs, and dairy products, all destined for sale on the urban market. Profits could also be made by selling timber, either for the construction of houses or for the production of charcoal. The lands of the Kikuyu were also endowed with a climate and ecology that offered prospects of riches for those who could produce cattle, coffee, tea, or other commercial products.[44] Before investing in the capacity to produce agricultural commodities, prospective entrepreneurs had first to be certain that they would be entitled to reap the benefits of their outlays. They therefore demanded clarification of their rights to land.

The result of both transformations was the rise of a profound political struggle within the Kikuyu nation. For incentives had been created to transform property rights. As argued most persuasively, perhaps, by Gluckman, property rights do not represent rights over material objects; rather, they represent rights with respect to people.[45] A person's rights in property represent the power to limit the ability of other persons to enjoy the benefits to be secured from the use and enjoyment of a material good. The corollary is clear: to alter property rights is to redefine social relationships. And by litigation and political struggle, the Kikuyu undertook to redefine the juridical element in their kin relations.

In Kikuyu society, as we have seen, kin relations had been defined inclusively; the larger the family, the more powerful and prestigious the family head and the more certain his soul of repose. But now, with old lands crowded and rights to new lands no longer available, the incentives were to exclude: to restrictively define kin relations and thereby to circumscribe who was or was not entitled to claims to land. Changes in land law therefore led to the coercive delimitation of kinship entitlements.

The result was rising volumes of litigation, as those who sought to secure land and the gains to be reaped from its commercial use sought to demarcate their rights and to exclude the claims of others.

A variety of traditional principles validated land claims. Land could rightfully be appropriated by first clearance, first settlement, or purchase. Land rights could also derive from inheritance. When applied to particular cases, these principles often conflicted. The legitimacy of claims based upon inheritance, moreover, depended on the relative standing given the initial act of appropriation; and these acts often had taken place in the distant past. Given the increased desire to establish land rights, conflicting versions of the primacy of means of establishing land claims, and the uncertain knowledge of past acts, it was inevitable that the volume of litigation would rise. Rise it did, and the legal struggles fragmented families and kin relations. As Kershaw describes the situation:

Inside the *Kikuyu* area a struggle was taking place, fought with great bitterness, to maximize the rights to land while at the same time minimizing the number of people who had rights to it. This conflict was fought through the use of past history and the rights which were associated with the growth of membership of the local group... [A] people for whom a line of descent, traced with precision to delineate legal access to land had always been of minor importance, went in search of its lineage to fight for survival, claiming precise and invariable traditional rights....[46]

The conflicts took place within the councils of the tribe. Families who saw their land claims best validated by village law pushed their cases through the councils specializing in village disputes; those who saw their strongest claims as arising from marriage lay their claims before the councils that dealt with that subject. The councils, as we have seen, were dominated by those who had been wealthy enough to finance the accumulation of dependents and thus power. They now used their elite standing to delimit and clarify the claims of land based upon family membership.

The legal struggle in the reserves was of profound significance to the emigrés from the White Highlands. Many returned to find the residents of the reserves invoking the power of the courts to claim exclusive rights over every patch of land; having been absent during the legal struggles and with but weak claims to ownership in any case, many now found themselves landless. The powerful family heads who were pressing the land cases found it costly to exercise compassion; the relative value of land had risen too high, and they were under strong pressure to exclude as many claims as possible. Increasingly therefore they used their positions of power to reject claims to land. Those who had been victims of the clearances on the Highlands now found themselves victims of the politics of economic change in the tribal reserves.[47]

Distributional consequences

Changes in the value of land rights, then, precipitated a struggle over family law. This struggle took place within a context that helped to determine the distributional outcome. The context consisted not only of tribal but also of colonial institutions. The colonial context generated an array of economic and political attributes that influenced both the benefits

29

to be secured from land litigation and the costs of processing claims. The result was that the inequality that had characterized Kikuyu tribal society in the precolonial period assumed the character of class divisions in the colonial era.

Colonialism generated new forms of economic opportunities. There arose a demand for such commodities as English potatoes, for consumption in Nairobi; wheat, for sale to the large European farms or directly to millers; and wattle, the wood of which was used in the construction of fences, burned by railways, or transformed into charcoal, and the bark of which was processed for export. As already noted, those who invested in the production of such commodities wanted, and demanded, secure land rights. They stood to benefit more than others from them. They therefore took the lead in securing the transformation of family law.[48]

The colonial incursion produced as well a change in the market for labor. Within that market, educated labor could command a substantial wage premium. Persons proficient in English could secure jobs as translators or clerks in the bureaucracy, as foremen in the industries and commercial farms, or as salesmen and assistants in the new commercial establishments. As Cowen, Kitching, and others have noted, there was no clear separation between these new educateds, earning money in commerce, industry, and the public service, and those who invested heavily in the production of agricultural commodities.[49] The funds generated off the farm were often invested on it. In addition, those earning incomes from wages and salaries were better able to invest in the costs of litigation necessary to clarify land rights and thereby enhance the expected value of the streams of income being generated by the rise of commercial agriculture.

Certain social categories, then – rural entrepreneurs and the educated, sometimes called the *athomi* (those who can read) – were specially motivated to engage in the legal struggle to redefine entitlements to real property. As Cowen has phrased it:

It was the *athomi* who by resurrecting the depth and width of the links of lineage from the original claims to land...pitched sub-clan against sub-clan. From the base of a resurrected sub-clan, each *muthomi* [a spokesman for a *mbari*] set litigation in motion, made the largest contribution towards the case and planted wattle to secure claims to "disputed" land. The *athomi* were cast as the defenders of the sub-clan interests to land and were rewarded with land accordingly.[50]

Not only did the educated possess strong incentives to demand legal changes; but also, within the context of the colonial order, they confronted lower costs in pushing legal claims. The educated spoke the language of the colonizers and the colonizers were dependent upon them for insight into local law and custom. Land litigation was pressed through the tribal councils that conducted their affairs in Kikuyu. It drew upon the knowledge of genealogies, which fell within the province of the elder traditionalists rather than the young educateds. Nonetheless, in dealing with the legal and administrative apparatus of the colonial state – the clerks, record keepers, registrars, and other elements of the bureaucracy – those who were educated and spoke English were better able to advocate their claims than were those who lacked proficiency in the language.

Within the context of colonial institutions, then, those families with a foot in the new social order – the urban job market, the colonial bureaucracy, or the ranks of the literate – were particularly active and effective in seeking the transformation of family law. The redefinition of the legal structure therefore resulted in an unequal apportionment of land endowments.[51]

The polarization of rural society in the Kikuyu reserves was noted by the colonial administrators of the time. In 1941, for example, the District Commissioner at Kiambu reported that "hundreds, possibly even thousands of acres have changed hands . . . during the past ten or fifteen years, and most of this has gone into the hands of a very few people, including chiefs, tribunal elders, and the educated minority."[52]

A statistical portrayal of these arguments, albeit a thin one, is offered in data collected in Kiambu in the early 1950s by Sluiter. Her data document a close relationship between education, income, and the holding of land. Over 40 percent of those with more than a form II education reside in the top income group; over 40 percent of the illiterates reside in the bottom income grouping (Table 1.3). Moreover, three-quarters of the top income group own plots of seven acres or more; over 70 percent of the lowest income group own plots of less than two acres (Table 1.4).

The transformation to Mau Mau

The course of political events leading to demands for constitutional progress in Kenya has been amply described elsewhere.[53] Politicians at the national level sought to accelerate the decolonization of Kenya by searching for political issues that would mobilize popular support and raise the costs of continued foreign occupation. As the stridency of their demands increased, the politicians sought to expand their political base. They began to recruit those who would take radical action to overturn the colonial order. When they sought such militants in the countryside, they tapped the reservoir of those who had lost out in the transformation of property rights in the reserves.

The Mau Mau wing of the nationalist revolt specialized in assassination. Near the end of 1953, the District Commissioner of Kiambu "ad-

Table 1.3. *Income and education in Sluiter's sample*

Education	Income			
	Low	Medium	Upper	High
Illiterate	129	128	45	8
Standard 1–6	36	36	20	8
Forms I & II	31	35	13	15
Higher	—	1	4	4

Note: The midpoints for the four categories are: low: Ksh. 222; medium: Ksh. 483; upper: Ksh. 987; high: Ksh. 2,000.
Chi-Square: 52.506, $p = 0.0001$. Gamma: 0.241, with an asymptotic standard error of 0.061. Somer's D (columns, given rows): 0.167, asymptotic standard error of 0.044.
Source: Greet Sluiter, "Confidential Report on Migrant Labour and Connected Matters in Four Villages in the Kiambu Reserve of Kenya," Department of Social Services, Training and Research of the Christian Council of Kenya, Mimeo, n.d., Kenya National Archives.

Table 1.4. *Average land endowments by income*

Average income	Average land holdings (acres)					
	<0.5	0.5–3.9	3.9–6.9	6.9–13.9	13.9–25	>25
Low	173	68	2	1	0	0
Medium	59	106	53	20	4	0
Upper	4	31	23	36	10	2
High	2	1	7	17	11	5

Chi-square: 423.569, $df = 15$, $p = 0.0001$. Gamma: 0.806, asymptotic standard error of 0.021. Somer's D (columns, given rows): 0.639, asymptotic standard error of 0.023.
Source: Sluiter, "Confidential Report."

mitted that half the murders in the district during the past year had been due to land cases."[54]

The Mau Mau wing of the nationalist movement recruited by oathing; the more militant the convert, the greater the number of oaths taken. As seen in Sluiter's data (Table 1.5), 74 percent of the richest members of her sample took no oath, whereas 20 percent took one or more. Of those taking more than one oath, 59 percent were drawn from the poorest segment of her sample. Its members suffered detention and jail. Over 90 percent of those from the highest income category were *not* detained;

The agrarian origins of Mau Mau

Table 1.5. *Average income and oath taking among males*

Average income (shillings per year)	No oath	One oath	More than one oath
Low	57	82	35
Medium	77	101	13
Upper	31	44	10
High	25	8	1

Chi-square: 33.547, *df* = 6, *p* = 0.0001. Gamma: −0.232, asymptotic standard error of 0.064. Somer's D (columns, given rows): −0.139, asymptotic error 0.039. *Source*: Sluiter, "Confidential Report."

Table 1.6. *Detention history by income, late 1950s*

Average income (shillings per year)	Not detained	Has been detained	Still detained
Low	139	35	22
Medium	169	19	12
Upper	76	9	2
High	30	0	1

Chi-square: 33.547, *df* = 6, *p* = 0.0001. Gamma: −0.232, asymptotic standard error of 0.064. Somer's D (columns, given rows): −0.139, asymptotic error 0.039. *Source*: Sluiter, "Confidential Report."

nearly 30 percent of those from the lowest income category were (Table 1.6). Of those who were detained, over one-half came from the very poorest segment of society.

The data thus confirm what Sorrenson, Lamb, Njonjo, and others have argued: that in the reserves, Mau Mau represented a civil war, which pitted those who had established a "rightful stake" in commercialized agriculture against those who had been disinherited of their legal entitlements.

CONCLUSION

In this chapter, we have launched our study of the contemporary political history of Kenya; of the politics and economics of agriculture; and of the political economy of development.

With respect to the last, we have focused on the significance of institutions. In particular, we have looked "beneath" markets, as it were, to

33

see how markets are formed. Thus, we have analyzed the way in which the vesting of property rights in the Highlands promoted the formation of a market for labor, and how the creation of property rights in the reserves promoted the production of commodities for sale in the city and abroad. And we have noted as well how the formation of institutions overrode incentives to behave opportunistically, thereby making possible the attainment of higher levels of welfare through exchange – of risks, credit, and commodities – between farmers and the state.

In probing the institutional foundation for exchange, this chapter has found much that supports an economic theory of institutions.[55] By introducing coercion into economic life, institutions enhance the capacity of individuals to make efficient choices. They curtail perverse incentives, as in the case of the settler farmers who might desire to cheat on loans; reduce uncertainty, as by creating reputations for probity; or equate the social with private returns to economic decisions, as by vesting property rights. Economic institutions make it in the private interests of individuals to use scarce resources productively.

Our analysis has brought us out of the world of market economics and into a world in which institutions have been forged in order to make possible the formation of markets. In so doing, it has moved beyond the realm of conventional economics. Indeed, it has moved it into the realm of politics. For, by focusing on institutions, the chapter has also brought us out of a world in which private parties make self-interested decisions from which all gain and into a world in which people possess the capacity for coercive acts – acts which extract involuntary transfers of wealth, privatize the benefits of economic progress, and inflict the costs of economic change upon others.

The history of settler agriculture illustrates that by creating centralized means for regulating economic activity, economic institutions may endow actors with the capacity to organize. They thereby may endow them with political power and set the stage for actions aimed not at the securing of joint gains but rather at the redistribution of income. The implications are ironic. For while often created to promote the capacity to secure mutually enhancing gains, economic institutions also promote the capacity to secure involuntary redistributions of income. The very agencies that underpin the market promote the means to violate its welfare-enhancing properties. This irony was most vividly dramatized by the manner in which those who dominated the institutions of Highlands agriculture failed to organize means of "trading around" the externalities prevalent in the dairy industry, with the winners compensating the losers – as the Coase Theorem would have it. Instead, they used the power conferred upon them to avoid paying compensation and to secure the benefits of the new farming system for free.

34

The agrarian origins of Mau Mau

The study of institutions leads not only to an appreciation of their impact upon the securing of efficiency at a given time. It also leads to an understanding of their impact upon economic change. This lesson too we learned by examining the introduction of dairying into settler agriculture. Those who controlled the economic institutions regulating commercial farming used their position of power to appropriate the benefits and avoid the costs of economic change. It was by appreciating the significance of such facts that we came to understand how the growth of prosperity that marked economic change in Kenya led as well to political violence.

Our examination of the role of institutions led to another insight, one which calls for further revisions in the contemporary theory of institutions. In an effort to apply economic reasoning to the analysis of institutions, contemporary economists — such as Feeny, North and Thomas, or Hayami and Ruttan[56] — have argued that shifts in the physical proportionality of factors lead to subsequent adjustments in institutional structures. By analogy with price theory in the study of markets, changes in the physical quantities of productive factors, they hold, alter relative prices and thus induce a demand for institutional change.

The Kenyan materials demonstrate the need for a more political interpretation. Rather than reasoning in terms of relative physical abundance, they suggest, the analysis should stress the role of legal entitlements. For, in the case of the Kikuyu, the colonial incursion, while *limiting* access to land rights, *increased* access to land. The colonial settlers promoted the migration of the Kikuyu into the White Highlands; they thereby radically expanded the range of Kikuyu settlement. What they restricted was the possibility of establishing land rights. It was thus not any diminishing of physical quantities of land that led to the restructuring of tribal institutions among the Kikuyu. Rather, it was diminishing access to land *rights*. It was politics that determined who possessed such rights; the issue was resolved by the white colonists and by the tribal elites, i.e., those who held power under colonialism. By shifting attention away from physical proportionalities to rights, the Kenyan materials once again underscore the significance of the political element in economic institutions.

The chapter focuses as well on the second major subject of the book: the study of agrarian politics and, in particular, agrarian revolution. In the literature on the developing areas, one approach sees rural rebellion as being part of the rise of nationalism. This approach has been applied to the developing world generally by Rupert Emerson[57] and to Africa by a host of scholars;[58] most relevant to this work, it has been applied to Kenya by Carl Rosberg and John Nottingham in their classic study of Mau Mau.[59] In the African context, the nationalist interpretation takes on tones of racial liberalism, as political conflict is seen as a struggle for racial justice and an end to discrimination based upon color.

Our interpretation of Mau Mau dissents from the nationalist interpretation by revealing that while the struggle may have been between whites and blacks, its origins did not lie in a preference for racial exclusion. The Europeans did not want a *white* Highlands. They wanted high land values; when importing labor augmented such values, they brought in more blacks and when land values could be raised by clearing land of blacks and their cattle, then blacks were chased away. Moreover, the colonial settlers did not form a uniform bloc, as the language of white against black, or colonial occupier and African native, would imply. The struggle between owners and laborers followed a previous struggle among the colonists themselves: between dairy farmer and grain grower, for example. The political struggles thus followed a logic that was not racial. And the subsequent violence was therefore caused by forces other than those highlighted by a nationalist account of political protest in the developing areas.

Other theories of rural violence have been put forward by the dependency school, and these too have been applied to Kenya.[60] A schematic account of the dependency interpretation would hold that through imperialism, foreign capital secured domination of the Kenyan economy; that, by seizing land and using the power of the state to regulate labor contracts, foreign capital was able to extract surplus value. Mau Mau is therefore to be seen as but another instance of a worldwide struggle against capitalism. Our account reveals two major deficiencies in this interpretation. Insofar as Mau Mau involved a struggle between workers and foreign owners of capital, it did so on the Highlands; but that struggle represented but one wing of the rebellion. The theory is therefore a weak one, accounting for but part of what it seeks to explain. In addition, the theory is misleading. For, as with the nationalist account, it imputes a uniformity to the interests of the parties in conflict; foreign capitalists fall neatly into the ranks of the exploiters and Africans into the ranks of the exploited. But, as we have seen, both segments of the population were in fact divided. The Europeans quarreled among themselves and internal differentiation had emerged among the colonized. In the reserves, there was no uniformity of interests; the battle was being fought within the ranks of those subject to colonial occupation.

The analysis calls into question a third prominent stream of the literature on rural violence: that of the moral economists. This approach also strives to account for rural violence in terms of opposition to the spread of capitalism; but it places greater emphasis on the way in which the market economy leads to a restructuring of pre-capitalist social forms.

The agrarian origins of Mau Mau

Traditional societies are held to be integrative. Through patterns of sharing, reciprocity, and mutual obligation, they secure a fundamental form of equality: they guarantee to all the entitlements by which to secure their subsistence. With the rise of the market, however, traditional elites come to seek personal gains and to reject communal claims. Within the structure of traditional institutions, patterns of inequality thus arise; the institutions lose their moral force; and they become subject to attacks by disadvantaged outcasts, often in the cause of the traditional values that they now violate.[61]

Our account dramatically confirms what the moral economists assert: that the rise of commercial agriculture leads to a rejection of claims to economic entitlements. But it also reveals a major weakness. For the basic logic of the moral economists presumes that communities stand in opposition to markets. It also assumes that communities are incorporative.

Our analysis challenges both assumptions. For we found that the stimulus of market incentives led to the formation of communities. This was true among the European settlers; it was also true in the reserves, where lineages acquired renewed importance. And neither form of community was incorporative. The settler community sought to liquidate the entitlements of squatters; the lineages to disinherit kin.

The Kenyan materials thus offer much to support the moral economy approach to the study of rural change. But they also highlight its limitations. In particular, they suggest that the approach could be strengthened by recognizing that those who seek the benefits of markets can also seek the benefits of communities, if only the better to secure market-generated outcomes. Communities are not anti-market; by supporting reputations and promoting trust, they can enhance market forces. Nor are they "social facts" that stand inherently opposed to individual self-interest; they are organized by individuals. The moral economy approach, in short, should be more firmly grounded on microfoundations.[62]

Among those criticizing the dependency and moral economy schools are the class conflict theorists. These too have written on the Kenyan materials. Kitching, Cowen, Sorrenson, and others stress the role of "accumulators" in Kikuyu rural life and locate the principal source of conflict in the efforts of these agents to secure land.[63] The account of the class theorists strongly parallels our own. But it shares some of the weaknesses of the other theories and it evidences a weakness unique to itself. This last proves particularly instructive because it so strongly affects the use of the theory in historical interpretation.

The class analytic theory shares with others the limitation of being incomplete. Those who have applied it to Kenya have generated powerful insights into one wing of the rural rebellion – that in the reserves – but they have failed to integrate that analysis with their treatment of the squatter wing. More significantly, they have also failed to take into account the importance of institutions: to examine the dynamics of class formation within the social institutions of the tribe.

Kitching and others explore the role of what they call the rural petit bourgeoisie; but they analyze this class as if it existed in an institutional vacuum. Clearly, however, the "accumulators" operated within an ethnographic structure. By appreciating the significance of tribal institutions, our analysis has been able to incorporate into its account both wings of the Mau Mau rebellion. It has also enabled us to achieve greater insight into the mechanics of class formation and into its historical significance.

Sahlins's notion of a predatory lineage system, briefly noted above, provides a basis for analyzing the process of rural class formation in terms of the ethnographic context within which economic change took place during the colonial period. Predatory (or segmentary) lineage systems exist, Sahlins theorizes, in poor societies where the ecological setting makes for a relatively uniform but highly uncertain range of opportunities. In such a setting, lineages spread out and colonize diverse "niches." As analyzed by Sahlins, these niches tend to be ecological – areas of better than average grazing, for example; but viewed in a broader framework, they could be economic (e.g., a line of trade) or political (a "colonizable" bureaucracy, for example). Under initial conditions of Sahlins's model, it makes sense for an individual to maintain a highly ramified kinship network. For the acknowledgment of a wide range of kin facilitates access to a broad range of opportunities. The web of kinship serves as a diversified portfolio. It serves as a form of insurance.

This model becomes a model of social change when the initial conditions alter. Say that an activity – or niche – becomes especially attractive, offering a stream of income that is more lucrative or more certain than that offered by others. Following such a change, persons may want to concentrate their holdings in this one, high-yielding asset. Rather than dispersing their holdings by acknowledging a wide range of kinship obligations, they may, for example, prefer instead to concentrate them and to divest themselves of unwanted hangers-on.

Our analysis suggests that such a transition happened in Kenya.[64] It has also happened elsewhere. Kinship and lineage systems have been transformed from systems of access to systems of accumulation, in which property and wealth are closely held by subsets of family members. The result is the economic ascendancy of some lineage segments and the subordination of others. In Europe, most dramatically, people who in former times would have been treated as kin instead came to be treated as laborers or serfs. Their former kin, in turn, became gentry.[65]

The chapter has demonstrated how taking into account the social institutions of the tribe enables us to integrate the squatter and the reserve

The agrarian origins of Mau Mau

wing of the Mau Mau rebellion. It also leads us fundamentally to rein-
terpret the historical significance of the revolt. While Kitching and others
see in the transformation of rural society that led to Mau Mau the
formation of a petit bourgeoisie, we instead see the formation of a different class. What was emerging from the combination of an agrarian
economic base and a lineage-based social context was not a nascent
bourgeoisie but rather a group more akin to an incipient gentry – managers not of individually owned, industrial corporations but rather of
family-owned, agricultural estates.

This reinterpretation bears significantly upon the third theme of this
book: the development experience of Kenya. In the fight against Mau
Mau, the British cleared the Highlands of Kikuyu squatters; they cleared
Nairobi of Kikuyu laborers. And, moving northward along the foot of
the Aberdares, they severed the connection between the mountains and
reserves, isolating the armed forces in the mountains forests from their
sources of information, recruits, and weapons. They then reestablished
military and administrative control of each of the Kikuyu districts. In
each district, they sought allies. The colonial government readily enlisted
the support of those whom the insurgents had attacked: the wealthy, the
landed, and those educated in mission schools.

While applying the stick on the one hand, the government offered the
carrot on the other. With the cooperation of the Kikuyu elites, the government implemented an intensive program of rural development: one
designed to bring prosperity to the reserves through the growing and
marketing of cash crops.[66] In the fight against Mau Mau, the aggressive
elites of the Kikuyu reserves thus gained even greater access to the coercive
power and economic resources of the colonial government.[67]

Mau Mau convinced the British that no white minority could hold
power in Kenya. The Mau Mau rebellion therefore brought independence
to Kenya. And the defeat of Mau Mau meant that when power was seized
by the indigenous inhabitants of Kenya, it was seized by the conservative
fraction of Kenya's rural society: those with a commitment to accumulation, investment, and private property.

Indeed, when Jomo Kenyatta, the leader of the Kikuyu, seized control
of independent Kenya, he allied the state with the fortunes of the incipient
gentry. Lineage ties bound rural elites to State House in the capital city.[68]
In contrast to other African governments, whose policies have favored
their urban, industrial interests, the government of postindependence
Kenya therefore possessed strong incentives instead to manage its national
economy out of a regard for rural, landed interests.

As we shall see in the chapters that follow, after independence there
remained the task of defining the institutions that would structure economic and political life in Kenya, and radicals and conservatives fun-

39

damentally disagreed as to how they should be structured. But Kenya's conservative core ran very deep. As this chapter has shown, it had been laid down in the very political struggles that had brought the nation to independence. Our analysis of these struggles thus helps to account for the characteristic and exceptional features of Kenya's postindependence development.

Appendix 1A: Kinship and stratification[1]

I have stressed the isomorphism between Sahlins's model of a predatory lineage system[2] and the holding of a diversified portfolio of income-generating assets. This appendix elaborates the argument and explores its implications.

THE MODEL

Assume that economic actors seek to maximize the expected value of their incomes, but that they are also risk averse. Assume that the nature of the society is such that rights to income-yielding assets are defined in terms of kin relations. And assume that the economic environment is marginal, by which is meant that (1) the stream of income generated by each asset is risky, i.e., possesses a large variance; and (2) the lower value of the variance of the income streams falls below the subsistence level.

Under such circumstances, risk averse economic agents would seek access to diversified portfolios of economic assets; each actor will seek to create claims to income streams whose risks are uncorrelated. Given that economic rights are defined in terms of kin relations, these implications follow:

1. Investments in rights to income can best be made by investing in the maintenance of family relations.

2. In (evolutionary) equilibrium:

(a) Persons will do better whose families ramify over many economic "niches," i.e., who possess assets whose risks are uncorrelated.

(b) And insofar as large families can occupy a greater diversity of economic niches, persons will do better who are members of large families.

Such a system would lead to a social structure characterized by openness, sharing, and the transfer of resources from those who are (mo-

41

mentarily) privileged to those who are not. The maintenance of ties with large numbers of kin is costly. But the payments purchase the benefits of insurance.

Now assume that there is a change in the economic environment. In particular, assume that the nature of the economy changes such that assets located in one particular niche now generate income streams that dominate in value those generated by other assets. This change could result from a reduction in the variance of the income stream, while preserving its mean; a shift in the expected value of the income stream, such that the utility generated by its mean more than compensates for its variance; or, what is less likely, both an increase in the mean and a decline in the variance.

Such a change in the economic environment could lead to changes in economic strategies. Those who are members of family segments that control the preferred asset no longer would possess an incentive to invest in the maintenance of kinship ties with family members who occupy other economic niches. For the better endowed family segments, the maintenance of ties with large numbers of kin remains costly but generates fewer benefits. The less fortunately endowed kin would now find that contributions that in former times generated a right to share in the income streams controlled by their brethren would now fail to elicit acknowledgment; they would find their claims excluded. Insofar as rights to assets are allocated by kin relations, the range of kinship would thus be foreshortened. And some kinship segments would become wealthy; they would possess "private" assets, which generate superior streams of income. Others would become poor; they would find their claims to share in the superior assets rejected by those who control them.

Shifts in the economic environment would thus transform kinship from an open system of lineage relations, which provides a diversified portfolio of economic assets, to a closed system of family property, which protects the rise of privilege. Rather than being a universalistic and leveling institution, kinship would instead become exclusionary. It would become a source of inequality.

IMPLICATIONS

This analysis offers insight into divergent patterns of social stratification and political conflict.

Differences within Kenya

The works of Cowen, Kitching, Njonjo, and others provoked a recognition of the exceptional nature of Central Province and of the Kikuyu.

Appendix 1A: Kinship and stratification

Others hastened to point out that in other regions and ethnic groups, far less accumulation had taken place; "communal" institutions remained comparatively strong; and far more opposition had been expressed to the formation of private property.[3] So, too, in the world of politics. As will be seen in Chapter 2, ideologies promoting economic accumulation and private property found favor in much of the Central Province and among many of the Kikuyu; persons from other regions and other ethnic groups, however, often favored economic equality and socialism.[4]

As will become clear in the next chapter, the rhetoric that dominates the scholarship and politics of Kenya would suggest that these differences arise from contrasting levels of prosperity. Richer regions and peoples favor private property and accumulation, whereas poorer ones favor communal rights and sharing. The analysis advocated herein suggests that this relationship between wealth and political preference arises from a common grounding in the structure of risk.

The richer regions of Kenya lie at higher elevations, with greater and more reliable rainfalls; the poorer groups lie at lower elevations with less and less certain rain. In addition, the groups living at higher elevations inhabit an environment favoring the production of cash crops; at lower elevations fewer crops of high value can be grown. A consequence of these differences is that those living in the more risky ecological zones possess stronger incentives to maintain widely ramified families so as to guarantee access to a wider distribution of farm sites, grazing zones, and ecological settings. And those dwelling in more favored environments possess stronger incentives to restructure kin relations: to exclude and to accumulate, rather than to purchase social insurance.

As Parker Shipton has argued concerning the Luo, a group that lives in a marginal ecological zone, nothing in Luo culture opposes the seeking of wealth; the Luo are consummate traders, for example. "But [wealth] must be shared with kin. . . . "[5] And a major reason for this, he argues, is that kinship represents a mechanism for dealing with the high level of risk characteristic of their economic environment.

Cross-national differences

Not only does our argument help to account for differences within Kenya, as between the Kikuyu and Luo; it clarifies as well differences that arise cross nationally.

Studying the Yoruba of Western Nigeria, Sara Berry offers an analysis similar to that advanced here, but of a situation that resulted in the strengthening of lineages and the erosion of class differences.[6]

We have argued that with the rise of commercial agriculture, land achieved new value among the Kikuyu: cash crops could be grown profitably for sale in Nairobi and abroad. As will be demonstrated later, the returns to the most profitable of these crops – such as coffee and tea – remained largely untaxed. Berry argues, by contrast, that in Western Nigeria the returns to agricultural production remained marginal and uncertain; this has been particularly true since the oil price rise of the 1970s. She also argues that in both the colonial and postindependence periods the government severely depressed the profitability of cocoa production. The result was that "West African cultivators sought flexibility. ... Their strategy ... has been to diversify their options, rather than to specialize completely. ... "[7] They maintain "a diversified portfolio of assets and access to markets,"[8] and they do so by investing in kinship and communal ties.

One result was the strengthening of the lineage system; the other, a weakening of the structure of stratification. For, in Berry's words, "class interests exist and are perceived, but ... diversification reinforces social relationships, some of which may cut across or dilute the emergence of class ... solidarity."[9]

CONCLUSION

In any agrarian society, family and kinship constitute primary elements of social organization. Kinship allocates access to productive assets and to streams of income. This analysis has sought to show how different economic environments and in particular different structures of risk promote the selection of different strategies toward the use of kinship and thus the creation of different social forms. It has also sought to demonstrate how such differences could result in contrasting patterns of social stratification and political conflict. It has thereby sought to explain why different social and political patterns emerge in different rural settings.[10]

2

Material interest and political preference:
the agrarian origins of political conflict

This chapter advances the historical narrative begun in the last. It covers the period from the Mau Mau rebellion to the early years of independence. In doing so, it moves beyond a discussion of the local politics of the Kikuyu to an analysis of politics at the national level.

At the time of independence, Kenya was swept by controversy. Party competition provided one source of conflict; ideological differences furnished a second; disputes concerning the constitutional order provided a third, as some Kenyans favored a centralized state while others favored a federal form of government. By exploring these issues and the way in which they were resolved, the chapter accounts for the basic institutional endowment bequeathed to postindependence Kenya. It gives further insight into the foundations for the distinctly antiradical commitment in Kenyan politics. And it lays the groundwork for understanding characteristic patterns of postindependence politics: the rivalries between interests and factions within the context of a single national party system.

While centrally preoccupied with the analysis of Kenya's contemporary political history, this chapter also pursues broader themes. It continues the study of agrarian politics. And it returns once again to the political economy of development. Here it breaks new ground.

In the multitude of studies of contemporary Kenya, two kinds of works stand out. Some analyze Kenya's development in terms of economics, and explore the impact of such factors as the systems of agrarian production, foreign investment, and multinational firms.[1] Others stress the role of politics, dwelling on the personality of politicians or on critical elections or party conferences.[2] This chapter seeks to integrate the two literatures. The focus on institutions, and the blending of economic and political analysis that the study of institutions promotes, permits it to do so.

On the one hand, the chapter advances strongly materialistic claims. The preferences of key actors concerning the kinds of institutions that

45

should prevail in independent Kenya, it argues, were shaped by their location in Kenya's agrarian economy. On the other, it argues that institutions stand autonomous – albeit, but partially so – from their economic base. Politicians compete for power by exploiting the opportunities offered by political institutions. Economic interests receive organized political expression because they are aggregated and processed by politicians. By affecting the calculations of political entrepreneurs, institutions thereby shape the way in which economic interests receive effective definition. What constitutes an economic interest, in short, becomes politically determined.

The impact of economic interests upon politics and the impact of institutions upon economic interests: the discussion of these themes moves the book toward an institutionally centered variant of political economy.

THE POLITICS OF TRANSITION: AN OVERVIEW

Because of Mau Mau, the British government decided to withdraw from Kenya. To do so successfully, it had first to pacify the forces of opposition. It therefore had first to resolve basic controversies surrounding the allocation of land rights and the institutional structure of power.

In the civil war that engulfed the Kikuyu, the counterrevolutionaries prevailed. But it was in their interests to revive, and indeed to champion, the demands for land that had fueled the rebellion. For the counterrevolutionary elites sought, above all, to stabilize their claims to land in the reserves; and they feared the political machinations of the landless. Those who had helped the British to defeat the insurgents therefore formed common cause with the vanquished in demanding access to land. And the British, in an effort to stabilize the central portions of Kenya, agreed to end racial exclusivity in the Highlands and to settle African farmers there.

When the colonial government agreed to promote African settlement, it immediately encountered rival land claims. With different groups competing for the fruits of independence, the land issue became the major source of political controversy at the time of the transition to African rule. The issue was contested within a rapidly altering structure of political power. The anticolonial militants remained in detention. But in 1954, under the Lyttleton Constitution, eight Africans were elected to the Legislature; and under the Lennox-Boyd Constitution of 1958, the number increased to fourteen.

Beginning in 1959, the pace of change accelerated even more. In that year the British formally announced their commitment to a resettlement program. And while negotiating with the African leaders in the Legislative

46

The agrarian origins of political conflict

Council the specifics of land resettlement, they agreed in 1960 to give Africans a majority of sixty-five seats in the Legislative Council and a majority of ministries in the Executive Council. The result was a scramble for power among competing local elites, who formed two political parties: the Kenya African National Union (KANU) and the Kenya African Democratic Union (KADU). At the center of their differences lay conflicts over land.

KANU won the series of elections in the pre-independence maneuvering for political domination in Kenya. At pivotal times in the negotiations, however, KANU leaders boycotted the proceedings, protesting the continued detention of nationalist militants, particularly Jomo Kenyatta. KADU, while a minority party, established close ties with the governmental administration in Kenya and with powerful economic interests, including those of the white settlers.[3] Because of KANU's electoral victories, it was a KANU run government to which the British ultimately surrendered power; and they did so while allowing Kenyatta to assume the presidency. But KADU extracted significant concessions of its own. In particular, it secured a federal structure of government, in which power devolved upon a series of regional assemblies – assemblies whose most significant duty was the administration of land rights.

During this period, disputes over land provoked national political controversies. Political preferences were dictated by material factors, such as access to land, physical location, or group size. But preferences were also dictated, and the course of alliances shaped, by the emerging structure of political institutions, and in particular, the bureaucracy, the electoral system, and the federal structure of government. All three institutions shaped the course of the land issue. And all three were themselves shaped by interests in land.

THE SHAPING OF MATERIAL INTERESTS: THE INSTITUTIONAL ORIGINS OF "TRIBAL" CLAIMS

The structure of political institutions helped to ensure that the economic interest in land assumed political form in the guise of ethnic claims.

African administration

As elsewhere in Africa, the British had attempted to set up in Kenya a system of rule based upon traditional political structures. The absence of centralized traditional states and the presence of settler colonists made it more difficult than elsewhere to institute the system of indirect rule.[4] Nonetheless, the British established "tribal" reserves; they structured administrative and legal services into units corresponding to "tribal"

47

groups.[5] Administrative districts bore names such as Kikuyu, Kamba, Elgeyo, or Marakwet, suggesting the effort to create administrative boundaries that corresponded to ethnic groupings. Particularly given the flux characteristic of ethnic identifications,[6] such efforts to identify tribal groups were often fantastical. Nonetheless, once the colonizers had established juridical facts in accord with their ethnographic fantasies, Africans subject to these jurisdictions had no choice but to behave as if the theories were true.

This initial pattern of administration proved critical to the evolution of conflicts over land. For the British vested control over land rights in the hands of the local governments; and if African subjects wanted to claim land, they had to prove to their overlords that they were a member of the relevant tribe. Entitlements to real property were allocated through an administrative structure that defined property rights in ethnic terms.[7]

The electoral system

Following Mau Mau, the British government sought to divest itself of the costs of imperial rule; it therefore sought means of transferring political power to local representatives. The problem then became how best to pick those Africans to whom power was to be transferred.[8]

As elsewhere in Africa, the British chose elections as instruments for orchestrating their retreat from imperial rule[9]: they conferred power upon those who proved able to command an electoral majority. Tactical considerations constrained the form of election chosen, however. In the mid 1950s, one factor was the need for the support of the white colonists while fighting a black uprising. Another was that during the rebellion means had to be found for allowing political competition while restricting the spread of dissent. The need to placate the settlers and to avoid the spread of sedition led the British to restrict the range and scope of electoral competition. Until the 1960s, candidates for national office in the Legislative Assembly could compete for votes; but candidates were permitted to campaign *within their own districts only*. By preventing the formation by African politicians of national political organizations, this form of election reduced the level of threat to the settler minority; it also prevented "political agitators" from moving from the "hot" districts – i.e., the districts of the Kikuyu – to the districts occupied by "peaceful" tribes.[10]

During the period in which the British Government was organizing its political retreat from Kenya, then, it laid the institutional foundation for an African political profession: a stratum of persons who sought high office and who could achieve positions of power by winning votes. But the manner in which the British formed this profession left each national level politician in Kenya beholden to voters who were drawn from a specific administrative district and thus from a particular tribe. When in 1960 the Highlands were thrown open and African citizens sought to expand the magnitude of their property holdings, they had to press their claims through a political leadership whose prospects for office were contingent upon ethnic service. Material interests were therefore pressed forward as ethnic claims.

The structure of political institutions thus influenced the way in which economic interests – the demands for land – received organized political expression.

ECONOMIC INTERESTS AND PARTISAN ALLIANCES

Land is a fixed resource; a group's physical location therefore influences its economic interests. Groups adjoining the Highlands had often used them for grazing; they also had members "on the ground," as it were: laborers, tenants, and their families, who lived on the farmlands of the European settlers. Physical proximity to the Highlands therefore motivated claims to the lands being vacated by the colonists (see Map 2.1).

Physical location played another role. Groups adjacent to each other were more likely to advance competing claims to land and more likely therefore to see each other as adversaries than as allies.

Population density also shaped interests. All else being equal, the greater the number of people in a particular group, the more crowded its land endowment. Being relatively more scarce in crowded groups, land was more highly valued. Crowded populations exhibited greater land hunger. For other groups seeking land, large groups therefore appeared dangerous. On the other hand, in the political competition for scarce resources, their large numbers made these groups valued allies.

A third factor was wealth. A prime source of wealth was location in the material environment; another was access to the streams of income generated by the commercialization of agriculture. Those who lived at high elevations, where rainfall was reliable and abundant and temperatures moderate, prospered more than those who lived in semi-arid zones; for coffee, tea, pyrethrum, and other cash crops of high value did better at high elevations. And those who lived close to transport routes or urban markets possessed opportunities for incomes not available to others. Groups that were prosperous as a result of these physical and economic advantages possessed the financial resources with which to back up their claims to land. Being weighted by income, their claims registered more persuasively.

Material factors, such as location, size, and wealth, thus defined interests in the struggle for land. The institutional environment structured

49

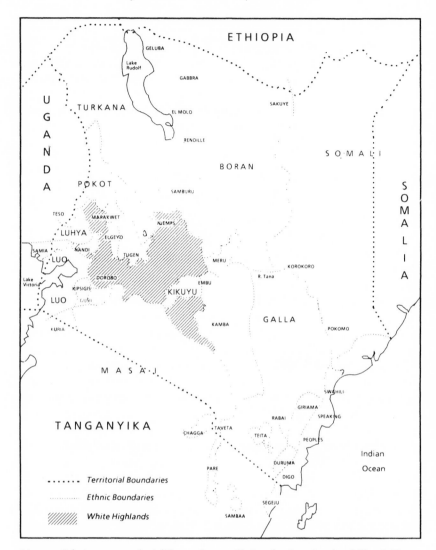

Map 2.1. Ethnic groups, colonial Kenya. *Source*: Christopher Leo, *Land and Class in Kenya* (Toronto: University of Toronto Press, 1984). From a map drawn by J. K. Mbazira, Makerere Institute of Social Research; used by permission.

the course of the resultant political controversy. In particular, rules for election shaped the way in which political organizers mobilized groups whose interests were defined by such material factors. The impact of political institutions was most clearly revealed when the rules for elections changed.

The agrarian origins of political conflict

Table 2.1. *Population of ethnic groups, 1969*

	Total	Percentage
Kikuyu	2,201,632	20.0
Abaluhya	1,453,302	13.3
Luo	1,521,595	13.9
Kalenjin	1,203,999	11.0
Kamba	1,050,177	9.6
Kisii	701,697	6.4
Coastal	708,849	6.5
Non-African	207,516	2.0
Total	10,956,501	

Source: Republic of Kenya, *Compendium to Volume 1: 1979 Population Census* (Nairobi: Central Bureau of Statistics, July 1981), p. 8. The figures for the Kamba represent the sum of the population of Machakos and Kitui districts.

Initial rivalries

Location, size, and wealth: all three factors helped to render the Kikuyu a powerful competitor for land. Prior to Mau Mau, as we have seen, nearly one-third of the Kikuyu lived on the Highlands. Following their clearance from the Highlands and the subsequent military emergency, many reinfiltrated the Highland districts – Nyandarua, Naivasha, and Nakuru – adjacent to their homelands. Kikuyu communities sprang up as well along the forested rim, particularly in Burnet Forest, the Cherangani and Nandi Hills, Molo, Njoro, and Tinderet. Not only did physical location strengthen the land claims of the Kikuyu; so too did their numbers. Best estimates suggest that they accounted for 20 percent of Kenya's total population, making them the largest single ethnic group in Kenya (Table 2.1). In addition, the Kikuyu were wealthy. They lived in highly productive ecological zones and so possessed access to the most valuable of Kenya's cash crops. They lived near the Nairobi market and could supply it at lower cost, and therefore with higher profits, than could others. They had reaped benefits from military occupation, albeit at high cost. The security forces had created a dense network of rural roads. And pacification had featured the carrot as well as the stick, the carrot being a crash program of small farmer development.[11] Politically subdued the Kikuyu may have been; but economically, they emerged from the period of reconstruction following the Mau Mau rebellion centrally positioned in Kenya's growing rural economy. The Kikuyu therefore had both the desire and the means to register their demands for land.

Most threatened by the claims of the Kikuyu were those who resided at higher elevations in the Rift Valley or near the districts bordering on the Kikuyu homelands – that is, in the areas that the Kikuyu tended to colonize – or who had grazed their cattle in the Highlands or worked there as laborers. The groups most directly threatened were the Kalenjin speakers – the Nandi, Elgeyo, Tugen, Kipsigis, Marakwet, and Njemps. The Abaluhya and the Luo were less close and therefore less threatened.

Incentives for cooperation

After the military defeat of Mau Mau, the colonial government had less need for a quiescent settler population. And with the end of the insurgency, it feared less the contagion of sedition. In 1959 the British therefore legalized the formation of national political organizations by African subjects; and in 1960 the Colonial Office agreed that African politicians could hold a majority of the seats in the Kenyan parliament.

These institutional changes made an immediate impact on the way in which economic interests in land assumed organized political expression. The issue was no longer purely conflictual. Given that power was now to devolve upon that team of African politicians who were capable of securing a *national* political majority, the issue now generated mixed motives. Being valued but fixed in quantity, land continued to generate conflict; one group's gains necessarily represented another group's loss. But because the allocation of this resource was to be determined by government policy, the land issue also promoted cooperation. In order to acquire the power to govern the allocation of this resource, competing groups had first to form political alliances that could generate numeric majorities at the polls. Groups whose economic interests had rendered them rivals therefore began – for political reasons – to form alliances.

A variety of factors helped to determine the resulting coalitional structure.[12] Basic were factors that shaped the choice of whether to ally with the Kikuyu and their claims to the White Highlands or with the Kalenjin in opposition to the Kikuyu. Two groups proved pivotal in the maneuvering: the Abaluhya and the Luo. The Abaluhya claimed Trans Nzoia, where Kikuyu had worked as farm laborers and therefore claimed land; the Luo possessed no land claims that conflicted with those of the Kikuyu. The Luo did, however, possess claims conflicting with those of the Abaluhya, as in the area of Maseno, and with the Kalenjin, in the areas bordering the Kipsigis and Nandi Hills.[13] In the search for partners in the competition for political power in Kenya, the Luo therefore allied with the Kikuyu; they joined KANU. The other groups combined into KADU and sought to forestall efforts by their rivals to secure a political majority. Both parties sought allies from groups that did not live directly adjacent the Highlands: persons in the semi-arid zones of the East and North and people along the Coast.

ECONOMIC INTERESTS AND PREFERENCES CONCERNING INSTITUTIONS

The analysis thus far has stressed the impact of political institutions upon the course of economic conflict. But it must also be recognized that institutions are themselves chosen. And the controversies sweeping Kenya at the time of independence offer ample evidence of the power of material interests in structuring preferences concerning institutions. Economic interests strongly influenced convictions as to what institutions were appropriate for the governance of economic and political life in independent Kenya.

While access to land endowments helps to determine economic interests in an agrarian economy, so too does wealth: entitlement to a portion of the streams of income originating from the commercialization of agriculture. Differential access to such income streams further refined political preferences in the postindependence period.

Two groups, for example, could possess near identical positions with respect to the White Highlands; they could, as a consequence, fall equally under the shadow of the Kikuyu threat and so agree to ally. But they could differ in terms of the degree to which they had participated in the commercial transformation of agriculture. In Kenya, geography is destiny, to a significant degree. Higher elevations yield greater and more reliable rains and more moderate temperatures, and valuable cash crops tend to be produced on the sides of the mountains and hills (see Figure 2.1). One group could dwell at elevations that supported the rise of smallholder coffee, pyrethrum, tea, or dairy farms, for example. The other might struggle at lower elevations, eking out a bare subsistence. Put short, the one could be rich, the other poor. Politically, this difference would matter.

KANU included the Kikuyu; and of all the groups in Kenya, the Kikuyu were the richest. Their physical and economic location, as well as their history, endowed them with advantages unattainable by others. KADU, by contrast, contained many groups that lived outside the zones yielding riches from cash cropping. The Pokot and the Masai, for example, dwelt within the semi-arid zones. Other groups, such as the Abaluhya, lived in more favored climes; but their fortunes were limited by the costs incurred in moving goods from their farm sites to major urban markets. None of the KADU groups had reaped the rewards of the programs for the intensive development of smallholder agriculture mounted as part of the pacification program in the central portions of Kenya.

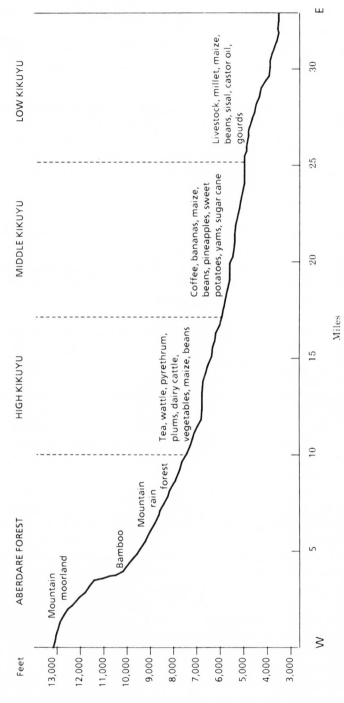

Figure 2.1. Agricultural cross section. *Source:* D. R. J. Taylor, "Agricultural Change in Kikuyuland," in *Environment and Land Use in Africa,* eds. M. F. Thomas and G. W. Whittington (London: Methuen, 1959), p. 485.

The agrarian origins of political conflict

There were variations *within* KANU and KADU, however, and these must also be stressed. Allied with the Kikuyu in KANU, after all, were the Luo, who occupied territories ill-favored for commercial agricultural production. They lived at low elevations, in relatively hot and arid zones; their soils were difficult to till; and many of their lands were infested by tsetse fly, thus limiting their ability to raise stock. They could grow none of the major cash crops that had brought prosperity to the Highlands of Kenya; nor, as a consequence of the fly, could they profitably raise dairy cattle. What wealth they had came largely from the export of manpower. And within the Kikuyu large differentials of income prevailed between landowners and the landless, growers of cash crops and labor migrants, and the residents of districts occupying favorable agricultural zones and those with inferior natural endowments.

Similar variations arose within KADU. Allied with the Abaluhya in KADU were some, like the Nandi, who were among the most prosperous in Kenya's agrarian economy. They had established individualized land rights in the 1950s and invested heavily in commercial farming. They specialized in particular in dairy production and the breeding of grade cattle. While in no way producing commodities that in quantity or value totaled the same magnitudes as those that flowed from the Kikuyu, the Nandi did produce a level of output that in *per capita* terms served to make them among the richest groups in Kenya (see Table 2.2).

As with access to land, access to the stream of income generated by commercially based agricultural industries shaped fundamental political preferences. These differences affected the content of the programs that were adapted by the two party alliances. In particular, in the early stages of the KANU/KADU rivalry, they affected the parties' stands on the structure of government and the scope of the market.

KADU contained groups that had grazed cattle on the Highlands and lived on its rim; it particularly drew its members from groups that had lived proximate to the districts colonized by the Kikuyu. While containing some who, like the Nandi, were wealthy, KADU also contained others, such as the Abaluhya, who were not. The groups incorporated into KADU wanted as much of the land vacated by the Europeans as they could get; they feared the competition of the Kikuyu, who, as tenants and laborers, were established on the ground, were numerous and driven by "land hunger," and were rich. The party responded by advocating the adoption of a federal constitution, in which regional barriers would be erected to land settlement;[14] within these divisions, the land market would be allowed to operate subject to oversight by regional political authorities. KADU thus advocated an organization of state power and a relationship between the government and the market that would protect and enhance the economic prospects of its constituents.

55

Table 2.2. *Total marketed output, 1969*

	K£ (thousands)	K£ per capita
Kakamega	1,039	1.32
Bungoma	877	2.48
Busia	331	1.66
Kisii	2,082	3.08
S. Nyanza	1,291	1.95
C. Nyanza	n.a.	n.a.
Siaya	579	0.74
Nyeri	1,907	5.28
Kiambu	2,500	5.25
Nyandarua	2,000	11.30
Kirinyaga	1,160	5.34
Murang'a	1,436	3.20
Nandi	1,165	5.58
Kericho	930	1.94
Elgeyo	70	0.44
Baringo	n.a.	n.a.
Uasin Gishu	n.a.	n.a.
Nakuru	n.a.	n.a.
Machakos	2,783	3.93
Kitui	257	0.74
Meru	2,664	4.46
Embu	978	5.46
Kwale	397	1.93
Kilifi	945	3.07
Taita	485	4.37

Computed from: Judith Heyer, "The Origins of Regional Inequalities in Smallholder Agriculture in Kenya, 1920–1973," *East African Journal of Rural Development* 8(1973):142–81.

KANU, quite naturally, did the same. But KANU was based upon the Kikuyu. They sought to colonize the Highlands and resisted all political impediments to their expansion to new territories. Many, moreover, were wealthy, and sought to increase commercial production by converting past earnings into new land holdings. It is not surprising, then, that KANU favored a constitution that created a centralized state – one without regional governments that could regulate access to land – and the un-impaired play of national market forces. Differences in agrarian endowments and material interests thus led to the formation of distinctive preferences with respect to political and economic institutions.

The agrarian origins of political conflict

As indicated earlier, KANU, by winning elections, won as well the right to seize the mantle of power from the retreating British. But it did so within a constitution that accommodated KADU's fears by providing a federal structure of government. The partitioning and settlement of the former White Highlands took place within a political framework in which KANU controlled power at the national level while KADU dominated the regional government of the Rift Valley. A centralized bureaucracy – the Land Development and Settlement Board – planned and administered the resettlement program; but because of the federal structure of the government, the agency was subject to political oversight by politicians at both the national and regional level. The latter group of politicians operated virtually on the ground, as it were; in the Rift Valley, they acted as "single issue" politicians, focusing on the issue of land; and, at least as important, they held the constitutional power to monitor the actual selection of settlers.

Because of the fundamental conflicts of interest surrounding the land issue, the reallocation of the Highlands threatened to provoke political violence. That it did not is in part due to the influence of political incentives that operated separate from the economic interests in land. Political institutions created incentives for politicians that rendered them less than perfect agents for their constituents. As a consequence, political entrepreneurs could play on the interests of political leaders, separating them from their constituents and diverting them along courses that were surprising, given the economic interests that had initially propelled them to prominence. Given the opportunity to maneuver, political entrepreneurs were able to defuse the threat of violence generated by the land issue. One result was a peaceful transition to independence; another was the wholesale restructuring of Kenya's institutional endowment; and a third was the rise of political forces that were keyed less to the issue of land and more to the issue of inequality.

Bureaucratic institutions

As their subsequent memoirs and reminiscences made clear,[15] the technocrats working in the Land Development and Settlement Boards possessed a clear sense of mission: They sought to enhance the productive potential of the Highlands. During the colonial period, they had promoted its intensive settlement. They had pioneered the introduction of new farming practices. And they had lobbied for the expansion of credit and farming services so as to enhance the productive use of land resources.

The technocrats had been politically astute. To advance their mission, they had aligned with the white settlers after World War II and promoted the importation of demobilized military officers. The result for the colonists was higher land values; for the technocrats, an expanded program and the more efficient use of Kenya's farmland. When African protest added a political element to the economic problems of postwar adjustment, the bureaucrats prescribed programs designed to address that problem as well. They offered a diagnosis: The political problem in the African reserves originated from overcrowding. And they prescribed a cure: the resettlement of Africans from the crowded reserves to less densely populated areas. They thus anticipated – and indeed stole a march on – the evolution of political forces in Kenya. By the time that revolutionary forces from below and the pressures of Whitehall from above had made independence inevitable, the Department of Lands and Settlement had crafted plans for the transfer of lands from European to African ownership in such detail that they could be circulated in international capital markets, appraised, and funded to the tune of over £20 million – all within a few months' time.[16]

In implementing the resettlement program, the administrators exhibited a judicious understanding of the economics of Kenyan agriculture and of the political environment within which they functioned. They recognized that economies of scale varied across commodities and that the production of some crops most economically took place in larger units (see Chapter 3). They recognized as well the imperfection of capital markets; large land units could not be bought by poor people, for poor people would be unable to secure adequate loans. On these grounds, they partitioned the Highlands into some areas exempt from and others subject to resettlement. Sisal estates and cattle ranches possessed scale economies and were expensive to purchase in large, single units; they therefore were exempted from settlement by small farmers. Maize and dairying were not subject to significant economies of scale, and dairy herds and maize fields could be purchased in small units; lands on which they could be raised or grown were therefore allocated to the resettlement program.

Having employed economic criteria in their initial partitioning, the bureaucrats then invoked political criteria for making subsequent decisions. To forestall European opposition to the programs, and the possibility of economic sabotage, they valued lands at 1959 prices – prices reflecting expectations that European hegemony would be underpinned, rather than compromised, by the power of the British state. They (correctly) assumed that they would be subject to political pressures from the leaders of each of the major ethnic groups proximate to the Highlands; they therefore designed settlement schemes for each. They appraised the Kikuyu as the most powerful and threatening group and apportioned to them 40 percent of the land zoned for settlement. Other groups too

The agrarian origins of political conflict

claimed "spheres of influence," and settlements were designed to accommodate them. For each group, they developed two kinds of schemes. Low-density schemes offered larger farms to more prosperous Africans; people taking up such farms had to be vetted as experienced farmers by the officers of the agricultural department and had to advance substantial cash deposits in order to qualify for plots. In high-density schemes for the poor, each farm was designed to achieve a target income; and depending on the land and climate, a farm plan was designed that would secure that target. The officers then advanced credit and services designed to enable the farmers to secure their target income, and therefore to be in a position to repay the debt engendered by buying out the Europeans at prices that they could not refuse.

Representative institutions

The bureaucracy in charge of the resettlement program operated within an environment of political institutions. Most relevant to this analysis was the Rift Valley Regional Assembly. Within the Assembly, KADU outnumbered KANU by two to one. The majority of those elected came from Kalenjin speaking areas. The most prominent leaders of the Kalenjin peoples (Murgor, Seroney, and Moi, for example), some of whom (such as Moi) also held national offices in KADU, took seats in the Assembly. Moi, the Chairman of KADU and the leader of Kalenjin Political Alliance, became the Assembly's president.

The Assembly leased a hall in Nakuru, the largest town in the Rift Valley, and designated Nakuru as the regional capital. It designed a regional seal and adopted a regional flag. The Assembly became a major source of political patronage. It drew its membership from the ethnic political machines that, taken together, made up KADU. And its leadership oiled those machines by proposing housing and vehicle allowances for the members of the Assembly and sitting and travel fees to offset the costs of attending public business. Twice within eighteen months the leaders proposed raises in the members' salaries; not surprisingly, both proposals passed.

Through the regional authorities, ethnic interests in the land settlement program gained a political base. Under the federal constitution, the regions held the right to approve settlers moving into the settlement schemes. The evidence suggests that the right of approval was in fact exercised by the KADU leaders of the Assembly and, in particular, by the Assembly's president.[17] The politicians of the Assembly became increasingly aggressive in pushing the land claims of their constituents against those of "outsiders," by which of course they meant the Kikuyu.

59

Beyond the miracle of the market

The threat of violence

KADU leaders used the regional government to resist the Kikuyu incursion. From its forum they made public threats; as one politician declared in a speech in the Western Regional Assembly:

My constituents asked me if it were time to use our spears and arrows but I told them to wait until I blow my whistle. We shall not allow Mr. Kenyatta to bring Kikuyu settlers from Kiambu to come and take over our farms.[18]

And through the power conferred on them by public office, they pressed for the eviction of Kikuyu who had stayed on in hopes of securing plots on farms where they had once served as laborers.[19]

The Kikuyu reacted to these threats. In August 1962, reports of oathing resurfaced in Molo, Kinagop, and Nakuru.[20] In October 1962, a former leader of Mau Mau spoke out publicly on behalf of the Kikuyu: "Has anyone thought about the security of tens of thousands of . . . agricultural workers employed on European farms in the Rift Valley Province?" wrote Bildad Kaggia in the *East African Standard*; "KADU leaders have been . . . telling [their followers] that when the settlers vacate the Highlands all the land will be for the Kalenjin and Masai. . . . Is there any sense in turning out thousands of . . . laborers, many of whom have been working on their farms for 15 years, in order to make room for Africans from elsewhere?"[21]

Soon reports began to surface of land seizures, illegal squatting, fights between ethnic groups, and armed conflict. The Kikuyu "infiltrators" assembled into an armed, if loosely organized, military movement. The Kalenjin and others, cheered on by their political leaders, fought back. As noted in one account:

Thousands of Nandi massed on Sunday along the Nandi escarpment after Nandis rounded up a Land Freedom Army gang near the Siret Tea Estate on Saturday.

The Nandi had formed themselves into bands varying from 200 to 600. They were all disbanded by police but one band told the police that if the Government was reluctant to clear the Kikuyu out of Kalenjin areas, the Nandi would do it themselves.

Similar anti-Kikuyu feeling also flared among the Tugen tribesmen and yesterday a band of 600 armed with spears, shields, bows and arrows was discovered at Solai. The police reported that they had arrived in the European farming area to "fight the Kikuyu." They were dispersed.[22]

The diffusion of conflict

Championing the interests of their constituents, the KADU elite of the Rift Valley Assembly thus threatened to plunge the nation into civil war. However, Kenya in fact experienced a peaceful transition to independence. One factor explaining this peaceful transition is the mixture of motives surrounding the land issue; another is that politicians possess independent political interests separate from the economic interests of their constituents. Lastly, the structure of the political institutions governing the land settlement program enabled national politicians to exploit the mixture of motives to disorganize regional political opposition.

The competition over land divided groups from each other; the need to capture the political power with which to control land rights impelled them to cohere. The motives of the constituent groups were therefore mixed, and political parties operated more as alliances than as disciplined organizations. Also mixed were the interests of the political leaders. At times, the interests of the party leaders corresponded with those of their constituents.[23] But at other times the desire to hold political office could – as we shall see – best be served by trading away, rather than servicing, the interests of constituents. The mixed motives within party alliances and the distinctive interests of politicians provided room for political maneuver.

The opportunity was seized by the top tacticians of KANU. KANU held power at the national level; the Land Development and Settlement Board had to operate in consultation with the Regional Assembly but was funded by the national government and headed by a KANU minister. The national politicians in KANU, in league with the technocrats of the Board, sought to fragment the KADU opposition. And they did so by exploiting the interests that divided groups within KADU and the independent interests of the KADU politicians.

A key issue exploited by KANU and the national bureaucrats was the status of Trans Nzoia, a prosperous farming district in the north of the Rift Valley. KADU contained two major blocs: the Abaluhya of Western Kenya and the Kalenjin of Rift Valley Province. Groups in each laid claim to the rich farmlands of Trans Nzoia, and the senior officers in KADU fought over whether Trans Nzoia was to go within Western Province, thus to be settled by the Abaluhya; or to remain in Rift Valley Province, the heartland of the Kalenjin. The issue put the leaders of KADU in a difficult dilemma. For to secure national office they had to preserve party unity and thus the prospects of winning a numeric majority of votes in a national election. But given the conflicts over land dividing the constituent groups within the party, party unity proved difficult to achieve.

It was the KADU leaders in Rift Valley Province who acted as political "statesmen": transcending their own ethnic base for the sake of party unity, they endorsed the transfer of Trans Nzoia to Western Province.[24] The KANU leadership then intervened: They threatened to run a slate of candidates in Rift Valley constituencies that would remain faithful to tribal sentiments opposing the loss of the rich farmlands. This deft counter was orchestrated by the Parliamentary Secretary for Local Government and Regional Affairs in Nairobi, within whose portfolio fell control over elections to local and regional bodies.[25] He further curried favor with the Kalenjin electorate while threatening the KADU leadership by vigorously lobbying the Regional Boundaries Commission – a body put in place by the British to resolve jurisdictional disputes when power was devolved to indigenous politicians – to retain Trans Nzoia within the Rift Valley Province. The efforts were successful; the Kalenjin leaders of KADU failed aggressively to oppose KANU before the Commission, and the Commission ruled that Trans Nzoia should remain within Rift Valley Province.

Through this maneuver, the KANU leaders weakened KADU. The western wing of KADU lost faith in the ability of the party to "deliver the goods" on the issue of greatest importance to them: access to land in the Rift Valley. Prominent leaders of the Abaluhya therefore began to negotiate terms for their surrender to KANU; they then crossed the floor and joined the ranks of KANU in Parliament, where they were rewarded by being placed in ministerial positions of junior rank and on the boards of statutory corporations.[26]

Interests within Kenya's agrarian society are defined not only by land but also by income. As Table 2.2 indicates, in terms of income, the Kalenjin speakers from an area like Nandi had more in common with the Kikuyu barons from Kiambu than they had with backwoods Abaluhya from Kakamega. In their attacks on the political opposition and in their efforts to disorganize collective resistance to the land policies of the national government, the wily tacticians of KANU and the bureaucrats in charge of land settlement also played upon the economic interests of the Kalenjin elite.[27] They maneuvered several counters in this campaign.

One was "technical" advice. With the vigorous approval of their KANU ministers, the settlement officials filed an important ruling: that the farming systems of the Trans Nzoia – mixed maize, wheat, and dairy – "were fundamentally suited to large-scale farming" and therefore should be "excluded from the settlement schemes."[28] The territory was therefore made available for private purchase.

The plunder of Trans Nzoia had thus been denied the Abaluhya. But the district was made available for sale to the prosperous Kalenjin. Having largely been excluded from the resettlement program, most of the lands of Trans Nzoia were to be sold in the market, rather than apportioned politically, and in lot sizes that only the wealthy could afford.

The political managers of the land program moved a second counter: they reconfigured the lot sizes on existing settlement schemes. In a modification of their plans, they created so-called Z-plots, which included

The agrarian origins of political conflict

the homes and major buildings of a farm plus one hundred acres about them; the remainder of the farm was then apportioned for dense settlement. As noted by Ruthenberg, who served as a government advisor in this period:

> By direction of the Cabinet, a new policy was started ... whereby the better class houses on large-scale farms had a 100 acre holding planned around them, regardless of the size of the plots in the remainder of the scheme. This was done so that the house and 100 acre holdings could be sold to a leader of the community such as a member of the Central Assembly. ... [29]

Land policy was thus redefined to make available lot sizes that would gratify the elite's desire for land, and on attractive terms. And in terms of wealth, the Kalenjin leadership constituted the largest portion of the economic elite in the Rift Valley. The KANU political managers and their bureaucrats thus used their management of the land program to generate side payments – material incentives to undermine the commitment of the Kalenjin elite to KADU.

These maneuvers provided a basis for political compromise, one worked out among the contending political leaders. In the summer months of 1964, individual politicians in KADU began to defect to KANU. In November 1964, KADU itself dissolved; its leaders were rewarded with prestigious postings in the central government.[30] In December 1964, Kenya became an independent republic. With the end of KADU, the regional assemblies were dismantled; Kenya therefore became a centralized state. And with the end of the regional form of government, Kenya constituted a national market. The allocation of that most sought after commodity in Kenya's agrarian economy – land in the former White Highlands – was now to be left to market forces.

RADICALISM

The merger of KADU and KANU removed one economic source of political conflict: the distribution of the Highlands. Another source remained, however: access to the riches to be made from commercial agriculture.

Sources of inequality

The roots of radicalism lay in economic inequality. Variations arose both within and across regions. And both operated powerfully during the period of party competition, generating political conflict within and between political parties.

As noted in Table 2.2, there were two worlds in KANU: the world of Central and Eastern Provinces on the one hand and the world of Nyanza on the other. The Central and Eastern Province people benefited from the intensification of agriculture. They gained access to coffee trees; added tea plantations; and, following Mau Mau, were assisted in acquiring, breeding, and husbanding grade cattle. They marketed their products in nearby Nairobi, using the roads built by the security forces. In examining the rise of smallholder production in the 1950s and 1960s, Heyer notes: "the districts that have really contributed to the tremendous growth of marketed output . . . are Kisii, Nyeri, Kiambu, and Meru, and to a lesser extent Embu and Kericho."[31] All but Kisii and Kericho lie in the central portion of the nation. As Heyer concludes:

Thus, behind the impressive growth of the small farm sector there emerges a pattern of substantial inequality. The growth has been concentrated in the high potential areas with plenty of rain, and among them it has been concentrated more in the central Kenyan districts with good infrastructure and access to markets around Nairobi.[32]

The fortunes of these regions stood in marked contrast with those with whom they were united politically, particularly Nyanza. Not only did the Luo live in an area in which it was prohibitively costly to produce coffee or tea and prohibitively risky to raise grade cattle; but also they lacked access to major markets and quality infrastructure. They therefore remained largely untouched by the prosperity brought on by the surge of smallholder production.[33] The disparity in fortunes of the two groups was further enlarged by the differences in their experiences in the settlement programs. Not only did the Central Province people get more land; the quality of lands secured by the Luo rendered their development expensive and long delayed. The settlement schemes of the Luo lay in the heavy clay soils below the western escarpments. Sugar was the sole profitable crop; it took the administration several years to secure the capital necessary to finance the expansion of the sugar industry and it took still further years before the investments began to pay off for the Luo settlers.[34]

It is not surprising, therefore, that a radical faction grew within KANU or that it drew heavily from KANU's Luo wing – a faction that rejected government policies emphasizing growth at the expense of equity; opposed the concentration and accumulation of resources; and sought the political management of the economy so as to forestall the rise of privileges.[35] The faction was led by Oginga Odinga, one of the Luo's leading spokesmen.

Economic fortunes varied *within* regions as well. As revealed in the 1963 survey of income and expenditures in the Central Province, the incomes of the Kikuyu differed dramatically between districts. The modal income in Kiambu, for example, was nearly three times that of Murang'a. And significant disparities of income existed within particular districts.

The agrarian origins of political conflict

The standard deviation of income within Murang'a, for example, exceeded the value of the mean.[36]

Particularly among the Kikuyu, these *within* group differences fanned political passions, for they strongly resonated with the trauma of that group's political history. Land, literacy, and income had correlated with political affiliation during the Mau Mau insurgency. Kiambu, by far the wealthiest district, had furnished the bulk of the Home Guards and loyalists; Murang'a, among the poorest, had provided a focal point for the insurrection. And within each district, the rebels tended to come from the poor, the uneducated, and the landless; their opponents tended to be drawn from the ranks of the wealthy. During the course of the emergency and the subsequent pacification campaign, the loyalists had seized additional economic advantages.[37] The postinsurrectionary program of agrarian reform, which had so benefited the Central Province as a whole, had benefited first and foremost those who had collaborated during the state of emergency. It was the loyalists who were first allowed to grow coffee or who first received the capital, technical advice, and licenses to raise dairy cattle.

Economic growth in Central Province had benefited some more than others. And the political determinants of economic fortunes were sufficiently visible that prosperity could be equated with the betrayal of the nationalist revolution. In the postindependence period, those advocating equality and socialism could thus draw upon the tradition of radical nationalism formed in the colonial period.

The structure of political competition

Politicians competed for power within Kenya. But Kenya was located within an international political system that increasingly intruded into the domestic politics of Eastern Africa. The domestic and international political arenas provided opportunities and imposed constraints, and these strongly shaped the way in which the issue of inequality assumed political form.

The presidency is the highest political office in Kenya. Following independence, the presidency of Kenya was held by the president of KANU, the party in power. Competition therefore focused on the vice presidency of KANU; the president, Jomo Kenyatta, was too securely in office for anyone credibly to threaten him. In this competition, two KANU politicians stood out: Oginga Odinga, the incumbent vice president, and Tom Mboya, his colleague and rival. While both Luo politicians, Odinga and Mboya forged contrasting domestic coalitions. Odinga's electoral constituency was in the rural areas; Mboya's in Nairobi. Odinga remained close to the radical nationalists who had been detained by the

British, Kaggia and Oneko, for example. Mboya, by contrast, had entered politics following the emergency; and the ties he forged were with African politicians who had been selected into the African ruling class through the electoral reforms put in place by the British during their strategic retreat from Kenya.[38]

What precipitated the *ideological* separation of the two rivals, however, was their competition for support in the international political arena. In negotiating for the transition from colonial rule, Mboya shrewdly and skillfully cultivated a reputation in Western political circles as a tough and skillful spokesman for "responsible" African interests; he was willing to trade off the support of political militants within Kenya for the support of allies from abroad. Mboya quickly became the preferred Kenyan spokesman among progressives and liberals in the West, as well as among government agencies who sought to build a stable and secure future for western interests in Third World nations. Odinga pursued an alternative course; he sought to promote a reputation for flamboyance and militancy in western political opinion and to convert that reputation into mass political popularity in Kenya. When, at a later stage, he saw that Mboya was converting foreign assets – money, fellowship programs, opportunities to attend international conferences, and so forth – into domestic political support, he too sought access to external resources. Given the reputation he had cultivated, however, Odinga had little choice but to seek these resources from socialist countries. The political maneuvering between the two major rivals for the second highest office in Kenya thus led them increasingly to diverge in their political positions – and to diverge in ways that were interpretable along a left-right, East-West, or Marxist-Liberal dimension.

Reinforcing this tendency was the extent to which the foreign political interests played upon the rivalries in Kenya. During the 1960s the cold war had spread to Africa. China, the Soviet Union, and the United States – each sought the support of African governments and, within given nations, the support of leading politicians.[39] East Africa, in particular, represented a locus for rivalry among the major powers; and prominent politicians in several East African countries played a major role in supplying financial and military support to rebellions in the Sudan and Zaire on behalf of rival world powers. Pressures therefore mounted for those contesting for prominence in Kenyan politics to clarify the extent to which they subscribed to the political doctrines of one or another of the foreign powers.

Political ambition thus tapped regional interests. And ambition sparked the formation of international alliances, drawing ideologically polarized interests from the international system into the interior of Kenyan politics.

The agrarian origins of political conflict

Table 2.3. *Parliamentary voting, 1963–68*

	Number of seats	Number of "dissidents"	Potential votes
KANU	104	45	59
KADU	23	0	68

Source: Cherry Gertzel, *The Politics of Independent Kenya 1963–68* (Nairobi: East African Publishing House, 1970), pp. 125ff.

Political competition in parliament

The dissidents that grouped about Odinga advanced their radical program within Parliament; their particular forum was the backbenchers group – a semiformal coalition of members who lacked ministerial positions. The tactic they employed was to pivot between KADU, the official opposition, and KANU, the governing party, using threats to defect to the opposition to elicit concessions from the government. KANU held 104 seats, KADU 23; the "hard core" radicals held 19 seats, but could command up to 45 votes, depending on the issue.[40] As noted by Gertzel, the radicals "sought to use [their] pivotal position in the two-party House to influence the Executive . . . ,"[41] demonstrating in at least one case their tactical power by defeating the government on the issue of federation with Uganda and Tanzania.

The rules of the House of Assembly gave the radicals power beyond their numbers, for they were able strategically to deploy their votes so as to create or to break legislative majorities. They employed that power to evoke from government commitments to policies they cared about: to subsidize loans for those willing to invest in depressed regions; to locate new projects outside Nairobi; to increase the level of services – schools, clinics, roads – in the less prosperous areas; to target new projects to the West of Kenya or in the semi-arid zones; to demand more rapid Africanization in the civil service; to limit foreign ownership and to promote local participation in multinational firms; to restrict foreign investments and assist African businessmen; and so forth. Above all, they lobbied intensively on the land issue. The aim of all groups in the nationalist period had been to seize back the White Highlands. National liberation had been achieved. Why, then, did Kenya have to borrow to buy back the White Highlands? And why did the settlers have to repay these loans? In the words of one member of Parliament: "We fought so that we could have our land back. . . . The Africans now are forced to pay for it. . . . [T]here is no reason why. . . . "[42] Moreover, should land be bought and sold? Should rich people, and especially political leaders, be able to ac-

67

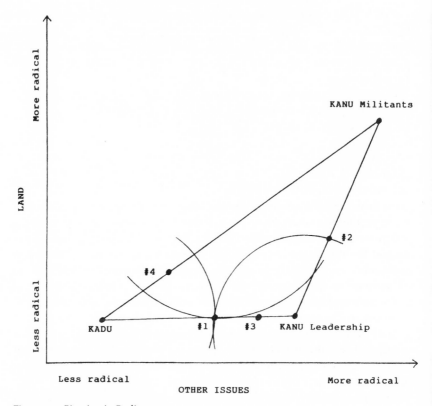

Figure 2.2. Pivoting in Parliament.

cumulate large acreages? The radicals thought not, and repeatedly con-
demned the government ministers and other elites who were taking over
the farms of their colonial predecessors.

The merger of KADU and KANU devalued the radicals' position. Given
the predisposition of KADU to vote against KANU in Parliament, the
radicals, although a minority of KANU, could threaten to defect, and
thereby evoke concessions from the government. But once KADU merged
with KANU, they lost the power that went with this capacity to "pivot."
To advance their position, they were thus forced to create a new party.

The tactical position of the radicals is portrayed in Figure 2.2. The
diagram portrays a two-dimensional issue space: one dimension por-
traying positions on the land issue and the other dimension positions on
other issues. Points further from the origin represent points of greater
radicalism. The KADU delegation occupied the least radical position
in Parliament; the "KANU militants" took the most radical stand on
both sets of issues; and the KANU leadership is shown as resembling

68

The agrarian origins of political conflict

that of KADU on the land issue but occupying an intermediate position on other issues. The shape of the indifference curve for the KANU militants suggests the strength of their feelings on the land issue; the slope of the indifference curve suggests their willingness to trade away a substantial amount on other issues to gain small concessions on land policy.

As the figure suggests, the militants, while a minority, could use their position to influence government policy and, more specifically, to move the government "to the left." By the rules of Westminster, the program of the majority party in Parliament became the program of the government. Assuming the status quo to be point #1 in the diagram, the militants could offer in the KANU party caucus a program, such as point #2, that was more radical in both directions. Should the KANU leadership agree to the deal, the party could use its majority in Parliament to make program #2 government policy. Should the KANU leadership refuse, however, and move a program such as #3, which they would prefer to both point #2 and the status quo but which the militants would not, then the latter could join KADU and pass program #4, which they would prefer to the status quo but which the government would not. This credible threat enabled the militants to exploit the Parliamentary setting to pressure the government "leftward" in its policies.

After the merger of the two parties, however, the position of the radicals changed. The radicals were still driven by economic interest and political ideology to favor government intervention to overcome economic inequalities; but the shift in their political environment dictated a change in strategy. They could no longer exploit the rules of Parliament and the government's need to secure majorities to shift public policy in a preferred direction. The radicals therefore changed strategies. Unable to convert their minority position in KANU into a majority position in Parliament, they therefore withdrew from KANU and formed a new party: the Kenya People's Union (KPU).

The new party proved short-lived. Folklore suggests and data substantiate that many Kenyans want high incomes and wealth; they want to accumulate, to invest, and to prosper; and they enjoy exhibiting the accoutrements of prosperity: good clothes, handsome homes, and properly turned out families.[43] All want land. The KPU proposed, or appeared to propose, limits upon accumulation. Save in a small number of regions and in a few particularly frustrated locations, it therefore possessed limited appeal.[44] Another reason for the party's failure was that it was internally divided. In Murang'a, for example, former detainees who sought parliamentary seats were denounced by others, who accused them of betraying fellow revolutionaries while in jail.[45] Lastly, the KPU was repressed. It was harassed by the public administration: its candidates' papers declared invalid, its meetings banned, and its organizers intimidated with impunity.[46] Ultimately, the party was banned. In the face of the evidence of the risks incurred in launching an opposition party, few leaders have since been willing to invest in so risky a venture. A major legacy of the defeat of organized radicalism was the creation, de facto, of a single-party state.

CONCLUSION

This chapter has advanced our understanding of the history of Kenya, the politics of agriculture, and the political economy of development.

The chapter has taken us from the Mau Mau rebellion to the postindependence period. The retreat of the British in the face of the Mau Mau insurrection, it has shown, precipitated a struggle over land and material goods; it also precipitated a struggle for political power, as politicians formed political alliances and competed to capture control over the institutions abandoned by the British. This struggle bequeathed to independent Kenya a legacy of institutional commitments: a dominant party, KANU; a unitary form of government; and an economy based in major part on market forces. The events of this period also bequeathed a legacy of defeated radicalism. In contrast to other African nations, the radical movement in Kenya had been channeled out of the governing party and into the political periphery, where it was divided, isolated, and repressed. The transition to independence left Kenya governed by political forces unlike those of her African neighbors, where those who captured control over government were committed to the use of political power to redress grievances generated by the market.

This chapter has also advanced our understanding of the politics of agriculture. It has explored the origins and dynamics of land hunger, showing how struggles over land threatened political violence. It has shown how location in commercial markets shaped political preferences and ideological orientations in agrarian societies. And it has studied the ways in which agrarian endowments and positions of economic advantage generated economic inequalities in rural societies that then spawned political conflict.

While exploring these themes, the chapter has focused in particular on political economy. Two schools dominate the literature on Kenyan development. One emphasizes economic factors; the other, the role of politics. This chapter has argued that the two schools must be combined. And it has focused on the role of institutions in an effort to integrate the two forms of analysis.

Because this chapter has centered on the agrarian origins of Kenyan politics, it has advanced strongly materialistic claims. Time and again, however, the materials uncovered in this chapter drove us to a more complex analysis. The rules for elections; the structure of party competition; and the ways in which legislation gained passage in the national assembly – all generated political incentives that operated independently of economic incentives. And these incentives shaped the way in which political organizers imparted ideological expression and organized form to material claims.

The chapter has stressed how material interests define political preferences; institutions are created and forged, it has shown, to advance the economic interests of particular groups. They are thus endogenous to economic analysis. But it has also stressed the (partial) autonomy of institutions and demonstrated how they structure the manner in which economic interests gain political expression.[47] The economic interests that count are those that gain ideological coherence and political organization. And the ideologies that are elaborated and the organizations that are formed are those that enable politicians to capitalize on the political opportunities offered by political institutions. Economic interests are thus defined by the political environment.

Material factors, particularly those in the agrarian economy, thus promoted the formation of commitments to particular institutional forms. But the institutions themselves generated incentives that shaped the way in which economic interests were defined and organized.

The argument of this chapter thus suggests that the course of political conflict in Kenya constitutes a political-economic dialectic. The initial institutional legacy promoted the formation of certain kinds of economic interests, as about the issue of land; these interests then formed preferences concerning the appropriate structure of institutions; and the way in which they restructured institutions was in part determined by the political resources and political opportunities that the institutions themselves conferred to politicians. The path of political change was strongly influenced by the way in which economic interests shaped, and were shaped by, the initial institutional endowment.

Understanding the interplay between material interests and political institutions enables us to comprehend the origins of Kenyan exceptionalism. Despite the predictions of many, Kenya did not disintegrate into ethnic violence. Nor was power captured by those dedicated to using the government to overturn the opportunities offered by the market. Kenya emerged from this period, then, different from many of its African neighbors. It experienced little of the violence that engulfed Uganda to the west or the more distant Zaire or Nigeria. And it exhibited little of the commitment to economic redistribution that marked Tanzania to the south, Ethiopia to the north, or the more distant Angola, Ghana, or Mozambique.

The political struggles of this period did, however, endow Kenya with

71

a legacy shared with others: a single-party system.[48] The conflicts over land, wealth, and power left Kenya, de facto, a one-party state. As we shall argue in Chapter 3, the shift to a single-party system generated a fundamental change in the structure of political incentives. It thereby altered the substance and style of politics in Kenya.

3

Institutional structure, agricultural development, and political conflict

This chapter continues our exploration of the foundations of Kenya's development by examining the institutions that underlie agriculture. It explores as well the politics of Kenya's single-party system. And it studies the interaction between economic institutions and politics, arguing that the institutions put in place to enhance the productive growth of agriculture furnish as well resources which help the managers of Kenya's single national party to maintain themselves in power.[1]

THE ORIGINS OF ECONOMIC INSTITUTIONS

Anyone studying Kenyan agriculture quickly notices the limited role for competitive markets. In many industries, vertical integration is the rule, with production, processing, and sales concentrated in a single firm. Public agencies commonly regulate the production and marketing of crops. And where one might expect decentralized trading in open markets, one often finds bureaucracies instead. An observer would also note that the different agricultural industries are structured in contrasting ways. A major purpose of this chapter is to employ this diversity to construct explanations for the origins of economic institutions.[2]

Three factors appear to have been critical: risk in capital markets, costs of information, and economies of scale.

The role of capital

Assuming the presidency of the American Economics Association in 1974, Kenneth Arrow noted one of the enduring puzzles for neoclassical economic theory: the continuing disparity in income between nations. In an extraordinary essay, he focused on the difficulties uniquely associated with the transfer of capital.[3] Many of the organizational forms found in

73

Kenyan agriculture appear to have been formed to counter the deficiencies in incentives in capital markets noted and stressed by Arrow.

Capital is inherently intertemporal; it redistributes resources over time. Its creation involves forgoing consumption at one time in order to enhance consumption at later periods; and its use involves present expenditures for the sake of higher future earnings. An important consequence of the intertemporal nature of capital is uncertainty: Present decisions are made out of a regard for future, and therefore inherently unknowable, returns.

Because most people are risk averse, uncertainty imposes costs. Suppliers of capital will seek compensation for these costs; and demanders of capital, in efforts to secure this scarce resource more cheaply, will seek to reduce them. Were capital markets perfect, such efforts would be of no consequence for economic organization. For every potential risk, there could be created a financial asset that could be traded among those with differing preferences for risk or differing assessments of their probabilities. But such markets are difficult to organize, if only because not all contingencies can be foreseen. The result is that suppliers and demanders of capital possess an incentive to cooperate in devising nonmarket means of providing assurances to investments.

Capital markets are therefore likely to serve as fertile sources for innovative forms of contracting. Particularly for those interested in the political economy of growth and development, the search for the origins of economic institutions can therefore profitably be directed at the behavior of those who demand and supply investments.

One of the clearest illustrations of the structuring power of risk comes from the so-called resettlement program, introduced in Chapter 2. The purchase and repeopling of the Highlands proved to be extremely expensive.[4] A total of £11.7 million was required for land purchases alone; an additional £13.7 million for the subdivision of the land and the establishment of new settlers. In the words of Ruthenberg, "this [was] a colossal injection of capital. . . . "[5] Raised from Britain, Germany, and the World Bank, the loans for the resettlement program represented the greatest single investment in the history of the territory.

The problem was: How were the loans to be secured? Debts could not be secured through personal bondage; that was unthinkable. Nor at the time of the resettlement program could land stand as collateral. The recently subdivided lands had not yet been officially surveyed and registered. And even when they had been registered, it was politically costly to seize the lands of defaulters. The cry of land hunger had fed the nationalist rebellion that had brought the government to power. To turn people off the lands that they had fought to capture would be to risk the wrath of the true believers in the nationalist revolution.[6]

Institutions, economics, and politics

Given these constraints, those seeking to reduce the risks to capital elaborated structures and rules to provide assurance for lenders. They drew up detailed production programs designed to guarantee the generation of a flow of revenues sufficient to repay the costs of capital. And they mounted and staffed a bureaucracy whose job it was to use administrative controls to enforce adherence to the production programs.

The department that administered the settlement schemes devised intensive farm plans. Associated with each farm plan was a "target income." Reasoning backwards, as it were, the plan prescribed detailed production programs to guarantee the attainment of the income targets. The farm plans varied according to the elevation and climate, as different crops and farming systems were optimal under different physical conditions; they also varied according to the size of the farm. They contained such details as the siting of farm buildings; the layout of the lands; the crops to be grown and the proportion of land to be devoted to each crop; the rotations to be followed; and the off-farm inputs to be employed.[7] The department then recruited an unprecedented number of staff – settlement officers, cooperative officers, extension officers, and farm managers – to cajole and persuade the new settlers to adopt the approved farming practices.

The result was an intensive infusion of bureaucratic regulation into Kenya's rural society. The prescribing of farm practices, their monitoring, and their enforcement – these forms of nonmarket controls became a significant feature of agrarian life in Kenya.

The bureaucratic structuring took a second form: the attempt to secure legal control over crops. If neither land nor labor could be used to secure farm loans, title to the crop could. The farmers on settlement schemes were compelled to market their produce through state-sponsored cooperatives. On the one hand, the societies distributed the farm inputs required to produce at a level that would repay the loans; on the other, they served as the sole legal purchaser of the produce of the farms, deducting loan repayments from their payments for the crops. It is interesting to note the reaction of one spokesman for the government's program to criticism of this arrangement:

The security for loans has to be the crop, and unless suitable arrangements are made for marketing by the organization which gives out the loan, the likelihood of recovering is greatly reduced.... For this reason it may ... be permissible to query [Ms. Whetham's] conclusion that private traders should operate freely ... on the Kenya Land Settlements.[8]

Forces emanating from the market for capital thus had an impact on the structure of rural society. And they introduced regimentation and bureaucracy in settings where one might expect markets normally to prevail.[9]

Beyond the miracle of the market

Kenya stands as a paradox.[10] On the one hand, since the defeat of organized radicalism, the government maintains a strong commitment to private investment; on the other, particularly in agriculture, it intervenes actively in markets and maintains a dense network of regulatory controls. The grounds for unraveling this paradox lie in understanding that the elaboration of administrative controls need not be antithetical to the promotion of investment. For the visible commitment to planning, the precommitment on the part of the borrower to planned production programs, the creation of the administrative capacity to compel the use of approved farm inputs, and the securing of legal title to the crop and public control over marketing – such measures may reduce risks to lenders and thereby secure greater infusions of capital.

Information costs and the problem of quality

A second factor has operated to promote the growth of nonmarket institutions in rural Kenya: costs of information.[11] These costs confound the capacity of the market to elicit product quality, thus creating a demand for nonmarket means of securing attributes which consumers desire. Information costs often operate in conjunction with incentives promoted by capital markets and by scale – the two other factors examined in this chapter – to promote the creation of economic institutions.

For many commodities, it costs more to produce products of higher quality. The "market's solution" for the securing of desired levels of quality is to generate a dispersion of prices. Through price dispersion, those who prefer a higher quality product can reward those who incur the costs of producing it. A variety of factors prevents the attainment of this solution, however. And the failure of the pricing mechanism has contributed to the creation of economic institutions in Kenya.

A factor that commonly bedevils the emergence of price dispersion is the costliness of measurement. Often quality is not observable at the time of production; it is observed only at later stages. The quality of coffee, for example, is but imperfectly related to the observable attributes of the coffee bean, i.e., its size or color; only when the bean is processed and tested "in the cup" can its quality fully be determined. Similarly, the sucrose content of sugar cane cannot be determined at the time of harvesting; only upon processing can its value be known.

In the face of such difficulties, economic agents have created market-like solutions. They have, for example, split payments to farmers. They initially pay by the quantity of production, which is easily measured; farmers are paid by the kilogram, for example. They then make subsequent payments on the basis of the earnings realized from the sale of the crop, where the price fetched reflects the quality attributes incorporated into the product. This method of payment has been adopted for both coffee and tea in Kenya.[12] But even in these cases it is still imperfect and it has not been applied in the case of other commodities. A primary factor confounding its adoption is the phenomenon of scale.

Scale economies can arise at the level of processing; the output of tens of thousands of farmers must be aggregated in order to run a sugar plant at volumes sufficient to secure low unit costs. Such economies can also arise at the level of marketing. Coffee and tea sales, for example, take place in standardized lots. These lots bear the mark of a particular factory; but the output of that factory represents the amalgamation of the production of hundreds of peasant farms. The result of scale economies in processing or marketing is that when producers receive a quality premium, it represents the market's evaluation of the *average* quality of production as generated by all farmers. The *individual* farmer is thus not rewarded for the quality of his or her production. Indeed, those who have expended the resources necessary to produce above-average quality fail to secure compensation for their efforts; they get paid a price that reflects but the average. And those who have shirked in efforts to enhance the quality of their produce are rewarded; they too receive a price based on the average quality of output by all farmers. The result is the erosion of incentives to produce goods of high quality.

Under such circumstances, it may be cheaper to monitor and control inputs into production than to develop a spectrum of prices based upon the quality of outputs. Bureaucratic controls may replace market mechanisms.

An example is furnished by the sugar industry, where farmers growing sugar sign contracts compelling them to replant at intervals prescribed by the company (the sucrose content of cane declines with the number of ratoons[13]); to accept from the company and apply a prescribed level of fertilizers; to weed with a specified frequency or to accept and pay for the company's supply of manpower for weeding.[14] Another example is furnished by the tea industry, which is regulated in part by the Kenya Tea Development Authority (KTDA). By law, the KTDA possesses a monopoly on the purchase of green leaf from smallholders. When it was promoting the initial development of small-holder tea in Kenya, it retained as well a monopoly over the nurseries from which smallholders obtained planting materials. The KTDA used these controls to ensure that farmers would employ approved tea varieties and growing practices. The KTDA thereby sought to ensure the production of tea of high quality.[15]

Given the high costs of monitoring the quality of products, control over farm inputs thus replaces the evaluation of outputs, and rules and regulations replace markets in efforts to enforce quality standards.[16]

77

Beyond the miracle of the market

The demand for quality, as analyzed in this section, reinforces the effect of the investors' demand for ex-ante guarantees of returns to their capital, as analyzed in the section above. By designing into crop development schemes constraints to guarantee the quality of products, crop development authorities are able to render higher returns more certain and thereby render investments more attractive. By imposing such regulations, they exhibit to investors a precommitment to the use of production practices that will secure output of sufficient quality to reward their ventures of capital. The requirements of capital, linked with the costs of information, thus help to promote the intrusion of law into the day-to-day life of Kenyan farmers.[17]

Scale economies

A third factor – scale – has promoted the regulation of economic life in rural Kenya. In so doing, it has also affected the structure of economic organization.

In Kenya, as in other developing countries, public policy and political influence have promoted the subsidization of capital. In particular, foreign capital has been privileged by government. The government has overvalued the exchange rate, lowering the costs of capital goods. And through a variety of tax benefits and other measures, it has subsidized investment.[18] The result is that investments in agriculture have often been large, often inappropriately so.

Investors in large-scale projects face the risk of insufficient throughput; they need to process large volumes of raw materials in order to reduce unit costs to profitable levels. And the government, eager to secure investments, has therefore imposed market controls so as to guarantee profitable levels of production.

One example is provided by the cotton industry in the 1920s. To secure investments in ginning, the government had to assure investors of a volume of raw materials sufficient to enable the factories to operate at high levels of capacity and at low unit costs. It therefore created zones in which each gin could, by law, serve as the sole purchaser of the farmers' cotton crop.[19] Within each zone, the factory could legally function as a monopsonist. To safeguard the profitability of the new firms, the government therefore restricted the economic options of peasant producers.

Another example is provided by the government's effort to promote investments in the sugar industry in the 1970s. To promote investments in sugar processing, it once again created zones wherein particular factories exercised by law exclusive rights to purchase products. Other factories could not compete for sugar within these zones; nor could local entrepreneurs, who sought to purchase cane for processing into jaggery,

78

a relatively crudely refined product consumed locally and used for the brewing of intoxicants.[20] By restricting competition for raw materials, the government thereby sought to guarantee a sufficient volume of throughput that the factories could generate profits for their investors.

Economies of scale not only promote the regulation of rural life. They also influence the structure of the industrial organizations that emerge when rural resources are channeled into the production of crops for commercial markets.

Static arguments. One impact is upon the size of farms.[21] Variations in scale economies help to determine the farm size associated with different crops, for different crops impose different demands upon farm management.[22]

The value of some crops may be more strongly affected than the value of others by the ability to make a consistent stream of precisely timed and finely tuned decisions; optimizing farmers who produce different crops may therefore choose to operate farms of different size. A contrast may be drawn, for example, between the production of tea and coffee on the one hand and of wheat on the other. In the case of tea and coffee, care in planting is crucial; each bush must be individually trained so as to enhance lifetime yields and pruned annually so as to increase yields and lower the costs of pest control. Both tea and coffee require careful and timely harvesting. In the case of tea, only certain portions of the plant (two leaves and a bud) should be picked; in the case of coffee, only berries of uniform ripeness.[23] Neither product, when harvested, stores well, with the result that care must be taken to secure rapid delivery to the processing unit. In the case of wheat, by contrast, planting can be done by broadcasting seed; in no conceivable way do the individual wheat plants demand the farmer's attention. Wheat does require careful attention for pests, particularly rusts, given the moisture levels in Kenya; but little manipulation of the plant is required to make wheat amenable to the application of chemicals, and researchers have developed strains that are largely resistant to rust infestation. Domestication has resulted in plants of uniform height; the crop can therefore be harvested mechanically. And wheat, like other grains, stores well; timeliness of harvesting and delivery therefore have less of an impact on the values of production than they do in the case of tea and coffee.

Wheat farms can therefore be of a larger size than those on which farmers grow coffee and tea, for the latter require more intensive monitoring and management.[24]

Scale economies also arise at the level of processing. In the case of sugar the average capacity of processing plants is in the range of 50,000 tons per annum; when further capacity is added, it is added in increments of 15,000 tons. In the case of tea or coffee, processing plants are far smaller. The minimum economic unit for a tea factory tends to require 1,000 tons of throughput per annum; and processing units are sufficiently divisible that new capacity can be added to existing plants in units of 500 tons. In the case of coffee, throughputs of 100 to 200 metric tons per pulpery are regarded as economic; smaller sizes produce congestion and larger sizes require the addition of new management, as the processing of coffee is a delicate and skilled task, requiring the careful control of the rate and extent of chemical changes in the fruit and bean.

Scale economies at the levels of production and processing generate characteristic social organizations in agriculture and characteristic patterns of social conflict. When there are economies of scale in processing but not in production, the result is the domination of the rural landscape by a large factory, surrounded by a multitude of small-scale farms.[25] Factory meets peasant in the rural countryside, and economic conflict assumes the form of relations between industry and labor. An illustration is offered by the sugar industry. When economies of scale are weak in both production and processing, the result is a mixture of artisan and peasant production, as small-scale factory units lie widely dispersed among a multitude of peasant farms. Economic conflict then takes on the cast of rural populism. An illustration is offered by the coffee industry. When there are significant scale economies in both production and processing, the result is what observers would characterize as "modern" agriculture: large farms, conjoined with large-scale, factory-like processing units. In such settings, economic conflict tends to assume the form of bargaining between associations and firms.

Because of variations in economies of scale, then, the producers and processors of different crops inhabit distinctive social universes. The distribution of scale economies within an industry helps to determine its social structure and political dynamics.

Dynamic arguments. Scale economies also have a dynamic effect on the structure of rural industry: The existence of scale economies in one part of an industry induces changes in other parts, with the result that the industry is transformed. This effect can best be illustrated by examining the impact of scale economies in processing.

Because economies of scale in processing result in large fixed capacities, reductions in throughput increase unit costs and, all else being equal, thereby lower profits. One way of securing profitable volumes of throughput is therefore to invest in transportation so as to forage, as it were, for raw materials. All else being equal, however, a transporter finds it cheaper to make fewer stops. The result is that there is a natural affinity between large-scale processors who maintain transport services and large-scale farmers, and this affinity helps to transform the structure of the industry.

A telling illustration is provided by the KTDA, the agricultural agency most vocally promoting a small farmer strategy in Kenyan commercial agriculture. In the 1970s, the tea authority sought to expand its productive capacity. A factor limiting the expansion of tea processing was the greater transport costs incurred in securing green leaf. To capture the economies available from larger processing plants, the authority therefore sought to increase production *not* by increasing the numbers of producers (a "spreading" strategy) but rather by allowing each farmer to work a larger number of tea bushes (a "thickening" strategy). In this way it was not necessary to extend transport routes in order to secure increased throughput, nor did vehicles have to make more frequent stops. As argued by Steves, this change in strategy led to the emergence of a large farm bias in the operations of the tea authority, despite its egalitarian rhetoric.[26]

The effects of scale in inducing a preference for dealing with larger farmers are also revealed in the structure of rural contracts. The most vivid illustration is offered by the creameries of the dairy industry.

Within that industry, economies of scale arise in processing; in Kenya as a whole, fewer than a dozen creameries process the output of several hundred dairy herds. To maintain a high and consistent level of production, the creameries require a large and constant level of deliveries of raw milk. But because of fluctuations in rainfall, the costs of milk production vary with the season; and unless compensated for the higher costs of producing in the dry season, farmers would curtail production, thereby imposing higher unit costs upon the processors. The creameries therefore devised a contract wherein they compensated producers for the costs they incurred for milk production in the dry season. Should a producer contract for off-season deliveries, the dairy would pay a higher price for that producer's milk throughout the year; should the producer fail to perform, then the dairy would cancel the contract, assigning it instead to another producer. The result was the creation of a two-tier milk market, wherein higher prices were paid to those producers with access to sufficient capital to incur the costs of irrigating grazing pasturage, storing feed, or purchasing supplementary foodstuffs in the dry season, thereby keeping their herd in milk throughout the year.[27]

The existence of economies of scale in the processing portion of an industry thus appears to set in motion forces that bind the processor to distinctive segments of the producers: those who are larger in scale and who have access to the capital necessary to finance large volumes of production. The effect has been the creation of an alliance between large-scale processors and large-scale producers. This alliance is often described as the "modern" portion of Kenya's agricultural industry. The analysis thus offers insight into the dynamics underlying the modernization of agriculture.

Discussion

The materials in this section suggest that economic institutions have been created in efforts to rectify problems that inhibit the operation of markets. Legal powers and administrative authority have been put in place to reduce risks, avoid information costs, and insure against potential market failures arising from economies of scale. Incentives arising from capital markets, the economics of information, and scale economies help to account for the creation and structuring of Kenya's agrarian institutions.

The materials thus support an economic theory of institutions: one that imputes their origins to the gains in efficiency that they make possible. But they also support a more political interpretation. For time and again they reveal the influence of large interests. The institutions have clearly been designed not only to increase production but to do so by safeguarding the interests of the owners of capital, large-scale plants, and foreign purchasers of local farm products. The result is a distribution of privilege that many find repugnant.

INDUSTRIAL STRUGGLES IN KENYAN AGRICULTURE

Although created for reasons of efficiency, economic institutions provide the locus for political struggles. For while all agents in an industry share an interest in maximizing the value of production, their interests concerning its distribution conflict. In this section, we focus on the ways in which economic interests use the power of the institutions that they have created to capture the benefits to be derived from commercial agriculture.

Struggles over markets

Economic interests sometimes find it desirable to alter the structure of markets. Particularly when an industry is politically regulated, they find it plausible to believe that by lobbying they can succeed in doing so.

The natural endowment of Kenya creates circumstances under which the capture of markets becomes a feasible objective. A combination of altitude, temperature, and labor supply confers upon Kenya a relative advantage in the production of pyrethrum, for example, sufficient to leave it virtually uncontested in world markets, save by the manufacture of synthetics.[28] Pyrethrum is a flower that yields chemicals toxic to insects, and Kenya produces 60 to 80 percent of the world's supply.

Kenyan processors have used the political power given them to regulate the industry to exploit this market position and to extract resources from foreign consumers. They first attempted to restrict competition on a decentralized basis; they merged with new entrants in the industry and retired their factories from production. This method proved unsatisfactory, for it allowed rivals to threaten entry and thereby extract the noncompetitive rent deriving from Kenya's market position. The processors therefore demanded an alternative way of restricting entry: they secured legislation creating a policeman for the market – an official statutory board, with the power to license, or to ban, the creation of new capacity. Because pyrethrum generates foreign exchange, the government deemed it in the national interest to confer statutory authority to restrict competition and thereby preserve Kenya's ability to set international prices.[29]

Not only do natural endowments confer market power, as in the case of pyrethrum; so too do economies of scale. Where such economies reduce the number of agents in a market, it becomes plausible for the agents to believe that they possess sufficient market power to alter prices to their advantage. It also becomes less costly to police agreements, once formed. For given that the number of agents is small, each looms large in the market, with the consequence that the actions of any single agent will affect market prices; cheating is therefore publicly visible. In the presence of economies of scale, noncompetitive agreements may therefore appear both profitable and relatively inexpensive to police, and the small group of actors may be expected to attempt to form them.[30]

To see this, consider the Kenyan dairy industry.[31] In the early part of the century, farmers invested in creameries. Given the scale economies associated with milk processing, it took but a small number of creameries to process the output from the entire commercial dairy herd. With the downturn of dairy prices in the depression, the biggest of the creameries organized a merger of the existing creameries into a single entity called the Kenya Cooperative Creamery (KCC).

The KCC was formed during the colonial period. During that period, as we have seen, a variety of political and economic factors conferred power upon the dairy producers. And through the lobbying efforts of the KCC, they were able to secure legislation empowering the KCC to act as a monopolist in urban milk markets and to control entry by licensing the construction of creameries.

The KCC used these statutory powers to organize the processing and marketing of milk products so as to extract income from consumers. Milk represents a multitude of products, each with its own characteristics. The price elasticity of demand for whole milk is far smaller than that for processed products, such as butter or cheese. Whole milk is bulky and highly perishable, however; butter and cheese are less costly to transport and to store. When the KCC organized its operations so as to maximize its profits, it therefore limited the sales of whole milk and it did so by removing milk from the domestic market in the form of butter and cheese, which it stored or shipped to foreign markets.

In the cases examined thus far, struggles among interest groups have taken the form of rivalries among processors and between processors and consumers. Other fights within rural industries involve struggles between different categories of producers, and in particular those who are established – whose interests are sheltered by the existing industrial structure – and those who seek entry.

Perhaps the most vivid example is offered by the dairy industry, once again. In the immediate postindependence period, smallholders acquired dairy cattle and began to produce milk. They did so in particular in regions where prosperity from tea and coffee production had generated an increase in the demand for whole milk and an increase in the supply of capital necessary for the purchase of grade cattle. The growth of smallholder production took place most rapidly in Central Province.

As production for the rural market grew, prices in that market declined. The smallholders therefore sought to dispose of surplus milk in the urban market. Several features of the organization of the dairy industry frustrated the attempts of the smallholders to gain access to that market. One was that the small farmers supplied milk in small batches; the creameries were therefore unwilling themselves to handle their deliveries, for the costs of transport were too high. The small farmers therefore formed cooperatives, purchased their own transport equipment, and built their own processing facilities. At that point, however, they faced two other market barriers. Because the farmers were unable to supply whole milk in the dry season, their sales throughout the year were made to the KCC at lower prices than those of the large-scale farmers. In addition, the legal authority created to regulate the milk market, the Dairy Board, responded to pressures from the KCC and refused to license the small-holders' factories for direct delivery to the Nairobi market.[32] The Board thus protected the interests of the established producers at the expense of the interests of the new entrants.

The small farmers charged the KCC with discrimination. Some of the charges were cast in racial language, for many of the larger dairy herds remained in the hands of the white farmers. Other charges were phrased in the language of neocolonialism; the KCC was held to perpetuate the colonial pattern of favoring the large-scale farmer. Some, for obvious reasons, were in the language of class. Still others were phrased in the language of regionalism. For the new entrants who stood to gain the most from the abolition of barriers to entry were in the Central Province; the large-scale farmers tended to reside in the Rift Valley.[33] In this way, the fight over market structure animated larger political conflicts in Kenya.

THE POLITICS OF ECONOMIC INSTITUTIONS

The first section of this chapter explored the origins of rural institutions and emphasized the way in which they made possible levels of economic activity unattainable through markets. The second has stressed the way in which these institutions have provided a framework for economic competition among agrarian interests. While largely contractarian in spirit, the arguments in the first section nonetheless sufficiently emphasized the role of foreign capital, large investors, and scale to create the expectation that the interests of these actors should prevail in subsequent rivalries.

Such expectations are in accord with well-established reasoning; they conform to the predictions that would flow from the work of Olson, Stigler, and others.[34] Economic conditions are public goods, this reasoning holds; and the incentives to lobby are therefore confounded by the problem of free riding. The costs incurred in lobbying create benefits that are enjoyed by all; each actor therefore does better letting others pay these costs, while enjoying the benefits for free. But, as argued by Olson and others, the incentives to free ride decline as the size of the actors increases. For the benefits increase with the size of the actor; a price rise created by a tariff on textiles means more to the owners of a textile factory than to the owners of a handloom, for example. But if the costs of lobbying for the price rise do not increase proportionately with size, then it may pay a large actor to lobby, even though the benefits of his efforts are shared by others. The result is that we should expect large-size actors to dominate the process of lobbying and to shape government regulation of markets to their advantage.

As intimated above, economies of scale appear more often to characterize the processing of agricultural commodities than their production. There are seven sugar factories and over fifty thousand growers of sugar; thirty-nine tea factories and over one hundred thousand tea growers; seven hundred coffee factories, but over five hundred thousand coffee growers. And indeed, as expected, the processors act as vigorous lobbyists. They often secure monopsony rights over the produce of farmers. In the case of the creameries, they achieved monopoly standing in the major consumer markets. And in virtually every regulated industry, they have secured cost-plus agreements, allowing them to pass on their costs to others.

Beyond the miracle of the market

At first glance, then, it would appear that Olson-like arguments apply: in the interest group politics surrounding the regulated agricultural industries, the interests of the large processing firms would appear to prevail. A closer look, however, suggests that things are not so simple.

Instead of large-scale processors invariably prospering, they often experience losses; occasionally, they go bankrupt. In recent years, for example, the massive sugar companies have been technically bankrupt, avoiding foreclosure only because of the infusion of new loans and the rescheduling of old debts.[35] In the cotton regions, many of the gins have been accumulating losses; several factories are technically bankrupt; and many of the cooperative societies that own them have been put into receivership.[36] The grain milling companies frequently complain of the small markups allowed them; they occasionally run at a loss, sometimes ceasing production when they do so. As noted by Grosh, in a review of the finances of sixteen of the major companies in Kenyan agriculture:

> Throughout the period 1979–84, over half the firms for which data are available reported losses. Of the 16 agricultural firms which operated in that period, seven reported losses in every year for which data are available. In 1981 and 1982, nine of the firms for which data are available reported losses.[37]

As Olson and others would predict, the large-scale, capital-intensive units do in fact constitute organized, vocal, and active lobbyists. But it would appear that they are not effective ones.

The Kenyan materials therefore suggest that basic modifications are needed in the dominant theory of interest groups. For clearly the large-scale interests have been subject to economic predation. They suggest as well additional factors that need to be taken into consideration. One is the political setting within which the industry inheres. Quasi-rents constitute the other, as they affect incentives to engage in efforts to restructure markets.[38]

The politics of predation

The attacks on large-scale interests emanate from the political environment of the regulated industries. The relevant characteristics of this environment are that politicians compete for votes to secure office; that the competing politicians belong to the same political party – here KANU; and that, to contest elections, they must first be cleared by the KANU party committee in their constituency.

Electors. Politicians see in the small farmers a source of votes. In the politics of Western Kenya, for example, the more than 50,000 outgrowers of the sugar industry represent a major bloc of votes, one to whose needs and interests any politician would do well to attend. And the ten thousand or so pyrethrum growers in the escarpment overlooking the Rift Valley represent another potential constituency. As one would expect, politicians compete to achieve the status of spokesmen for such interests. Members of Parliament seek to defend their interests against the processors of the crop, and fight for higher and more prompt payments for crop deliveries and lower charges for farm inputs. And in the case of the strategically placed pyrethrum growers, the defense of their interests originates at the very highest levels of the government.[39]

Politicians often manipulate the regulatory authorities to pressure the large-scale processors to pay higher prices for raw materials and to impose lower charges for farm inputs. The processors cannot recover losses by charging higher export prices, for they would then be undercut by firms from other nations. And for crops marketed within Kenya, the processors face pressures from another source: consumers, themselves a highly vocal and highly organized political bloc, whose power we shall explore in the chapters that follow. The result is that the processors find themselves squeezed between politically organized economic interests and accumulate large losses.

Nominators. To win the right to run for elected office, a politician must first be nominated by the local KANU party committee. The committee is composed of local residents. Typically, many are politically ambitious and economically prominent; but lacking literacy in English, they cannot move upward politically or compete economically in major urban markets.[40] To fulfill their ambitions, they therefore mediate the careers of those who can operate effectively on the national stage. By the rules of the political game, those competing for positions in Kenya's national Parliament must first win their approval; they must be nominated and cleared by the local party organization. The local KANU officials employ this strategic advantage to extract political favors and economic benefits from aspirant politicians.

Many utilize their position to secure contributions to the formation of collective goods. Highlighting local needs, they organize meetings to promote community projects. Those who wish to succeed in the pursuit of office are well advised to attend these meetings and to contribute generously to the cause.[41]

Many use their position to extract private benefits as well. And it is here that the political process imposes costs upon rural industries. The national-level politicians compete to provide benefits to those local officials by using their influence over the regulated agricultural industries to do so. A member of parliament in Malaba Malikisi, for example, rewarded his election workers by placing them on the management committee of the local cotton factory. They issued "loans" to friends and hired on extra staff. In effect, they transformed the factory into a political machine, creating financial benefits for electors while promoting the political fortunes of the local member of Parliament and buying him popularity among his rural constituents.[42] Another example is offered by the cotton industry, where one factory in Kendu Bay was milked of over Ksh. 90,000 by a partisan management committee.[43]

The institutional structure of agriculture in Kenya thus provides a means for forming local political organizations. It also furnishes ways for integrating these rural political machines into organized political factions. The prescribed use of farm inputs, characteristic – as we have seen – of several of Kenya's agricultural industries, helps to make possible the building of national-level political organizations. The crop authorities rule that certain farm inputs must be purchased. And powerful figures at the national level issue the licenses to import them or influence appointments to the boards of firms that supply them. The economic benefits thereby created constitute a valuable resource for loyal followers. The procurement of fertilizers, chemicals, and farm equipment form the basis for political patronage networks.[44]

In the sugar industry, to illustrate, an inter-ministerial group repeatedly drew attention to the losses incurred by the "high costs resulting from unnecessarily large tractors and equipment."[45] The ordering of inappropriate equipment nonetheless persisted; and a key reason was that politicians at the very highest levels of the government possessed a financial interest in the firm that sold this equipment to the sugar companies. Similar patterns have been found in the coffee industry, where the owners of factories have been compelled to purchase inferior equipment, such as inappropriate kinds of coffee driers.[46] Grosh's analysis documents the inflation of costs in a variety of other agricultural industries.[47]

The market. We have already indicated that large firms are often unable to raise the prices they charge consumers. In addition, they have not been able to use their market power to reduce the costs of the raw materials provided by small-scale farmers. They are prevented from doing so not only by the political power of the rural electorate, but also by the strategic opportunities available to small-scale producers.[48]

Large processors possess large quasi-rents, whereas the small farmers do not. Quasi-rents represent the difference in value between what an input generates in its present use and the alternative, next-best use in which it can be employed. A factory may possess a large quasi-rent; if it is designed for a specific use, it may be of little value when employed

88

for other purposes. The result is that other actors in the industry may be able to extract the value of the quasi-rent, for the owners of the factory may be willing to sacrifice gains rather than to incur losses from redeploying the asset to its next best use.[49]

By comparison with the fixed assets of the factory owners, the inputs controlled by growers can be readily deployed into a variety of alternative uses. Particularly in the case of annual crops, they can be quickly diverted from a commodity whose value has declined to a commodity that is relatively lucrative by comparison. Thus we find growers in the Coast rapidly switching out of the production of cotton when the relative price of cotton declines; those in Eastern Province switching from cotton to maize; and those in Western and Nyanza Provinces switching from cotton to maize or sugar cane.[50] But the owners of cotton gins cannot switch into the processing of alternative crops. When confronted by adverse regulatory decisions regarding their cost margins, they must remain in the production of cotton. In this sense, the farmers, being more mobile, are less vulnerable than are the large-scale processors. Their strategic position is marked by an absence of the very quasi-rents that render the processors such easy targets.

The principal implication of this analysis is that the interest-group politics that dominate agrarian politics in Kenya need not result in the exploitation of the many by the few or the small by the large. Rather, the pattern may resemble one of plunder, wherein the large ineffectually oppose predation, for want of an ability to take refuge in economic alternatives. The Kenyan materials thereby compel us to revise the theory that is basic to the study of the politics of regulated industries: the theory of collective action.

CONCLUSION

From this chapter, we have learned much about the origins and structures of economic institutions, much about agrarian politics, and much about the evolution of political conflict in Kenya.

Institutions

The economic theory of institutions would have their origins lie in the efforts of economic agents to promote exchanges unattainable in markets. Capital markets exhibit risks that discourage investments from which lenders and borrowers both could gain. The costs of information restrict the profitability of agriculture by inhibiting the production of commodities of high quality. And scale economies create risks of inadequate throughput, thereby limiting investment in large enterprises. Many fea-

89

tures of the administrative structures governing Kenyan agriculture can be attributed to efforts to reduce the risks arising from intertemporal contracting, information costs, and scale, thereby supporting a greater volume of mutually beneficial transactions than would be attainable in unregulated markets.

There is thus much in the Kenyan materials to support an economic theory of institutions. And yet the materials also support a more political interpretation. Clearly, while the provision of institutions may have rendered agriculture more efficient, the constraints they put in place favored some groups more than others. Time after time, constraints designed into institutional rules were clearly supplied to assuage the concerns of big interests: most prominently, the investors of capital.

Upon reflection, this result is to be expected. It represents a dark side to the economic theory of institutions. For if the creation of institutions enhances the efficiency of markets, as economic theory would suggest, then the institution creates a public good. And if each agent is motivated by its own economic welfare, as economic reasoning would assume, then an agent would have to loom large in the market before being willing to incur the costs of organizing the new institution. Only then could it capture a portion of the benefits sufficient to cover the costs of organizing.

Lying behind the economic theory of institutions, then, is a political story, one in which big interests possess an initial advantage. The implication is that while many kinds of institutions may provide enhanced efficiency in markets, not just any set will be formed. Those institutions will be created that favor what have long been referred to as "special interests."[51]

This chapter has also illustrated how economic institutions, once put in place to secure greater prosperity, then provide the framework for struggles over the division of the gains. Economic institutions become the battlegrounds for interest-group politics.

Common sense and folk wisdom would suggest that the investors of capital, who played so prominent a role in the creation of these institutions, should provide the most active and most successful agents in the subsequent political struggles. The dominance of large-scale capital would be presumed by Marxists, dependency theorists, and the devotees of the theory of collective action as well. A major lesson of this chapter is that such expectations are wrong. The large interests do in fact constitute active lobbyists; but they do not constitute the most successful ones. For the strategic possibilities of large investors are constrained by their subsequent economic immobility, while those of small actors are not. And interest-group politics takes place in electoral environments, where politicians may be willing to bear the costs of organizing the numerous small and so subject the leaden-footed large to economic predation.[52] The power of large-scale economic interests in the Third World is eroded by forces originating from their political environment.

Economic institutions thus become political institutions. While formed to secure greater gains, they provide arenas for subsequent distributional struggles. And those who dominate the process of their creation often become victims of their subsequent operations. Institutions, once created, promote processes that take on a life of their own.

Agrarian politics

This chapter has also examined the interests that compete to control the organizations regulating commercial agriculture, the issues animating them, and the forces shaping their interplay. Fights over pricing, the structure of markets, the distribution of inputs, and the biasing of market operations – these controversies, we have seen, form much of the substance of rural politics.

Indeed, and this is the last major lesson of this chapter, these issues have come to dominate day-to-day politics in Kenya. Put more strongly, a qualitative shift has taken place in the politics of Kenya. And a major reason for this change, we argue, is the restructuring of the system of political parties. The shift from a competitive to a single-party system rendered distributional struggles and the factional rivalries that formed about them the major forms of political life.

Struggles among interest groups long antedated the change to a single-party system; many of the illustrations employed in this chapter were drawn from the preindependence period. But the era of competitive parties was marked by broader controversies as well. As documented in the last chapter, it was characterized by major debates concerning the shape and structure of institutions, the constitutional order, and the role and scope of the market. With the movement to a single-party system, however, ideological controversies no longer played a central role in electoral politics. What was left was normal politics: Little issues – those having to do with special interests – came to dominate the political agenda. The heroic period of Kenyan politics was over.

Changes in Kenyan political life

We conclude by attempting to explain why politics of special interests has become predominant. Adumbrated in V. O. Key's analysis of the politics of another agrarian society in another era and in another part of the world,[53] the explanation suggests the power of institutional environments to define the content of politics. The reasoning can best be elaborated from the citizen's point of view.

Under a competitive party system, it makes sense for citizens to pay attention to a candidate's stand on those issues affecting the entire national political system. For if a candidate is committed to a party, then her success could conceivably affect national policy; her performance at the polls would combine with the performance of other candidates from her party and their joint performance would help to define which team would subsequently control the government. Under a single-party, multiple-candidate system, however – the system found in Kenya after the banning of the KPU – it does not make sense for the voters to pay attention to the candidate's stand on national issues. Under this system, political competition remains; so too does electoral competition, but it takes the form of individual rivalries at the constituency level rather than national rivalries between organized teams. If successful, a candidate will become but one of over 100 members of Parliament; the candidate's success would therefore have little impact upon national policies. In the absence of a competitive party system, voters, behaving rationally, should therefore tend to pay more attention to the ability of candidates to do things of immediate, local value than to their stands on national issues. And candidates seeking votes would possess an incentive to compete in terms of their ability to deliver particular benefits.[54]

We can therefore comprehend the change in the substance of Kenyan politics: the move from contests over grand designs, forged by rival national alliances, as analyzed in the last chapter, to contests over particular issues, conducted by warring candidates in local constituencies, as analyzed in this.

4

From drought to famine: the dynamics of subsistence crises

Maize is grown by nearly 90 percent of Kenya's rural farm families. Expenditures on maize account for nearly two-thirds of all expenditures on cereals by Kenya's low-income, urban families and about 14 percent of their total expenditures.[1] Maize constitutes Kenya's staple food crop; shortages of this crop generate subsistence crises. In the period since independence, Kenya has repeatedly faced the prospects of famine. In each case, intense political controversy arose concerning the competence of public institutions, the wisdom of public policies, and, more centrally, the legitimacy of the national leadership. This chapter focuses on the crises of 1980 and 1984.

POLITICAL BACKGROUND

When the first of these crises hit, Daniel arap Moi was just establishing his hold on the presidency of Kenya. At the time of the second, he was consolidating his power.

As we have seen (Chapter 2), Moi was a leader of the Kalenjin-speaking people of the Rift Valley. A national officer in KADU, he served as the president of the Rift Valley Regional Assembly during the time of the land settlement programs. Having fought KANU and Kikuyu claims to the Highlands, Moi subsequently helped to negotiate the merger of the two parties. And like other leaders in KADU, he was rewarded with high governmental office.

Despite the merger of the two parties, the tensions between the major ethnic groups remained. Moi provided important political service by helping to mediate political disputes between them. In many areas in the Rift Valley, Kikuyu migrants sought to establish settlements, and local political leaders opposed their land claims. Among the most virulent of these disputes were those in Nandi, which represented one of the wealthiest of the Kalenjin-speaking areas. It was Moi who negotiated with the

93

leaders of the Nandi and quieted their militant opposition to the Kikuyu incursion.[2]

Moi thus proved a valuable ally to the KANU elite. And following the withdrawal of the radicals from the party, Jomo Kenyatta promoted Moi to the vice presidency of KANU and the nation. Whereas it had been the Luo who had provided the western leg of KANU, following the shift of the Luo into the KPU, it was now the Kalenjin, led by Moi.

During Kenyatta's administration, political rivalries tended to focus on the office of the vice president. The president possessed access to patronage that others could not rival. Having been the leader of the independence struggle, martyred by years in detention, and first president of the newly independent nation, Kenyatta possessed a stature that made direct political challenges unthinkable. In the struggle for political prominence in Kenya, then, ambitions focused on the vice presidency.

Kenyatta, as we have seen, ran a government that furnished a political base for the Kikuyu gentry. His cabinet was dominated by political allies from the Central Province in general and Kiambu district in particular. His administrative and security services systematically dismantled organized challenges to the resultant concentration of wealth and power in the postindependence period.[3]

From the point of view of those who had attached their fortunes to Kenyatta, Moi therefore represented a threat. For were he to succeed to the presidency, power would then shift from the hands of the privileged, largely concentrated in the Central Province, to the hands of others, largely based in western portions of the nation.

In the struggle for succession, the members of Kenyatta's inner circle therefore determined to weaken Moi's position.[4] Led by Dr. Njoroge Mungai, Kenyatta's nephew and most likely heir apparent, they sought to change the constitution so that Moi could not automatically succeed to the presidency but rather would serve as a figurehead while a new president was elected. Moi fought back. In his fight, he was supported by other "outsiders," such as Stanley Oloitiptip, a wealthy and influential leader of the Masai, and Shariff Nassir, the political boss of Mombasa. He was also aided by two key "insiders": Charles Njonjo from Kiambu and Mwai Kibaki from Nyeri. Both were long-term Cabinet members; both were from Central Province; and both felt that they would be more influential were they to succeed in installing their candidate, arap Moi, as president than they would be in a government dominated by the old guard.

In the political jockeying surrounding the "change the constitution" movement, Moi and his backers won out. Moi remained vice president. The constitution remained unchanged. As a consequence, when Jomo Kenyatta died in August 1978, Daniel arap Moi became the president of

Dynamics of subsistence crises

Kenya. Upon succeeding to the presidency, Moi retained Njonjo as attorney general and installed him as his closest political advisor. He picked Kibaki as his vice president.

In August 1978, Moi became president of Kenya. In 1979, drought hit Kenya. In 1980, there was a shortage of maize and people feared famine.

Where did these shortages come from? To what degree could the government be held accountable for them? And what was their impact upon the new Moi regime? These are the questions addressed in this and the following chapters.

DETERMINANTS OF THE TRANSFORMATION

An obvious answer to the first question is that food shortages were caused by the failure of the rains. But the record suggests that not all droughts become famines. A drought can be defined as a failure of the rains sufficiently great that crops also fail. A famine can be defined as hunger and/or starvation resulting from a lack of food. A relatively unsystematic reading of the evidence suggests the occurrence of major droughts in Kenya in 1889, 1894, 1898, 1914–19, 1928, 1931–34, 1939–40, 1943–44, 1948, 1954, 1960–61, 1964–65, 1970–71, 1973–74, 1979–80, and 1984.[5] Some, but far from all, of these droughts led to famines.

Droughts, and the resultant controversies over food policy, have played a major role in contemporary Kenyan politics. It is therefore worth devoting time to understanding what transforms them into food shortages.

Several sets of factors appear to influence the transformation. Of these, only one is in the short run under human control: the public policies and political institutions affecting the relationship between rainfall and food supply.

The magnitude of the drought

A major factor affecting the likelihood of a drought resulting in a food crisis is the magnitude of the drought. An appropriate measure is the number of plantings that fail to result in harvests.

One determinant of magnitude is duration. Most rural families store enough food to survive the loss of a season's planting. In Kenya, many store sufficient food to survive through a failure of both the long and short rains. In drought-prone regions, many manage their grain stocks in such a way that they can lose yet a third harvest while retaining sufficient seed to replant once again. When the rains fail a fourth time, however, even the most prudential managers of family grain stores face

Beyond the miracle of the market

the prospect of famine. The longer the duration of the drought, then, the more likely it is to result in food shortages.

A second determinant is geographic spread. The plantings of more farmers are at risk the broader the sweep of the drought. The Kenya drought of 1984–85 was a particularly dangerous one, for instance, not only because it led to a third loss of crop in the low lying areas but also because it ranged into areas lying at higher elevations. It spread into the densely populated Central Province, thereby leading to a far greater loss of harvest and a greater likelihood of famine.

Vulnerability to drought

Other factors increase the likelihood that drought will result in famine. These are linked not to the stimulus – that is, the duration or pattern of the rainfall – but rather to the population subject to that stimulus.

One is simply the skill of the farmers in managing their food stores or in employing strategies for handling food shortages.[6] Illustrative of the importance of these factors, once again, is the drought of 1984–85 in Kenya. When the drought penetrated the Central Province, it not only placed a larger number of harvests at peril; it also attacked a population not frequently subject to drought and therefore in possession of few skills for coping with shortfalls in the rains.

Also affecting the vulnerability of a population is its farm technology. Populations that have shifted to crop production are more vulnerable to fluctuations in the supply of moisture than are those engaging in pastoralism. Pastoralists can shift their enterprises to where rainfall *has* fallen; in the drought of 1984–85, for example, many herders shifted to the Coast, where rainfall levels had remained closer to normal levels. Farmers, by contrast, grow standing crops; unless the rain comes to the farm site, the crops are lost. Moreover, where arable production has significantly displaced grazing, livestock can no longer wander; many are stall fed and special grasses are grown for them. With the onset of drought, such grasses are lost; and because the livestock cannot forage, many perish. Populations are therefore more at risk when crop production replaces herding as the economic basis of rural life.

Characteristics of the population provide a third set of factors affecting the likelihood that famine will result from drought. One is its size; another, its rate of growth relative to the rate of growth of productivity in agriculture.

For a given agricultural technology, population size affects the transition of drought into famine by affecting the drought's magnitude: the larger the size of the population, the greater the number of harvests lost. The relationship between the rates of population and productivity growth affects the population's degree of vulnerability. If the population increases at a rate faster than technical change, farming must spread from areas of high-quality soils and abundant and reliable moisture supplies to more marginal agricultural regions. For in the absence of technical change, the old farming areas cannot produce sufficient food to support the larger population. The result of rapid population growth and static agricultural technology is thus an increase in the number of people at risk to climatic fluctuation. This dynamic is reflected in Kenya by the movement of farming from the Highlands into the semi-arid zones.[7]

As population increases, moreover, there is an acceleration in the shift from pastoral to arable production. Pastoralism requires a low ratio of people to land. Population can increase, but the quantity of land remains constant; as population increases, land becomes relatively scarce, pastoralism more costly to pursue, and arable production therefore increasingly attractive. The result of moving from herding to settled agriculture, once again, is an increase in vulnerability to drought.

The impact of these variables can perhaps best be seen by comparing two droughts of similar duration and geographic spread that take place in two different periods, the first prior to an increase in population and the second after. If the rate of population increase has exceeded that of the increase in the productivity of farming, then more people are at risk, greater numbers will have shifted to marginal agricultural zones, and crop production will have replaced the herding of livestock. The second drought would therefore pose a far greater threat, even though of the same duration and geographic spread as the first.

The analysis thus far has focused on the role of factors that are, in the short run, not governable by human agents. It has also suggested why food crises in Kenya may have become more frequent. With a rate of population growth that rivals the rate of technical change, the spread of arable production, and the movement of population from the well-watered Highlands into the semi-arid zones, a failure of the rains now poses a far greater risk to food supplies than before. Kenya's contemporary political leaders therefore may face a greater risk of food crises than did their colonial predecessors.

But what of the factors that are controllable? It is now time to turn to the role of human agents, and especially public institutions, as they affect the relationship between rainfall and food supplies in Kenya.

INSTITUTIONAL LINKS BETWEEN DROUGHT AND FAMINE

People can control population growth and invent new agricultural technologies; but neither in the short run can help to avoid the suffering

Table 4.1. *Dependent variable: Changes in stocks ('000 mt)*

Constant	−0.334
	(−0.009)
Rainfall (mm)	−0.001
	(−0.027)
$F = 0.000$ $R^2 = 0.000$ $DW = 1.714$	

t-statistics in parentheses. Eleven observations.

occasioned by a failure of the rains.[8] In the short run, it is the level of food stocks that can most effectively be controlled.

As Mbithi and others have documented, individual farm families in Kenya employ a variety of techniques for managing their food supplies.[9] The concern of this chapter is more with national policymakers than with individual farm families, however, and we therefore focus on the way in which government officials manage national food reserves.

A fruitful puzzle

We begin with a puzzle, one pertaining to the behavior of the national bureaucracy – called the Maize Board – that is charged with the maintenance of national food stocks.[10] The Maize Board possesses a legal monopsony over grain purchases. It alone can legally transport grain for sale in consumption centers or across international borders or manage the national grain stores.

Common sense suggests an intimate relationship between rainfall and grain reserves. It seems plausible that variations in rainfall would have a major impact on the reserves held by the Maize Board. In fact, contrary to expectations, there is *no* apparent statistical relationship between variations in the rainfall and in the level of stocks held by the Board, and no alteration of the lag structure in the measures employed altered this finding (Table 4.1).[11]

It also seems plausible that variations in the rainfall would have a major impact on the intake of grain by the Maize Board; that is, that the Board would be able to purchase more grain in years in which farmers experienced abundant rains. Once again, however, expectations are confounded. The data yield *no* apparent statistical relationship between variations in the rainfall and in the level of purchases by the Board. Whether the Board purchases a lot or a little maize is not significantly affected by the weather. Experimentation with a variety of alternative specifications failed to alter this finding (Table 4.2).

How, then, do droughts affect the national food stocks? Almost in

Table 4.2. *Dependent variable: Purchases by the Board ('ooo mt)*

Constant	524.008
	(3.041)***
Rainfall (mm)	−0.239
	(−0.963)
F = 0.830 R² = 0.192 DW = 1.347	

t-statistics in parentheses.   ***significant at .01 level.   Eleven observations.

Table 4.3. *Dependent variable: Sales by the Board ('ooo mt)*

Constant	738.685
	(8.239)***
Rainfall (mm)	−0.579
	(−4.362)***
F = 11.759 R² = 0.77 DW = 1.320	

t-statistics in parentheses.   *** significant at .01 level.   Eleven observations.

desperation, we turn to a third measure of the board's activities: its sales. And here, by contrast with our previous efforts, we find a large and highly significant relationship. In years of shortfall in the rains, sales by the Board rise dramatically. A 40 percent reduction in the rainfall over the period April to August in Kitale, these estimates suggest, leads to a roughly 150,000 mt increase in sales by the Board – or over 1.6 million bags[12] (Table 4.3).

The stocks of the Board can provide a buffer between drought and famine. And drought itself influences the activities of the Board. But it does not do so by affecting sales *to* the Board; rather, it affects the volume of sales *by* the Board. The Board can leave Kenya vulnerable to drought by failing to possess sufficient stocks of grain to cover the surge of consumer demand for its stocks at times when the rains fail.

Illustrative are the data contained in Figures 4.1–4.3, which portray the impact of the drought of 1984. As can be seen in Figure 4.1, despite the drought, purchases by the Board in 1984 initially exceeded those in previous years, although they fell off precipitously. As seen in Figure 4.2, sales by the Board in 1984 differed most strikingly from previous years, reaching the unprecedentedly high level of 300,000 bags a week by the end of July. The result, as seen in Figure 4.3, was a rapid draw-down in the Board's stocks, with levels plummeting toward zero by the month of September.

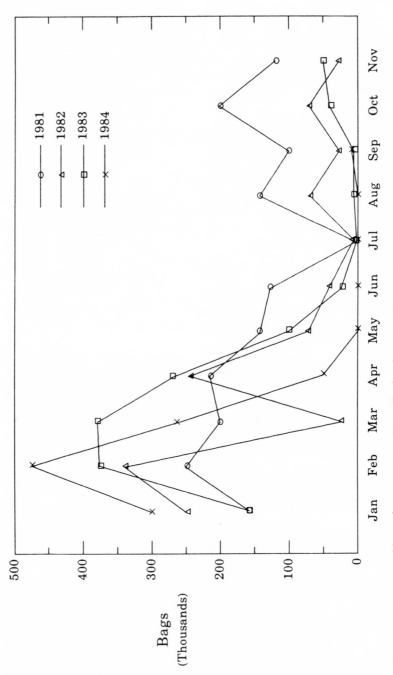

Figure 4.1. Average weekly purchases, 1981–84. *Note:* No data for 1984 following September.

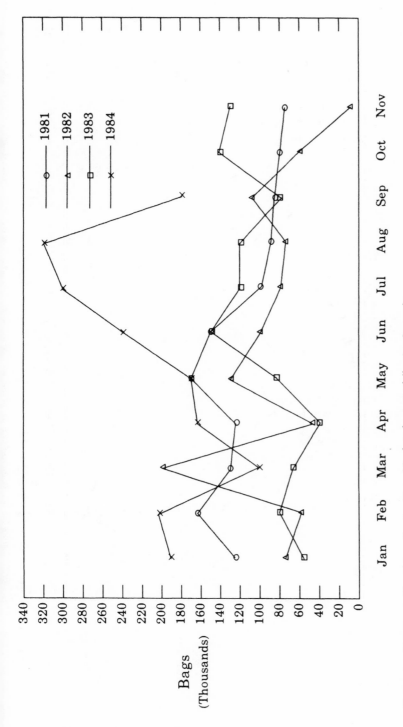

Figure 4.2. Average weekly sales, 1981–84. *Note*: No data for 1984 following September.

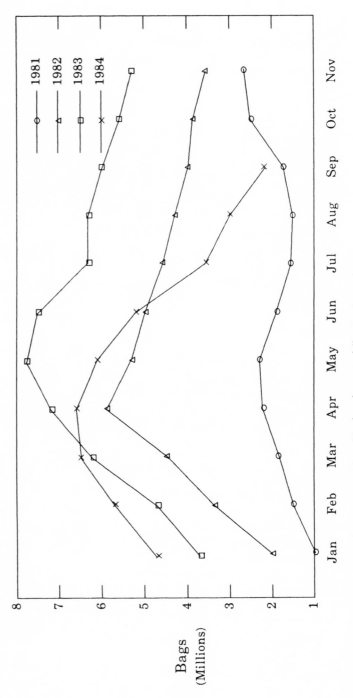

Figure 4.3. Average weekly stocks, 1981–84. *Note*: No data for 1984 following September.

Table 4.4. *Dependent variable: Imports ('ooo mt)*

Constant	-83.793
	$(-1.713)^*$
Sales	0.464
	$(3.333)^{***}$
$F = 6.685$ $R^2 = 0.49$ $DW = 1.420$	

t-statistics in parentheses.   * significant at .10 level.   *** significant at .01 level. Seventeen observations.

Unscrambling the puzzle

The data thus present a puzzle. Fluctuations in the rainfall do not affect the Board's stocks. Nor do they affect purchases by the Board. But they do affect Board sales.

The reason that the Board's stocks are not significantly affected by variations in the rainfall is straightforward: Increases in sales trigger imports by the Board. As seen in Table 4.4, an increase in sales of 100,000 mt (or slightly over one million bags) leads to imports of 46,000 mt (or slightly less than one half million bags). Because the Board calls for imports at times of high sales, the impact of drought on stocks is muted.

It is trickier to unscramble the reason why droughts affect sales but not purchases; but the lessons learned in doing so are highly informative. They underscore important elements of the basic structure of the maize industry.

Some elementary structures

The supply side. For purposes of analysis, maize producers can be divided into large, intermediate, and small farmers. The dividing line conventionally employed in Kenya is twenty hectares or greater for large farms; nine to twenty hectares for intermediate farms; and eight hectares or less for small farms. The large farms tend to be located in the former settler areas of the Rift Valley; maize production tends to be located in the western reaches of the valley, concentrating in Trans Nzoia and centering about Kitale. The intermediate sized farms also tend to be located in the Rift Valley or in areas immediately adjacent to it; many are the results of the subdivision of large-scale farms that took place with independence. Small-scale farms are to be found everywhere in Kenya. According to one report, the number of persons falling into each category in the mid 1970s were 20,000, 270,000 and 10,340,000 respectively.[13]

All categories of farms produce maize. Estimates suggest that the large

Beyond the miracle of the market

Table 4.5. *Distribution of total maize harvest by province and size of holding, 1981–82*

Size of holding	Percentages						
	Central	Coast	Eastern	Nyanza	Rift	Western	Total
Small	9	2	7	12	25	12	68
Intermediate	0	0	0	0	9	2	12
Large	0	0	0	0	19	1	20
Total	9	2	7	12	54	15	100

Source: Republic of Kenya, Ministry of Finance, *Grain Marketing Study, Interim Report*, vol. 1 (Nairobi: Githongo and Associates and Bookers International, July 1983), Appendix 2, Table 1.

and intermediate farms produce 20 to 30 percent of the total crop, and the multitude of small farms 70 to 80 percent.[14] It is tempting to think of the large and intermediate farmers as "commercial farmers" and the small farms as "subsistence" producers, and many people tend to do so. Indeed, the large farmers market in the order of 75 percent of what they produce; and while representing a very small fraction of the total farming population, the large farmers supply nearly one-half of the purchases by the Board. A breakdown of the sources of the 1983 maize crop is presented in Table 4.5.

Nonetheless – and this provides a crucial foundation for the argument being developed – studies suggest that smallholders also vigorously participate in the market, and in particular the market for food. Over 75 percent of the smallholders both buy and sell food.[15] Roughly one-half of the food consumed by smallholders is purchased off the farm, including 19 percent of the starchy staples, which include maize.[16]

The demand side. Over 80 percent of Kenya's maize consumers live in rural areas; the vast majority are small-scale farmers. The vast bulk of the maize that is marketed is therefore sold within the rural areas, largely among the smallholder families.

Also critical to the argument is that the maize consumed in the rural areas and that consumed in urban areas are of different forms. Maize sold in the rural areas tends to be purchased in *unprocessed* form. Of the maize consumed in the villages, less than 50 percent is commercially milled;[17] the percentage rises to over 60 percent in Central Province and falls to 15 percent in Western Province. By contrast, the vast bulk of the maize that is consumed in the urban areas is *processed* maize: maize that has been ground and/or sifted in the commercial maize mills, nearly all

Dynamics of subsistence crises

Table 4.6. Outline of the maize industry

Western Kenya	Urban Kenya	Eastern Kenya
Large and intermediate farmers	Consumers of milled maize	Smallholders
Altitude: 4,400 ft.	Negative trade balance vis-à-vis the Board	Altitude: 3–4,000 ft.
Rainfall: 650 mm		Rainfall: 3–400 mm
Positive trade balance vis-à-vis the Board		Few transactions with the Board

of which are located in the major towns: Nairobi, Mombasa, Nakuru, Kisumu, and Eldoret.

The millers receive their consignments from the Maize Board. Should they purchase from suppliers other than the Board, they would risk losing their licenses.

Perturbing the system. According to Acland, maize in Kenya requires roughly 200 mm of rainfall in the planting season. Less than that and yields decline; much less than that and crops fail.[18]

As we have seen, much of the maize that is marketed through the Maize Board originates from western Kenya and especially from the large farmers in and about Kitale and from the intermediate sized farmers in the former settlement schemes. Kitale lies at roughly 5,500 feet and on average 650 mm of rain falls during the growing period in Kitale – a figure that is exceeded in the areas of western Kenya lying in the "rain shadow" of Nyanza Victoria.

Many smallholders live in regions lying at lower elevations and receive lesser amounts of rain. The maize and cotton zones of Machakos, for example, lie between 3,000 and 4,000 feet and receive roughly 300 to 400 mm of precipitation during the growing season.[19] In these and other small holder areas, far more maize is grown than is marketed and what is marketed tends to be exchanged in unprocessed form.

Table 4.6 presents a schematic portrayal of the system thus outlined. Say, now, that there was a 35 percent reduction in the rainfall. The large and intermediate farmers would then receive roughly 420 mm of rain, which, according to Acland's figures, is enough to produce a crop. But the small farmers would receive but 195 to 260 mm of rain, barely enough to secure a crop. Being unable to secure unprocessed maize in the rural markets, the smallholders must instead purchase processed maize. This means that their demand – and rural consumers constitute by far the greatest portion of all consumers – shifts to commercial retailers. Rural businesses experience a rapid increase in demand for processed maize. Store owners therefore stream into town and purchase supplies from the maize mills. The mills are supplied by the Board. At times of drought, then, the Board experiences a growth in demand for its stocks of maize, for it has been hit with a shift in demand from Kenya's rural sector – the sector that contains over 80 percent of the nation's consumers.[20]

We can thus comprehend why drought might not affect Board purchases while nonetheless affecting the Board's sales. The explanation that unravels this puzzle also helps to show how droughts become food crises; for it illustrates how random perturbations in the weather can lead to a rapid run-down of the national stocks, as rural people start to purchase their food from the Board. Should the Board's stocks be low at a time of drought, then that drought could result in a food crisis.

In light of this lesson, it therefore becomes critical to understand how the Board manages the national food stocks. The results of such an examination prove disturbing. For they suggest that problems within the institution may generate pressures that convert abundance into dearth and therefore translate droughts into food crises.

THE DYNAMICS OF THE BOARD

For evidence for this assertion, we can examine the food crisis of 1979–80. If that crisis can be said to have a beginning, it was with the lobbying activities of the larger maize farmers, many of whom belong to the Kenya National Farmers' Union (KNFU). In 1975, they had submitted "detailed proposals and costings" to the government in an effort to secure a price rise for their products.[21] But they had been disappointed: The prices for maize and wheat had remained unchanged and the price increases for other commodities were considered to be too little and too late to be of major benefit to farmers. The Union therefore determined to do better. In September 1976, the KNFU "initiated a delegation to see His Excellency Mzee Jomo Kenyatta" and "a number of carefully prepared memoranda and proposals were prepared and submitted."[22] The results "far exceeded" expectation.[23] Maize prices increased 23 percent; the price of wheat, 20 percent; and that of beef between 15 and 23 percent, depending on the grade. The price rises were announced by the president on September 26, 1976, at a public meeting with the leaders of the farm delegation.

In the agricultural cycle for maize in Kenya, there is a long-rain and short-rain crop. The former is by far the larger. The long rains commence in March-April; the short rains toward October. The timing of the president's announcement of the new maize price therefore limited its initial

Dynamics of subsistence crises

impact; it was sufficiently late that it affected a limited portion of the short-rain crop. The full impact upon farmers came at the time of planting for the long rains of 1977; and its full impact upon the marketing system registered at the time of that crop's harvest.

The onset of abundance

In early 1977, those who harvested a short-rain crop found that "a bumper harvest . . . had an acute storage problem. . . . The Maize and Produce Board cannot buy any more maize owing to lack of storage facilities." "Maize growers are being forced to sell again at 'throw away prices,' " one newspaper reported.[24] In some areas, the Maize Board raised its standards for moisture content, allowing it to reject deliveries.[25] Reports circulated that some depot managers now demanded bribes to accept maize deliveries into their crowded store.[26] Having bought more maize than they had sold, the managers of the Maize Board lacked the cash to pay for new deliveries; farmers who sold to the Board had to wait weeks for payment.[27]

The harvest from the long rains indicated the full dimension of the problem. Headlines read: "MAIZE EMERGENCY HITS KEYNA."[28] The nature of the emergency was outlined in the body of the article:

Kenya has got too much maize, millions of bags are in danger of going to waste. The national stores are already full to bursting point, and a record crop of nearly eight million bags is to be harvested in the next few weeks. . . . The forthcoming bumper harvest would strain already extended transport and storage facilities beyond any credible capacity.[29]

Political pressures, moreover, were mounting from farmers seeking to utilize the government market for maize. As reported in the press, the provincial commissioner of the Western Province pleaded with the director of agriculture to "come forward and help maize farmers in the Western Province to market their surplus maize."[30]

In the face of such pressures, those in charge of maize marketing policy began to formulate plans for disposing of excess stocks of maize. Some they disposed of as famine relief; some as stock feed. Determined to sell three million bags to open up their stores for the new harvest, the Board began to plan for exports. But the decision to export was postponed.

There was a financial reason for postponing the decision: The Board stood to lose over Ksh. 40 per bag from exports. The government was unwilling to incur such losses. There were also political reasons. The Board spans a market – one in which there are not only maize producers but also maize consumers. The benefits to be gained from rewarding the interests of producers must be balanced against the costs of alienating consumers. The government's reluctance to export originated from its fear of future food shortages and their impact upon consumers. As the Minister of Agriculture declared:

we want...to ensure that being a staple good for the majority of Kenyans, everyone gets [maize] at a controlled price anytime wherever he may be in the Republic.

The Government intends to ensure that everyone gets maize...We would like to make sure that our people are well fed before we think of exporting outside at a loss.[31]

The perceived risks of dearth for consumers thus initially outweighed the magnitude of the economic losses resulting from glut, and the government therefore delayed maize exports.

The result was the continued accumulation of surpluses. As a consequence of large stocks, the Board experienced both administrative and financial difficulties. It was unable physically to store the crop; and with its economic resources tied up in inventories, it was unable to pay for new deliveries. It therefore began to reject them.

In July, the depot in South Nyanza lowered its moisture standard from a maximum of 13 percent to 11 percent, thereby enabling it to reject new deliveries of maize. The district chairman of KANU protested the measure on behalf of the farmers and asserted that "most of the farmers, particularly those living in Migori, will not be able to pay school fees for their children or repay government loans because they have nowhere to sell their maize."[32] In Eldoret North, the Maize Board lowered its moisture standard to 10 percent and refused to accept maize containing foreign matter, broken or discolored grains, or evidence of damage by insects.[33]

The administrative inability of the Board to manage abundance was matched by its financial inability to pay for it. As noted in a government review of the crisis:

The effect of Government's policy was that a storage of 5 million bags reserve would have to be financed as indicated in a letter to the Treasury.

The pressing seriousness of the financial implications prompted a series of papers to be presented [in June 1978] to the Ministry of Finance and Planning. These papers [noted] that without some solution ... Treasury would be faced with a request of K£40 million to support the maize industry. There was reported [sic] no funds ... to finance [the Maize Board] and an increasingly large bill for storage and losses through inadequate storage. An analysis showed that [the Maize Board] had debts of K£33.5 million and a stock of 5.4 million bags, i.e. near capacity under storage.[34]

In July 1978, the Maize Board exhausted its capital reserves; it was compelled to approach the Treasury for a subvention. The Board received an infusion of K£2.5 million; but because the Board continued to hold

Dynamics of subsistence crises

stocks of 5.6 million bags, the Ministers of Finance and of Agriculture combined to petition for a change in policy. They drafted a cabinet paper pressing for a financial solution: relieving stores by exporting. In late September 1978, their petition was approved; in October, tenders were placed for exports; and in March 1979, exports began and a run-down of stocks commenced.

It is to be noted and stressed that these meetings took place just weeks after the death of Kenyatta, when Moi was struggling to take control of the national government.

The costs of sustaining abundance also led to a change in pricing policy. The government reduced the maize price from Ksh. 80 per bag to Ksh. 60 per bag. The reduction in the maize price was announced in February. The announcement therefore took place in time to affect planting for the long rains.

The onset of dearth

In May of 1979, an official of the Maize Board toured the maize production regions. He filed the following memorandum:

Recently, the Government announced policy decisions on withdrawal of [the government's credit program] and reducing the producer price of maize. In view of these decisions, I carried out a brief field survey in the main commercial maize growing areas of Trans Nzoia, Uasin Gishu and Nakuru.

I visited some farmers and asked the farmers how much acreage they had planted [in] maize in 1978 and how much they have planted or are going to plant this year (1979). The response I got was that the commercial maize acreage in Trans Nzoia and Nakuru will be reduced by about 50 percent and by more than 50 percent in Uasin Gishu. The main reasons indicated are the withdrawal of GMR, the reduction in prices, and the marketing problem the farmers experienced in the 1977 season.

It seems that the 1978–79 maize intake by the Board will be slightly less than 3 million bags, probably around 2.7 million bags. This is partly because some farmers want to retain the 1978 crop for their animals rather than deliver at Ksh. 65 per bag. There were reasonably good rains in 1978 and the farmers who had no doubts got [government credit]. Thus, considering that 1978–79 intake will be about 2.7 million bags, it would be reasonable to assume that 2.5 million bags will be on the high side.[35]

Based on this observation, the Board's statistician calculated the expected food supply for 1980. As of October 31, 1979, given the end of the 1978–79 crop purchase program, there would be stocks of 3.6 million bags. With internal sales of 4.2 million bags per annum and a maize intake of 2.4 million bags, he warned, the maintenance of export commitments amounting to 1.8 million bags threatened to create a food deficit. "Maize exports should be stopped," he wrote, "to save the country from serious maize deficits by 1980."[36] The managing director of the Board notified the permanent secretary of the Office of the President of this forecast in July 1979; in November 1979, the general manager notified the permanent secretary of the Ministry of Agriculture that the situation had "deteriorated further"; "therefore," he wrote, "although we had forecast a critical position for next May or June 1980, on present form, we could now be critical in January or February 1980."[37]

The Board thus had advised the Office of the President and the Ministry of Agriculture of the problem of food shortages in May and again in July of 1979 (and once again in November). But by July, 163,170 tons of maize (1.8 million bags) had been exported.[38] By August 1979, grain reserves stood at 1.7 million bags. By December 1979, they stood at 400,000. And by May 1980, they were exhausted.

A food crisis thereupon broke out and it was marked by the articulation of vocal, bitter, and explosive political protest. The first signs of crisis were registered in the cities. Such headlines as "FURIOUS WANANCHI STORM INTO STORES: Near Riot at City Queue for 'Unga' "[39] suggest the nature and magnitude of the urban challenge. Even more striking than the political energies unleashed at the local level were those precipitated at the national level. The outbreak of protest shook the foundations of the new Moi government. By comparison with the political reactions to abundance, those accompanying dearth proved explosive.

Policy adjustments

The political pressures led to changes in public policy. Some took the form of structural changes. In conjunction with the strict enforcement of movement restrictions and heightened vigilance against smuggling, the government created grain purchasing monopsonies in several maize-producing districts. In others, it created and staffed over 400 local buying centers (see Appendix 4A). Banning private traders in most maize-growing regions, the government sought to leave its own marketing centers as the sole channel for the marketing of maize. The purpose of both measures was clear: to insure, in the words of the time, that "every grain of maize" ended up in the public stores.

The government also altered its maize prices. In November 1979, it raised the price of maize from Ksh. 65.00 to Ksh. 80.00 per bag; in July 1980, it raised the price once again, this time to Ksh. 90.00. It is notable, however, that in so doing the government continued to accommodate the interests of consumers; in February 1980, the Minister of Agriculture had announced a 30 percent increase in the price of wheat flour and bread; but on February 20, the Cabinet canceled these price increases "with immediate effect."[40] One group protested the producer price rise:

Dynamics of subsistence crises

the Sugar Authority, which feared the diversion of production from sugar to maize.[41] Another protested the failure to raise the consumer price: the millers, who stood to lose on the price margin allowed them under the new structure of prices. Aside from these protests, the government's tactic of raising producer prices while restraining consumer price increases elicited widespread assent. The economic costs of political accommodation were born by the public treasury. The Board lost over K£3.8 million on internal maize sales in 1980–81; in connection with its loss on imports, it amassed deficits totaling K£14.2 million.

Additional evidence

Investigations of the maize crises of 1964–65 and 1972–73 outline dynamics very similar to those discussed above.[42] As noted in the second report, the commission of inquiry noted "the familiar syndrome," which they described as:

... shortage produces a panic reaction and a rise in price for the following year; natural conditions return to normal and these, together with the rise in price, produce a surplus; the surplus has to be exported at considerable loss and pressure builds up for a reduction in price to make the farmers pay for the losses they have incurred; low prices then continue until the drought pushes them up again.[43]

A policy-induced food cycle?

Three investigations, then – our own in the 1980s, that of the commission of inquiry in 1966, and that of the parliamentary select committee of 1974 – suggest the existence of a characteristic institutional dynamic. Its structure can be summarized:

Period 1: Glut, with warehouses full to overflowing, generally resulting from high prices to farmers and fortuitous growing conditions, combined with stocks of imported grain carried over from a previous food emergency.

Problems of the Board: Physical congestion; money tied up in inventories; lack of room to store additional purchases and of money to finance them.

Responses by the Board: A raising of moisture and quality standards as a means of avoiding additional purchases. Delays in payments to farmers.

Responses by farmers: Increased frustration over rejected deliveries and delays in payments for deliveries made. Changes in production plans, substituting other crops for maize.

Beyond the miracle of the market

Period 2: Continued glut, as maize intake matches maize sales.

Problems of the Board: Physical congestion; money tied up in inventories; a lack of room to store additional purchases or of money to finance them.

Responses by the Board: Continued rejection of deliveries; lowering of prices offered farmers in real and sometimes nominal terms; the proposal of exports to clear the stores and to generate cash flow.

Response by the farmers: Cutbacks in planting in response to delays in payments for maize, reductions in prices, and the rejection of deliveries.

Period 3: Reduced inventories, as a consequence of reduced deliveries and increased exports.

Problems of the Board: Physical and cash flow problems alleviated by the export of maize and reduced domestic purchases.

Responses by the Board: Continued exports, as export contracts signed in the period of glut are honored.

Responses by the farmers: Continued caution in growing maize.

Abundance thus creates problems for the Board: administrative problems of managing physical stocks of grain and financial problems of paying farmers for deliveries to the Board. The response of the Board is to export and to behave in ways that weaken the incentives for farmers. Because of exports, the Board's stores are empty; because of weakened financial incentives, fewer deliveries flow in. Clearly, should there be a drought when the system is at this state, the Board might lack the stocks to cover the increase in its sales. A food crisis would result, and the nation would be vulnerable to famine.[44]

Unregulated markets would also produce fluctuations in supply. Behaving optimally, the Board could dampen them. It could purchase maize when prices were low, sell when they were high, and compensate for errors in its management of the domestic market by buying and selling in international markets where rainfalls in the various production centers remain uncorrelated, thus dampening weather-induced price fluctuations. But the Board acts so as to retard economic adjustments and thus may amplify the effects of dearth and abundance. Its lagged responses appear to exacerbate, rather than to dampen, the instability of markets.

POLITICAL SURVIVAL

The threat of famine that occurred in 1980 hit a regime that had been in power for but a little over one year. It precipitated elite-level maneuvering, as the new Moi regime sought to consolidate its position of power.

In February 1980, Moi, acting as commander in chief, called upon the

Dynamics of subsistence crises

Army to transport maize to Nairobi. The effort was dubbed "Operation Maize." As a news report phrased it:

Following the Presidential directive yesterday that army and National Youth Service trucks assist in the transportation of maize from Kitale to ... Nairobi and Mombasa, milling plants in these two towns have agreed to operate at full capacity throughout the weekend. The arrangement for the mills not to close during the weekend came with even better news that the Kenya Railways Corporation had managed by yesterday afternoon to transport over 6,000 bags of maize for Nairobi plants.... [45]

The exercise was repeated later in November. As noted by the newspaper:

UNGA TO FLOOD NAIROBI

A huge consignment of white and yellow maize meal under heavy police guard arrived in Nairobi yesterday. The 9,680 bags were sent from Eldoret to Nairobi yesterday under a "Presidential Directive."

The government is "to flood" all Nairobi ... with maize meal ... within the next few days, the Nairobi Area Provincial Commissioner ... said yesterday as he personally witnessed the off-loading of the consignment.

The Provincial Commissioner said: "We in the Government want to show our people we are capable and willing to feed them under the wise leadership of President Moi." [46]

The president thus sought credit for feeding the people. The new Moi government also sought to shift the blame for the food crisis onto others. Official accounts of the food shortage focused on the rains. They also featured populist themes by attacking "big men" who were supposedly hoarding or smuggling grain. As stated by one minister:

The food shortage had been caused by unscrupulous businessmen who were bent on getting rich over night.

He disclosed that such businessmen had purchased all the posho in urban areas and dumped it in rural areas, thus causing the shortage.

"As we all know" [he stated] "towns are the most sensitive areas." [47]

Dearth thus could be explained by the activity of those wealthy enough to own fleets of lorries. In the context of Kenya at the time, this could signify only two groups: the Asians and/or the wealthy Kiambu confederates of the old regime – Africans who had used their wealth and power to purchase transport fleets and so increase their fortunes.

It was of course well known that the Maize Board had been exporting maize prior to the food crisis. Strenuous efforts were therefore made to fix the blame for these exports. In particular, it was firmly believed that the national interest had been sacrificed to private interests and that an unwise level of exporting had taken place because people with influence over the Board's decisions could make money from grain deals.

Early in 1980 inquiries were made at the Maize Board asking for the

Beyond the miracle of the market

records concerning exports; the materials were hand delivered to the requesting party.⁴⁸ Shortly thereafter the records were leaked to the press. In an article published July 2, 1980, *The Standard* documented the dates, carriers, and destination of each shipment; the story listed as well the level of the national stocks at the dates on which the shipments took place. The implication was clear: The exports had put the nation at risk. Moi's close colleague and attorney general, Charles Njonjo, repeatedly demanded in Parliament the names of those who had negotiated the export deals. And increasingly he focused the blame on the man who had been minister of agriculture: Jeremiah Nyagah.⁴⁹ Circulating about the verbal thrusts of Njonjo was a rich complement of attendant rumors: that in authorizing the maize exports, Nyagah had allowed selected members of the old guard to serve as intermediaries for the foreign grain companies and thereby to profit from the deals.⁵⁰ Njonjo and his colleagues in the Moi regime thus used the export program to discredit those who had held power under Kenyatta.

Not only was the maize crisis used to advance the collective interests of the Moi regime, however. It was also used to secure powerful individual positions within it. In particular, it was used by Njonjo and his confederates to attack Mwai Kibaki, the vice president. The attacks began in the 1979 parliamentary elections, as Njonjo questioned the loyalty to Moi of candidates favored and sponsored by Kibaki. Shortly after the election and at the height of the maize crisis, rumors began to circulate that "groups" had been formed at the highest levels of government.⁵¹ Each group was organized about a political patron: Njonjo on the one side and Kibaki on the other. They both protested their loyalty to the president. And they both attacked those responsible for weakening the government by causing the "shortages of essential goods."⁵² The rumors orchestrated by the Njonjo faction accused its rivals of using underhanded political methods, convoking "illegal meetings in the night," with the implication of oath taking. The old guard, it was implied, which had lost out in the succession battle, was seeking to reinstate itself in power by promoting the fortunes of one of its own: Mwai Kibaki, the vice president and a Kikuyu from Central Province.⁵³ Kibaki's enemies also accused him of covering up or even abetting crimes of economic sabotage – crimes organized by rich businessmen with close ties to the Maize Board, businessmen who would smuggle for a profit the national stocks of grain.

By associating the program of exports with their political predecessors, those around Moi discredited those who had been close to Kenyatta. And by associating the vice president with this political faction, Charles Njonjo sought to muscle his way forward in the line of succession to the

114

Dynamics of subsistence crises

presidency. In the midst of the food crisis of 1980, the politics of the Moi regime had begun.

CONCLUSION

This chapter has taught us about subsistence crises. Drought transfers the demand for marketed food from the countryside to the towns. Drought causes rural dwellers, who make up the majority of the population of any developing nation, to eat from the government stores. If the public food stores lie barren, then drought becomes famine.

This chapter has also taught us about the importance of institutions. Food shortages, we have argued, were not the inevitable physical consequence of shortfalls in the rains. Rather, the transition from drought to famine is mediated by public institutions. Systematic tendencies in the behavior of the institutions regulating the maize marketing system, we hypothesized, transform the material condition of drought into the social outcome of famine.

Lastly, this chapter has focused on a third major theme: the agrarian foundations for politics. It has explored the political impact of food crises, showing how anxieties about food supplies can be used to win friends and to discredit enemies and thereby to consolidate political power.

In Chapter 5 we continue the investigation of this third theme. We examine how the crises of subsistence played out at the local level, giving the new Moi government a chance to implant itself into the structures of power at the district level.

Appendix 4A: The buying center program

As noted above, in response to the maize crisis of 1979–80, the government created a network of local buying centers. By offering the "into-depot" price for grain delivered to the local buying centers, the Board absorbed the costs of transport and sought thereby to make its services more attractive to small-scale farmers. Its objective was to increase production, reduce the level of retention of maize for on-farm consumption, and increase the level of sales to the Board.

The buying center program expanded rapidly. By 1982, there were over 500 local buying centers (Table 4A.1), and over 1,000 new staff had been added to the Board.

The centers proved expensive. The Kenya Farmers' Association (KFA), which served as the Board's agent for maize purchases in the Rift Valley, submitted a bill for over Ksh. 20 million to cover the costs of the buying centers for the year 1981–82. In 1984, a sample of twenty centers in Nandi yielded an average cost per center of Ksh. 62,285. A sample of eighteen buying centers in Trans Nzoia yielded an average cost of Ksh. 95,384. The KFA figures suggest that the costs per bag of maize purchased through the centers in 1981–82 was Ksh. 13.49. The two samples of buying centers yield an estimate of Ksh. 10.59 per bag in 1983–84. When added to the price paid producers, the costs of buying centers thus contributed an additional 10 percent to the procurement costs of maize.

Part of the costs of a buying center are fixed. They include the costs of construction (or rental), scales, drainage pallets, and tarpaulins. These costs average roughly Ksh. 20,000 per center. The variable costs are principally those of labor and transport. Board estimates suggest that total unit costs are lowest when a buying center processes 20,000 bags per season, though the optimum shifts depending on the distance of the center from its parent depot.

The costs of the buying center program have made it a point of controversy between the government and international agencies. Kenya's

Appendix 4A: The buying center program

Table 4A.1. Number of buying centers, 1982

District	Number of buying centers
Nakuru	40
Baringo	40
Narok	9
Kericho	74
Nandi	82
Uasin Gishu	54
Kakamega	42
Bungoma	44
Busia	17
Trans Nzoia	52
West Pokot	14
Elgeyo/Marakwet	22
Laikipia/Nyandarua	25
Loitokitok	5
Total	520

Source: From the files of NCPB, Nairobi.

donors have sought a reform in the maize-marketing system, including a comprehensive reevaluation of the local buying centers.

In debates with the World Bank, government representatives have stressed that many of the costly features of the buying center program generate benefits that are rarely noted by its critics. They stress that the centers strengthen the incentives for small farmers to plant maize, to sell it instead of retaining it on the farm, and, in particular, to sell it to the Maize Board. They also point to the sharp increase in the Board's purchases of maize in the year following the introduction of the local buying program, up first to 393,040 metric tons in 1980–81 and then to 550,000 metric tons in 1981–82 (the second largest volume purchased in the history of the Board) from 131,040 metric tons in 1979–80.

In an effort to measure the impact of the local buying centers, I worked with the staffs of the Central Bureau of Statistics and Maize Board. The Bureau generates detailed maps of the districts of Kenya and periodically surveys sample clusters of farmers in the rural areas. As part of these surveys, it determines the amount of maize grown, the total amount marketed, and the amount marketed to the Board. I randomly selected three districts from the maize surplus regions of Kenya: Nandi, Trans Nzoia, and Kakamega. With the help of officials from the Maize Board, I entered onto maps the location of the local buying centers. With the help of the staff of the Central Bureau of Statistics, I entered on the same maps the location of the clusters of farmers that were periodically interviewed as part of the crop forecast surveys. I then determined which of the Bureau's clusters lay close to a local buying center; these I labeled clusters characterized by "access" to the Board. I drew a random sample of the clusters with access and recovered from the storerooms of the Bureau as many as possible of the survey forms that enumerators had filled in when interviewing farmers in these clusters. To create a control group of farmers who lacked access to local buying centers, I located on the district maps clusters lying in the same ecological zones as those that had been chosen for my sample. For each cluster with access in my sample, I then picked another cluster that lay in the same zone but that lacked access to a buying center, and recovered survey sheets for farmers in these clusters as well.

All told, I collected data from fourteen clusters with and fourteen without access. The data were drawn from interviews with a total of 275 farmers, 116 with access and 159 without. The data record the planting and marketing behavior of these farmers for the years 1981–82, 1982–83, and 1983–84. The same farmers were not reinterviewed in each year.

Interviews with Board personnel suggest a preference for setting up buying centers in areas with larger farms so as to reduce unit costs of marketing. Interviews with politicians and local community leaders suggest a preference for locating buying centers in areas of small-scale farming, both because there are more small farmers than large and because of a desire for equity. The data suggests that the Board prevailed in Kakamega and Trans Nzoia, where farmers with access tended to have larger farms, whereas in Nandi politicians and local community leaders appear to have prevailed, as farmers with access tended to possess smaller acreages. As seen in Table 4A.2, however, when all farmers are pooled, there is no significant difference in farm sizes between those with and those without access to buying centers.

Comparison of the means of the two categories of observations – those taken from farmers with access and those taken from farmers without – reveals no significant difference in the tendency to grow maize (each grow roughly 21 bags); to retain maize for on-farm consumption (each retained roughly one-half of production); or, when selling maize, to sell it to the Board.

If access to the Board's facilities had no apparent effect on the behavior of farmers, then why did the intake of maize increase following the restructuring of the Board? The reason would appear to be that all farmers, those with and those without access, found conditions more favorable in the years following the introduction of the buying center than in 1979–80. In accounting for variation in output, retentions, and sales to the Board, we find that longitudinal effects – effects that vary for all farmers over time, such as prices and weather – are far stronger than cross-

Appendix 4A: The buying center program

Table 4A.2. *Comparisons of behavior among categories of farmers*

Farmers	Average farm size (ha)	Standard deviation	*t*-statistic	Average output (bags)	Standard deviation	*t*-statistic
With access	8.41	10.52	0.98	21.40	36.79	−0.19
Without access	10.00	16.27		20.49	44.08	
Total	9.08			21.02		

Farmers	Average retention (bags)	Standard deviation	*t*-statistic	Average sales to Board (bags)	Standard deviation	*t*-statistic
With access	10.92	8.99	−1.74	9.93	32.79	0.19
Without access	9.07	8.38		10.78	39.82	
Total	10.14			10.88		

Note: *t*-statistic derived from the means test. There are 273 observations.

sectional effects – effects that differ within given periods, such as those induced by giving some farmers but not others access to the Board's marketing facilities. Thus, whereas output, retention, and sales to the Board failed to vary with access, they did vary significantly by year (Table 4A.3).

It is possible, of course, that there are interactions between cross-sectional effects, such as access, and longitudinal effects, such as changes in prices or the weather. It is possible, for example, that farmers with access would respond more positively to favorable conditions than those without. To explore this conjecture, we fitted a covariance model to the data and estimated the relevant coefficients by regression methods. In doing so, we had to drop the data for 1980–81 from the sample, as in that year none of the farmers had yet been provided with a buying center by the Maize Board. The model is of the form:

$$Y = a_1 T_1 + a_2 T_1 A + a_3 T_2 + a_4 T_2 A$$

Where
Y = the dependent variable: output, retentions, or sales to the board.

Table 4A.3. *Comparisons of behavior by year*

Year	Average output (bags)	Standard deviation	t-statistic	Average retention (bags)	Standard deviation	t-statistic
1980–81	9.19	7.88		7.17	6.01	
1981–82	16.08	23.60		9.52	8.40	
1982–83	27.00	52.10	2.18	11.03	9.23	1.38

	Average sales to board (bags)	Standard deviation	t-statistic
1980–81	1.75	10.29	
1981–82	6.01	3.11	
1982–83	15.31	3.10	2.07

t-statistic: Tests for the difference between the means for 1981–82 and 1982–83 only. The data for 1980–81 contained no farmers with access to local buying centers.

Table 4A.4. *Estimated coefficients*

	Output	Retentions	Total sales	Sales to Board
a_1	7.66	5.83	1.83	1.08
	(1.14)	(4.01)	(0.30)	(0.18)
a_2	11.61	5.08	6.53	6.79
	(1.47)	(2.98)	(0.92)	(0.95)
a_3	29.28	11.12	18.16	17.50
	(5.97)	(10.53)	(4.12)	(3.96)
a_4	−4.71	−0.19	−4.52	−4.52
	(−0.66)	(−0.13)	(−0.71)	(−0.71)

t-statistics are in parentheses. There are 263 observations.

T_1 = a dummy variable for 1981–82, which captures the effects of weather, price, or some other factor that varies from year to year.

T_2 = a dummy variable for 1982–83.

A = a dummy variable for access. A is 1 if a farmer is drawn from a cluster of farmers who reside close to a buying center, 0 otherwise.

The estimated coefficients of this model are reported in Table 4A.4.

In 1981–82, farmers without access produced on average 7.66 bags of maize; those with access, over 19 bags. Large standard errors render this estimate of the positive effect of access statistically insignificant, however. In 1982–83, farmers without access produced 29 bags of maize; those with access produced fewer than 25. Again, the difference is statistically insignificant.

In 1981–82, farmers without access retained nearly 6 bags of maize; those with access, over 10 bags. Given that those with access produced more maize (19.27 bags as opposed to 7.7), these figures imply that access increased the rate of sales, with those with access selling over 40 percent of their production and those who lacked access, slightly less than 25 percent. In 1982–83, those with access retained slightly less than those without. As those with access produced roughly 5 bags less than those without, however, the result was that the two groups of farmers ended up marketing roughly the same percentage of their production: between 50 and 60 percent.

In 1981–82, those with access marketed to the Board an average of over 6 bags more than those without. The difference is not statistically significant, however. In 1982–83, those with access to the Board sold on average 4.52 bags of maize less to the Board than those who lacked access. Once again, however, the difference is not statistically significant. In percentage terms, in 1982–83, both groups sold 95 percent of what they marketed off the farm to the Board.

The data thus suggest that changes taking place in 1981–82 and 1982–83 led to increases in maize production, in total sales, and in sales to the Board. These effects were desired and intended by policymakers. But the analysis also suggests that the buying centers had very little to do with these effects. In some cases, those with access were more likely to make the production and marketing decisions that were desired by the government than were those who lacked access. In other cases, those with access were less likely to respond in positive ways than were those who lacked access. And in many instances, there simply was no statistically significant difference in the behavior of the two categories of farmers.

The data thus call into question whether the additional expenses incurred by the formation of local buying centers are worth the costs. Costs of transport could be conserved by locating buying centers near depots; labor costs, by confining the buying season to the peak of the harvest; and total costs, by closing buying centers with insufficient throughput.

Insofar as small farmers tend to live at some distance from the depots, the first measure might reduce the access of small farmers to the Board. It might also lead to higher unit costs from lower throughput, as the centers closer to the depots are more likely to have to compete for maize purchases with the depots themselves. By contrast, confining buying operations to the peak of the harvest appears both feasible and desirable. Given Kenya's geographical diversity, the harvest takes place at different times in different areas. The Board could therefore move buying teams from zone to zone throughout the year. This measure would reduce the costs of labor and, by maintaining buying teams intact, lead to higher labor productivity as the teams acquire experience and skill. The Board's willingness and ability to adjust its costs by taking the last measure – closing buying centers handling low volumes of maize – are discussed in Chapter 5.

5

The politics of food crises

This chapter examines the impact of the food shortages of 1979–80 and 1984–85 upon the politics of four districts: Trans Nzoia, Kakamega, Bungoma, and Nandi. It notes the common elements in the local responses to the food crises. And it examines as well the manner in which specific features of each district shaped the political challenges mounted at the time of stress. It ends by showing how Moi and his allies at the national center used the crises to neutralize political enemies, reward political friends, and thereby consolidate their hold upon power.

The districts selected for this study lie in the maize regions of Kenya. One, Trans Nzoia, contains large commercial farms and is situated in the Rift Valley. Two others, Kakamega and Bungoma, contain small-sized and intermediate-sized farms and lie in Western Province. The last, Nandi, lies in Rift Valley Province and contains both small and intermediate-sized farms. Under the new national government, Nandi's fortunes have risen. To use the local jargon, its leaders now stand in the "inner circle."

COMMONALITIES

Among the responses produced by the maize crisis of the 1980s, one was common to all four districts: the attempt by the national leadership to assert central control over the nation's grain supply.

The Maize Board, whose job is to guarantee food supplies, maintains a series of depots and purchasing centers around Kenya, concentrated – quite naturally – in Western and Rift Valley Provinces, where most of Kenya's maize is grown. Over 80 percent of the storage facilities of the Board lie on rail sidings in these two regions. The government also maintains a national administration, called the Provincial Administration, whose job is to preserve order. The head – or permanent secretary – of the Provincial Administration reports directly to the president; he directs

123

the police and internal security forces as well as civilian services. At the times of crisis in 1979–80 and 1984–85, the two bureaucracies merged, with the Provincial Administration superintending as a matter of national security the storage and distribution of the nation's maize supplies. The top civil servant in the Office of the President served as the chairman of the Maize Board, signifying the convergence.[1]

Among its first acts, the national center sealed and seized the Board's food stocks in the producing regions. Under the direction of the Provincial Administration, the Board's officers in Nairobi asserted their ownership of the stocks of grain held in its depots in the producing regions. They restricted the permissible levels of local consumption, thereby ensuring adequate reserves and their ability to transfer local supplies to consuming regions. By telegram, they informed the depot managers throughout the producing regions of the permissible quantities of local grain sales; they thereby imposed limits on the number of bags that the depot managers could release from their stocks each week for sale to local populations.[2]

Not only did the Kenyan bureaucracy seize physical control over the grain stocks of the producing regions; it also moved them from storage facilities in the farmlands to storage depots in the consuming areas. In both 1979–80 and 1984–85, the Board and the Provincial Administration initiated a strategic transfer of maize. They deployed railway wagons to transport grain from the depots of Western and Rift Valley Provinces to the storage houses of the Board and the maize milling companies in Nakuru, Kisumu, Mombasa, and Nairobi. The Treasury also allocated funds for the hiring of road transport, and the Provincial Administration and Board organized fleets of lorries to haul the grain to the maize mills located in the urban centers.[3]

The national administration sought not only to control and direct supplies already in its possession but also to accelerate the flow of grain from farm producers into the government's marketing facilities. Toward this end, it constructed a network of local buying centers and offered farmers the "into depot" price for grain delivered to these centers. The result, from the farmer's point of view, was a rise in the price offered by the government, as the government now paid for the costs of transport to its railway depots. Equally important, the administration and Board exercised their authority to approve movements of maize from out of the producing regions. The national officers of the Maize Board seized from its regional and district officers the right to issue movement permits for interregional shipments of grain.[4] No lorry could gain entry to a Board depot unless its driver possessed a permit authorized by the managing director in Nairobi. Orders from the center raised the level of vigilance of the police and border patrols; they were directed to stop and examine all lorries and to search for unauthorized movements of grain.

The politics of food crises

Lorries were forbidden to move at night, save as members of convoys escorted by the police, for fear that they might elude the efforts of the center to regulate the movement of food.[5]

VARIATIONS

The actions of the national center represent assertions of power; they also represent reactions to vulnerability. Following the droughts of 1979–80 and 1984–85, people feared famine and the center depended upon the grain producers to supply sufficient foodstuffs to quiet these fears. In each food-producing region, organized interests came forward to exploit the weakness of the center. The identity of these interests, their organization, and their strategies were specific to each district and depended upon its social, economic, and political composition.

Cooperative country: the lands of the small farmers

Kakamega and Bungoma lie in the Western Province. During the colonial period these districts exported labor to the European farming areas. This was particularly true of Kakamega, which registers some of the highest population densities in Africa.

Neither district possesses much industry. Sugar provides the principal cash crop, with cotton being grown at the lower elevations and coffee, milk, and tea being produced on the slopes of Mt. Elgon. Farmers tend to grow food crops, principally maize.

Numbering nearly two million in 1979, the population of Kakamega is composed overwhelmingly of smallholders. They buy and sell among each other, exchanging maize for cash in the multitude of market centers that dot the district. Bungoma, with a population of but half a million people in 1979, is far more sparsely settled. Farmers in Bungoma tend to operate medium-sized farms and to produce surpluses, which they then sell to the Maize Board.

In the competition to subdivide the Highlands at the time of independence, both Bungoma and Kakamega annexed lands formerly farmed by European settlers. The resultant settlement schemes produce surpluses of maize. The Maize Board maintains nine depots in the two districts. The preponderance of their intake originates from the intermediate-sized farms of Bungoma and the settlement schemes located in the two districts.[6]

When it became clear in 1979 that Kenya faced a major food shortage, the administration in both districts formed food supply committees. The committees comprised the heads of administrative departments and prominent individuals from the community, and they sought ways of

125

distributing food stocks. They also sought ways of increasing the quantities of maize sold to the Board. One way of fulfilling this objective was to restrict the marketing opportunities of farmers. The committees outlawed the sale of maize to private traders. They thereby left the Maize Board and the cooperative societies – the associations formed among the small and intermediate farmers – to compete for the grain produced by farmers.

Cooperative societies in the Western Province rank among the oldest in Kenya, many having been founded in the 1950s. In 1979, there were eighty-four registered societies in Bungoma; in Kakamega, fifty-four.[7] The cooperative movement maintains close ties with political elites – both bureaucrats in the Ministry of Cooperatives and elected political officials, who cultivate close ties with farm organizations.

The leaders of the cooperative movement, their patrons in the national bureaucracy, the officers of the Ministry of Cooperatives, and the Western Province politicians – all saw in the maize crisis the opportunity to form a powerful, local-level coalition. The leaders of the cooperative movement saw in it a chance to secure much-needed resources. The politicians perceived an opportunity to attract from the national government funds that could be channeled to their constituents. And both the politicians and the Ministry of Cooperatives saw in the maize crisis an opportunity to forge political bonds with the new national government – the government formed by Daniel arap Moi upon the death of Jomo Kenyatta.

As one loans officer in the Cooperative Bank responded to my query as to why funds were lavished upon the cooperatives of Western Kenya:

People in the region felt that the rest of Kenya had got their share and that this had been going on forever. So these funds were their right. So they took a ton of money. They had watched Central Province gobble up money. And the Ministry of Cooperatives lads, they went around saying: "You should be pleased with your government now . . . we have at last got you your share."[8]

The response to the crisis proceeded in two stages. The government had started a new seasonal credit program designed to replace the Guaranteed Minimum Return, a credit program that had been formed in colonial times and had been restricted to large farmers. In the face of the maize crisis, the government increased its funding for the new seasonal credit scheme and extended its lending to the multitude of small-scale farmers. In western Kenya, the government made the cooperatives the primary mechanism for distributing seasonal credit. It channeled funds for the production of maize through the Cooperative Bank of Kenya and thence to the individual farmers through the intermediary of the cooperative societies.

The politics of food crises

The second step was to seek, and to capture, monopoly standing in grain markets for the cooperative societies. Their champions argued that if the cooperatives were to advance loans from the national treasury, then there should be no rivals for the purchase of the farmers' crops; otherwise, they argued, farmers who owed loans to their societies could evade repayment.

The district food committees furnished the primary arena for the assertion of the cooperatives' power. The debates on the committees were strained, for the Board proved an adamant opponent. The cooperatives' demands provoked institutional jealousy, as the Board saw an erosion in its position as the government's marketing organization. Placing the cooperatives in control of the grain market also violated the Board's sense of professionalism. The Board appraised the competence of the cooperatives and found them wanting. In the Board's judgment, they lacked storage facilities, transport, manpower, and, above all, the funds with which to purchase the nation's food supplies. The intense pressure at the national level to replenish the national grain reserves strengthened the Board's opposition to the cooperatives' bid to secure a monopoly buying position.

Initially, despite the Board's opposition, the cooperatives won; in district after district, the food committees backed their demands. As resolved in the food committee for Bungoma, for example:

The National Cereals and Produce Board would cancel all licenses to private traders for the buying of produce in the Province and give all produce buying agencies to the cooperative Unions/Societies. This will facilitate early recovery of loans given by cooperatives and AFC. . . . [9]

In the initial period, then, the cooperative societies were able to use the food crisis to capture resources from an embattled government. And the Moi regime, threatened by fears of famine and the resistance of Kenyatta's old guard, saw in the crisis an opportunity to consolidate its political constituency in the western portions of the nation. By channeling loans through the cooperative societies and giving them monopoly standing in grain markets, it used the food crisis to generate benefits for its followers in Western Province – an area that had felt ignored under the Kenyatta regime.

The maize crisis provided a difficult vehicle for consolidating political support, however. For the benefits provided the food producers threatened the interests of consumers. The cooperatives proved inefficient purchasers of food. The Maize Board exploited this fact to prevail in its rivalry with the farmers' organizations.

In Kakamega the cooperatives began purchasing maize on September 1, 1980. One day later the area manager of the Board wrote the district commissioner that "it is worth noting that the Union has not delivered a single bag of maize . . . to our depots despite so much talk of monopoly buying."[10] In statement after statement, Board officials denigrated the performence of the cooperatives. A memorandum from the area manager of the Board concerning the maize-purchasing program in Kakamega exemplifies the campaign:

The [Cooperative] claims to have disbursed approximately 2 million [Ksh.] for this exercise. Even with the minimum "turn around" time of 5 days, the money would extend the buying season to about 30 weeks, i.e. till . . . 1981."[11]

Eliciting support from the Provincial Administration, which was increasingly concerned with the mounting sense of crisis in the national capital, the Board was finally able to break the cooperatives' monopoly. The nation must be fed, the district administrators determined, and they empowered the Board to begin its own purchasing operations and to compete for grain.

Organizational rivalry: large-farm country

The cooperative societies represented the organized expression of the interests of the small and intermediate-sized farmers of the grain-growing areas of Western Province. Among the commercial farmers of the Rift Valley, however, it was the Kenya Farmers' Association (KFA) that represented farm interests. The KFA also took advantage of the threat of famine. In so doing, it posed a significant challenge to the central government. In an effort to extend and augment its political power, Moi destroyed the KFA and its challenge to his suzerainty in the Rift Valley.

Trans Nzoia, a district in Rift Valley Province, forms the core of Kenya's commercial maize industry. Although one of Kenya's smallest districts, in terms of both land mass and population, Trans Nzoia furnishes over 20 percent of the Board's annual intake of maize. Kitale, the district capital, is the home of maize research. It also furnished the site for the production of maize hybrids, and the large farms of the area carry out the annual multiplication of hybrid seed. The Maize Board has invested heavily in Trans Nzoia. With storage capacity equivalent to nearly one and one-half million bags, the Board's facilities in this one district alone represent nearly 20 percent of its total national stores. The district is aptly referred to as the bread basket of Kenya.

Trans Nzoia provided one of the centers for the mixed farming economy of colonial Kenya. Some coffee was produced on the slopes of Mt. Elgon and some sisal at the lower elevations; but the mixture of maize and dairy production, or wheat and dairying, underpinned the district's settler economy. During the transition to independence, political maneuvering by politicians and bureaucrats largely sheltered the large farms of the area from subdivision under the resettlement programs that were mounted at the time of independence (see Chapter 2).[12] The subdivision that did take place in Trans Nzoia often took the form of low-density schemes. Large and intermediate-sized farms therefore characterize the district's maize industry.[13]

From colonial times until the mid 1980s, the Kenya Farmers' Association represented the interests of the commercial farmers of Trans Nzoia. As seen in Chapter 1, when during the Second World War colonial government imposed "maize control," the KFA became the government's agent. In that capacity the KFA administered loan programs for the government and took over the marketing and storage of grain delivered by the large-scale farmers.[14] Following independence, it continued to maintain a network of facilities providing services to its members. It imported fertilizer, distributed seeds, stocked spare parts and chemicals, and sold farm equipment. Above all, the KFA maintained its status as agent for major public programs.

As the Maize Board's sole agent in Rift Valley Province, the KFA constructed each and every warehouse; built and maintained each and every silo and storage bin; staffed and operated every depot; graded and inspected every delivery of grain; dried, fumigated, bagged and stored the crop; and contracted for its movement by road and rail. The funds for its massive operations came largely from its agency contract with the Maize Board.

From its relationship with the Board, there arose the potential for a conflict of interest between the Board as principal and the KFA as agent. Conflicts arose over operation of the maize driers that the Board had secured from foreign donors in the 1960s. Unless the driers were properly run, this major investment would be lost. The Board therefore decided to subject them to its own management and revoked the relevant portion of its agency contract with the KFA. A similar problem arose with the bulk storage facilities. To be run properly, they had to be run in tandem with the driers. Frustrated by problems of coordination with the KFA, the Board seized control over the bulk storage facilities as well.[15] In increments the Board thus began to take over the network of facilities run by its agents. The two organizations began to operate as rivals.

The tensions generated by these conflicts rose during the crisis of 1978–80; significantly, they were given a political cast. In response to the shortage of maize, the President authorized the construction of local buying centers. One purpose was to bypass the middlemen who bought from the farmers and who had sold at least a portion of their purchases to sources other than the Board. Another was to extend the government's "into depot" price virtually to the farm gate and so strengthen the incentives to produce, to sell, and, in particular, to sell to the government. As an agent of the Board, the KFA was in charge of the program in Trans Nzoia and elsewhere in the Rift Valley.

In financing the buying centers, the KFA opened an account, aptly named the "Strategic Areas Purchasing Account," and charged to that account "all expenditures concerned with the exercise."[16] Neither the KFA nor the Maize Board knew what the true costs of the buying centers would or should be; as a result, they began to quarrel over them. The managing director of the Board noted in September of 1980: "I have just returned to... find considerable concern here at the continuing level of expense claims being submitted by you to this office." He therefore proposed fixing an agency fee of Ksh. 3.50 per bag of maize purchased at the buying centers, whereas the KFA sought to collect over Ksh. 13.00 per bag.[17]

At first the KFA's management petitioned the Board by mail. Then its directors formed a delegation that traveled to Nairobi and pleaded their case. Finally, the KFA resorted to political blackmail. At the height of the food crisis, the KFA invoked its market power over the national food supplies. As its chief executive wrote to the Board:

If... you insist that we operate at Shs 3/50 per bag it is tantamount to telling us to stop the exercise of buying maize which we believe to be contrary to the Government's wish to buy all the maize available ...

... Since the inception of this exercise we have worked hand-in-hand with the Provincial Administration and I feel it only proper that I should copy this letter to... [the] Provincial Commissioner (RVP) because I believe that our withdrawal from the maize buying exercise in Rift Valley Province can have severe repercussions on the country's economy.

I hope in view of the above you can reconsider your decision failing which I will... be compelled to pull out all our maize buying teams by 30th September 1980. KFA should not then be held responsible for any consequences that may follow.[18]

In the face of this threat, the Maize Board backed down. The Board accepted the KFA's bill for Ksh. 20 million.[19] The association that represented the clearest institutional defense of the interests of the large farmers had thus successfully exploited the threat posed by the food crisis to defend its financial interests.

Adding to the tensions between the KFA and the national center was the KFA's control over the allocation of key farm inputs, particularly fertilizers. The rise of petroleum prices in the 1970s had led to a rise in the world price of fertilizers and to a decline in Kenya's ability to import them. The United States and other donors therefore added fertilizers to their foreign assistance programs. Impressed by the superiority of its accounting system, its storage facilities, and its broad distribution net-

The politics of food crises

work, the donors chose the KFA to distribute their fertilizers. The KFA's selection as the purveyor of concessional imports left it in control of over 75 percent of Kenya's fertilizer market.[20] Many outside the KFA – including prominent government officials who owned large farms – felt that the KFA used its control over the market to raise fertilizer prices. These suspicions were only exacerbated by the obvious wealth of some of the KFA directors.

Initially cast in terms of a clash between private interests and the national interest in food security, the conflict between the Association and the government became increasingly defined in more political terms. Not only were there fights between the elites over the price of farm inputs. But also there arose a struggle for political preeminence in the large farm centers of the Rift Valley. During the parliamentary elections of September 1983, one of the more prominent directors of the KFA contended for a seat in Parliament. He had the temerity to run against a candidate favored by the most senior of the Rift Valley politicians, arap Moi, the national president. While failing in his bid for office, the director nonetheless remained a prominent presence in the Rift Valley. His lavish donations to the political coffers of other politicians fueled rumors concerning his diversion of funds from the importation of fertilizers and – at least as important – the level of his political ambitions.

When in 1984 the rains again failed, the government was once again faced with a food crisis, and it was compelled to realize that control over food supplies still lay in the hands of its "agents," the KFA – a powerful and self-interested organization managed by a man regarded by many as a political enemy of the president. At the height of the maize crisis, the government therefore attacked. Using the powers conferred by the Cooperative Act, it replaced the Association's board of directors. Using its control over agreements with foreign governments, it set up an independent distribution network for fertilizers brought in by foreign donors. And using its control over the Maize Board, it terminated the agency agreement for the purchase of the maize crop.

The political tensions arising from the food crises thus led to the displacement of the most prominent and powerful defender of commercial farm interests in Kenya. And it left Moi and his loyal followers politically unrivaled in the large-farm country of the Rift Valley Province.

Politician country

In Nandi, the political tensions occasioned by the food crises of the 1980s took the form of conflict between local politicians and the Maize Board.

Nandi too lies in Rift Valley Province. Nandi never served as a center for white settlement, however, save for a small corner of the district.

Rather, it remained a reserve for the Nandi people, one of the Kalenjin-speaking tribes of central Kenya.[21]

The Nandi tend to accumulate capital in the form of cattle. Unlike their pastoralist counterparts in other parts of Kenya, the Nandi live in an area of abundant and reliable rainfall. Rather than accumulating large herds to ensure against losses from drought, they have tended instead to invest in herds of high quality, with cattle of large carcass weights, in the case of meat cattle, or high butterfat yields, in the case of dairy animals. As with other Kalenjin-speaking people in the Rift, they voluntarily divided their lands into family homesteads in the 1950s, registered them under individual title, and bought and sold land in efforts to upgrade their fortunes.[22] Fencing their lands, they began to invest in improvements: leys pasturage, cattle dips, forage crops, and dairy equipment. The cattle auctions in Nandi were attended by large buyers from neighboring districts, including the ranchers from the European Highlands. Their dairy products were sought by the creameries of the Rift Valley. And their relatively large farms yielded surpluses of grain, some of which they sold privately in the densely populated locations of neighboring Kakamega, the remainder to the Maize Board.

The Nandi therefore became one of the wealthiest groups in the Rift. More recently, they have also become one of the most powerful. At the time of independence, the Kalenjin leadership of KADU championed the KANU/KADU merger. The KADU leadership that had dominated the Rift Valley Assembly assumed leading positions in the Kenyatta government. With the death of Kenyatta, their leader, Daniel arap Moi, became national president. The District of Nandi, along with the other Kalenjin districts, thereupon moved into the heartland of Kenyan politics.

During the food crises of 1979–80 and 1984–85, Nandi, like other districts in the grain-growing areas, was called upon to supply increased deliveries of maize. The formation of local buying centers formed the keystone of the government's program in the area.

When the buying center program was launched at the height of the food crisis of 1979–80, members of Parliament, county councilors, and other local politicians quickly appreciated its political advantages. Thus, the area manager of the Maize Board in Western Province received a memorandum from "The Honorable Dr. A. Mukasa Mango, Ph.D., M.P., Minister for Health," concerning the "DISTRIBUTION OF BUYING CENTERS" in Busia. The memorandum transmitted but some of the many petitions, from farmers in every nook and cranny of his region, demanding that this idle plot or that village store be taken over by the Board and used to purchase maize.[23] Many such petitions carried political threats. On December 3, 1979, for example, the District Commissioner in Baringo wrote the Board's Area Manager, Nakuru, stating:

The politics of food crises

Our farmers in the Southern Division in Baringo have been experiencing great problems in selling their produce.

The problem is very much known to H.E. the President Hon. Daniel Arap Moi and he has directed me to ask you to find ways and means of establishing your Depots or Buying Centers at Maji Mazuri and Subukia.

I hope this request will receive your consideration.[24]

The area manager replied: "I am happy to inform you that our general manager has given the matter top priority.... Already we are negotiating with Kenya Railways to use their go-downs at Subukia and Maji Mazuri."[25]

Baringo is the president's home district. People in Nandi like to talk of their district as one adopted by the president. As a youth, he had attended school there. Nandi members of Parliament like to speak of the Moi government as "our government" and to exhibit their ready access to the top levels of power. Included in the top levels are the executives of the Maize Board.

During the food crisis of 1979–80, the politicians of Nandi invoked their political influence. The result was a barrage of orders from the center concerning the construction of buying centers. On October 6, 1980, for example, the Managing Director of the Board, responding to local initiatives, sent orders from Nairobi to open buying centers in Serem, Kapkangani, Kameloi, and Meteitei. And on the thirteenth, he ordered the opening of an additional four. On the twentieth, he telegraphed the local manager of the Board to communicate complaints he had received in Nairobi concerning the behavior of clerks at buying centers operating in these areas, hundreds of kilometers to the West.[26] As disclosed in the following telegram, his attentions rarely faltered:

It has come to my notice that the opening of buying centers in Nandi is quite slow and that our buying system is not effective.... [C]an you as a matter of urgency open the following centers within the week commencing Monday 13 December 1982:
1. Nandi Hills
2. Mbogo Valley
3. Baraton
and all centers in lower Nandi.[27]

Not only did the local politicians use their influence to open buying centers. They also sought to control who staffed them and who received contracts for transporting produce from them. Each buying center hired four staff; in addition, they recruited casual labor to fill maize sacks and to load them on vehicles. Rural jobs are difficult to find; the jobs are particularly desired by families who have invested in the education of their children but whose children have subsequently failed to find employment. The politicians of Nandi responded by compiling lists of suit-

133

able job applicants; they focused their recruiting efforts on "school leavers"; and they forwarded their lists to the Board's management in Nairobi. As indicated in the following letter, the central management then imposed their selection on the Board's officers in the field:

S.J. Karanga, Finance Manager, to Field Officer, NCPB, Kapsabet, 21 December 1982.

c.c. H.K. Kosgey

I attach a letter addressed to this office from the Minister from Transport and Communications, Hon. H.K. Kosgey, for your necessary action. The letter is being brought to you by Mr. Nelson Lelei of P.O. Box 257 Kapsabet who will identify the named people in the letter in order for you to ensure you have employed the correct people named therein. I should be extremely grateful if you could report back when the exercise is complete.[28]

Transport contracts provided another opportunity for political patronage. As indicated in a memorandum from the area manager, Western Province, to all depot managers, depot managers were held to be "unfair in allocating transport work. Some have even alleged that the work is dominated by 'foreigners' and the friends of the depot managers."[29] In local usage, the word "foreigner" means people from outside the district in general and more specifically Asians from Nakuru, Nairobi, or the Coast, or Kikuyu from Nakuru or the Central Province. Just as the politicians demanded that the Board hire local people, so did they demand that they contract locally as well.

The buying center program proved politically popular; but it also proved financially costly. The staff of the Board increased from roughly 1,000 before the commencement of the program to over 3,000 after its initiation. Transport costs escalated. So too did the fixed costs of the Board, as it built, bought, or leased over 500 purchasing centers. Following the end of food shortages in the early 1980s, the Board determined to reduce the costs of the program. The professionals of the Board sought to recapture control of their programs from the politicians. They attempted to operate the buying centers only during the peak of the harvest. They strove to reduce the Board's wages bill by hiring a smaller number of clerks to staff the centers and by then moving them from the lower elevations to the higher, following the harvest. For the crop year 1982–83, the Board proposed lowering the prices paid farmers for grain delivered to the buying centers, thereby transferring to them a portion of the costs. Lastly, the Board sought to close many of the centers. Following investigation of the costs of the program, it determined that only centers purchasing 20,000 or more bags per season should be kept in business. The Board thereby attempted to cut the number of centers from 520 in 1982–83 to 208 in 1983–84.[30]

The politics of food crises

The Board succeeded in implementing most of its measures. It established price differentials for the 1983–84 buying season; it began rotating its staff in 1982; and it reduced the number of centers from 551 in 1982–83 to 465 in 1983–84. Nonetheless, the Board's management did not succeed in all of its objectives. Nandi stood out as the most egregious instance of inflated costs from the operation of the buying centers.[31] The district had eighty-two centers; the size of the crop warranted twenty; and the centers were kept open far too long in the season, when the number of bags delivered no longer justified their continued operation. The Board therefore sought to close more than sixty of the Nandi centers, leaving open only those serving the settlement schemes where an intake of 20,000 bags would be assured.[32] In this it failed. As one officer expressed it: "We could not touch them. The political leaders there are part of the ruling class."

The economic impact of the political power of the Nandi politicians is illustrated in Figure 5.1, which portrays the actual costs per bag of a sample of buying centers as a function of the number of bags handled per year. The costs decline systematically with the number of bags, and the best fitting relationship is represented as a curve. Displacement from this curve is largely a function of transport costs, those buying centers that are distant from the parent depot having greater costs than ones that handle the same number of bags but that lie closer in. In light of the material presented in this discussion, however, what is significant about this figure is the location of the "200–number" centers. They are all depots in Nandi; and they all tend to cluster at the portion of the graph containing units with high average costs. The figure thus presents a visual portrayal of the economic costs of political manipulation of the buying center program, the principal policy response to the threat of famine in the early 1980s.

FORGING LOCAL ALLIANCES

When drought hit in 1979–80, President Daniel arap Moi had been in power for a little over one year. His right to succession had been fought for and won prior to Kenyatta's long-expected demise.[33] But he consolidated his power in the course of the political struggles precipitated by dearth. We have already seen how Moi and his supporters used the food crisis to claim credit from the urban consumers and to attribute blame to the old guard surrounding Kenyatta. In this chapter, we have seen as well how Moi recruited allies – and destroyed his enemies – at the local level, particularly in the portions of the nation that had formed his political constituency.

During the period of political consolidation, Moi drew support from

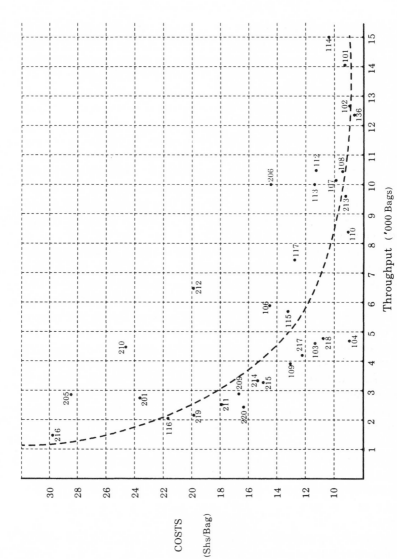

Figure 5.1. The costs of buying centers as a function of the number of bags handled. *Note:* Four buying centers are off the scale: 202 (102, 308); 203 (872, 63); 204 (349, 67); and 207 (601, 46).

the "backwoods" politicians of western Kenya: Mwangale, Shikuku, and Osogo, for example. They played key roles in the politics of the transition; and as western Kenyan populists, all retained close ties with local farmer organizations. It is not surprising, then, that during the food crisis, the national government channeled resources through cooperative movement in Western Province, binding local farm organizations to the new coalition being formed at the national political center.

Under Moi, the Kalenjin politicians moved into the top ranks of national politics. And they used their positions to push for their preferred solution to dearth: the multiplication of local buying centers and the transformation of government prices into farmgate prices for their constituents in the grain-growing regions. With a power base now located in State House, the Kalenjin political elite was able to quash those with an independent base in the Rift, such as those who promoted themselves through the Kenya Farmers' Association, and to build support among the local politicians, such as those in Nandi.

And as for the Central Province? The consumer interests of Nairobi held a veto, of course, on the life chances of any aspirant political faction; the Moi government, like any government in Kenya, had abundantly to provision, and to be seen to be provisioning, the capital city. But the political ascendancy of the Moi regime marked the political decline of those from the rich, cash-cropping hinterland of Central Province. Signifying the end of their primacy was the way in which the government sought to cover the losses made by the cooperatives in the West in their efforts to purchase grain. It required that the wealthy coffee and dairying cooperatives, most of which are located in the Central Province, shift their members' savings from commercial banks to the Cooperative Bank, which had run up large losses in loans for maize purchases.[34] Another measure of political decline, in the eyes of some, was the degree of suffering tolerated in the rural regions of that area during the disastrous drought of the mid-1980s (discussed in the Appendix 5A, which follows).[35]

The Central Province alliance between urban industry and rural export agriculture, which had underpinned the Kenyatta government, thus fractured, as the Moi presidency continued to placate the national capital but appeared willing to sacrifice the interests of the wealthy cash-cropping centers out of a regard for the interests of its own grain-growing constituency.

CONCLUSION

This book began with the chaos of the Mau Mau rebellion and the explosive act of self-assertion by the Kikuyu; it ends with the turmoil of food crisis and the political consolidation of power by those from the grain-growing regions. This chapter has completed our interpretation of the contemporary political history of Kenya.

While examining the contemporary politics of Kenya, this chapter has also explored the dynamics attending one of the most common forms of crisis in any underdeveloped society: the crisis of subsistence. It has shown that subsistence crises not only threaten political order but also promote the accumulation of influence. Parochial interests did indeed attempt to exploit the weakness of the center and to fracture the power of national bureaucracies; the Maize Board was challenged by local interests in each of the four districts studied in this chapter. But also, a wily national leader and politician of consummate skill, Daniel arap Moi, seized the opportunities created by the shifting of local coalitions to unseat political enemies, promote local allies, and thereby consolidate his control over the national political system. In Kenya, as in other nation states, crises of provisioning create opportunities to build absolutist political regimes.[36]

Appendix 5A: Famine: Meru, August 1984

PREFACE

In 1984–85, Kenya was hit by a one-in-a-century drought. In that year, the rains failed for a third consecutive time in the semi-arid zones. The rains also failed in the central regions of the country, where the population is dense and people employ farming systems highly vulnerable to drought. The Government of Kenya faced a challenge comparable in magnitude to those that had been faced by other African governments in Ethiopia and the Sahel.

Its response was extraordinary. In a display of administrative competence unparalleled in Africa, it procured, imported, and distributed sufficient food to feed its population. At the local level, the government located, registered, and fed the hungry. Subject to deep skepticism on the part of donors and persistent criticism on the part of relief organizations, the government succeeded in doing what no other government in Africa had done: compensating through public programs for deprivations inflicted by the failure of the rains.

This triumph, however, was not complete. For reasons I do not understand, Meru, a district in which I was conducting fieldwork, was initially bypassed by the government's efforts. Following my departure in August 1984, government provisions did reach the district. But they did not reach it in time to prevent the suffering I witnessed and recorded there.

The government's initial failure in Meru was noted by others. It has been used by those who wish to discredit the government in general and particular political leaders. I have no desire to contribute to such efforts. I present these results simply because they are true.

BACKGROUND

A district in the Eastern Province, Meru adheres to a pattern of environmental secession similar to that outlined in Figure 2.1 of Chapter 2.

Its topography ranges from the cold, moist peaks of Mt. Kenya in its western portions to the hot, arid plains in its eastern locations. The people of Meru raise cattle and livestock and grow sorghum, millet, pigeon peas, and other drought-resistant crops in the lower elevations; cotton and maize in areas with more rainfall; and coffee and tea in the higher zones. They also grow tobacco and *miraa*, a stimulant favored by certain ethnic groups in Kenya and in the horn of Africa, and breed dairy cattle. The people of Meru were allowed to grow coffee shortly after World War II because they were located distant from the European coffee estates and the settlers feared neither an unfavorable impact on their labor supplies nor the spread of disease. The coffee industry provides the district's economic foundation. Because of coffee, Meru is one of the wealthiest areas in all of rural Kenya.

A series of small towns dot the district, the largest being the town of Meru, the district capital. It contains hotels and boarding houses and over a hundred shops. The town also serves as a service center, particularly for merchants and transporters. Banks, telecommunications, and repair facilities for automobiles, buses, and tractors are located within its borders; so too are the headquarters of the public services. Lying on the forested slopes of Mt. Kenya, the town of Meru also contains sawmills and specialty shops that produce furniture, door frames, and other wood products.

Given the level of specialization in the production of cash crops and the density of manufacturing, governmental, and commercial establishments in the district, it is not surprising that Meru imports food. Most maize consumed in Meru *is* grown there; there is a vigorous private trade within the district. But much of the maize consumed in Meru is imported from outside. The Maize Board maintains a depot there, capable of storing 80,000 bags, which it provisions by road and rail with maize grown in the Rift Valley. And there is a modern maize mill in Meru, erected in 1977–78 by the Meru Central Cooperative Union, a cooperative grown wealthy during the boom in coffee prices in the mid-1970s. Restricted by law to employ maize furnished by the Board, the maize mill is the only major mill operating in the food-deficient areas of rural Kenya.

Lying east of the Rift Valley, Meru receives two rainfalls a year. When the plantings of spring 1984 failed, they joined those of March and October 1983; three successive crops had been lost. The people's stores were exhausted; they now had consumed their seeds. They faced the specter of famine.

As did their counterparts elsewhere in Kenya, the District administration convened a food committee. It collected estimates of the local supply

Appendix 5A: Famine: Meru, August 1984

Table 5A.1. *Agricultural estimates, Meru district, 1984*

Crop	Target (hectares)	Actual planted (ha.)^a	Original estimates (yields per ha.)	Revised estimates (yields per ha.)	Reasons for reduction
Maize	29,823	26,265	15 bags	0–2 bags	Drought
Beans	24,193	22,270	11 bags	0–1 bag	Drought
Wheat	7,500	6,700	17 bags	0–0.5 bgs	Drought

^{a}ha. = hectare
Source: Food Situation Report, Meru District, 19 June 1984.

and demand for food. The estimates for crop production are entered in Table 5A.1. The district livestock officer noted:

Weather: Dry and windy throughout the [period] under review.

Rainfall: Nil.

General review: Due to the above two factors, the situation during the week under review is going from bad to worse. Farmers have started ... grazing their animals in the maize fields in some areas as there will definitely be no harvest for this particular season.[1]

The figures presented represent district averages. The situation was much worse at the lower elevations than at the higher. For farms in the higher elevations would have gotten more rain, albeit less than in a normal year, and were more likely to have access to water running off the mountain. They could therefore produce crops on irrigated plots.

The food situation committee collected not only estimates of the supply of food but also estimates of food needs. It solicited from its district officers their calculations of the number of families affected by the famine – estimates which the officers compiled from the reports of location chiefs. Timau reported 1,120 families; Nithi, 5,000; Tharaka, 8,514; North Imenti, 3,720; South Imenti, 878; Tigania, 12,000; Igembe, 800.[2] These estimates were then forwarded to the Office of the President in Nairobi, where they became the basis for requests for food assistance and for planning the logistics of food distribution.[3]

The food committee also sought to secure supplies from outside the district. The principal agency for such supplies was the Maize Board. The Board initially targeted the Meru depot for 8,000 bags a week. The food committee responded with a bid for 15,000 bags a week for the depot plus another 1,600 a day for the maize mill, noting that both the

Table 5A.2. *Meru NCPB stores, 1984 (bags of maize)*

Week ending	Opening balance	Purchases	Transfers in	Sales	Closing balance
8 June	387	Nil	5,923	5,354	958
15 June	958	Nil	4,350	5,196	108
22 June	108	Nil	11,950	12,023	38
29 June	38	Nil	2,175	100	2,113
6 July	2,113	Nil	10,380	712	11,781
13 July	11,781	Nil	7,520	2,301	17,000
20 July	17,000	Nil	7,600	13,312	11,288
27 July	11,288	Nil	10,675	8,009	13,954
3 August	14,920	Nil	1,500	16,111	309
17 August	309	Nil	100	370	43
24 August	43	Nil	200	210	33

Source: Records of the NCPB, Meru.

depot and mill served not only Meru but also districts to the north and east: Isiolo, Marsabit, and Wajir.[4]

Formally, the committee won its request; the limits imposed by Nairobi were removed. In actuality, the quantity of maize that arrived failed to reach even the lesser of the two figures. Table 5A.2 presents data concerning grain movements by the Board. By August, shipments in were declining just as sales were mounting, with the result that stocks declined to several dozen bags – bags that the Board was unwilling or unable to sell as they were largely spoiled.

From August 24 until I left the field in late September 1984, no further shipments of maize were received by the Meru depot. As the depot manager said, "I cover up. I say maize is coming, it is on the way. . . . I cannot take away the hope."[5]

The maize mill faced a similar fate. In March, the Board ruled that the mill in Meru should contract for its supplies directly with the Board's Nairobi headquarters rather than with its Meru depot. It quickly became apparent that such transactions could not be done by mail; the mill therefore posted an emissary to Nairobi to "see to it that the payment is done and sales orders issued . . . and all the transactions are through to the final stage of loading."[6] The mill's demands mounted; its requests increased by 10,000 to 15,000 bags a month as rural consumers switched from farm purchases to the purchase of processed maize. But the mill failed to secure deliveries from the Board. Thus, the following minute of the purchasing manager in August 1984:

Appendix 5A: Famine: Meru, August 1984

Mr. G. Githonga has been to Nairobi the whole of this week to try and speed up maize delivery. He has paid for 5,000 bags....But he has reported to me there is no maize for us in Nairobi, although we are now promised 2,500 bags from Nakuru and 2,500 bags from Nairobi. Well by the look of things we are not likely to mill the whole of the coming week.

Please advise: May I send some workers on leave?[7]

Lacking maize to grind, the mill closed. In the midst of famine, it was unable to provide food for Meru's consuming population.

The harvest in Meru had failed and the government was unable to ship maize either to the depot of the Board or to the maize mill. The result was a massive food shortage. Maize was scarce; its price rose from roughly Ksh. 245 a bag in 1983 to roughly Ksh. 380 a bag in 1984. The price of beans – a food preferred to maize by many Meru speakers – rose from roughly Ksh. 560 a bag to over Ksh. 1,200 over the same period. Given the magnitude of the food shortage and the fact that food is an absolute necessity, one might have expected the price rises to have gone further. A major reason they did not was that drought brought with it a collapse in purchasing power.[8]

When the harvest failed, the farm families in Meru did what they always have done: they sold off their cattle and livestock. But so widespread was the drought that many sellers entered the market simultaneously and prices collapsed (Figure 5A.1). Goats, which had sold for Ksh. 300 a year before, now sold for Ksh. 25; and cattle which had sold for Ksh. 800, now sold for Ksh. 225. A farmer now had to sell more than fifteen goats to purchase a bag of grain, whereas a year before a single goat would easily have secured the same quantity. Cattle were considered a family's prized possession, their capital, and the object of their savings. That a single cow could not be exchanged for a bag of grain dramatized to Meru residents as nothing else could the severity of the disaster that had befallen them.

The farmers of Meru then took a second step: they began chopping down trees. They fed the leaves to their livestock; the wood they converted into charcoal. Again, the result was a collapse in prices. With hundreds of struggling farmers placing bags of charcoal by the roadsides in hopes of securing a sale, the price of charcoal plummeted from over Ksh. 40 to less than Ksh. 25 a bag.

The farmers then seized a last alternative: they left their farms and searched for employment. The overall pattern of labor migration was toward the higher elevations, where the drought had been less severe and where wealth had been accumulated from tea and coffee production. Old people and children begged; the young and middle-aged looked for jobs.

Because the drought was widespread, many people entered the labor market. The shift in the supply of labor pushed downward the average

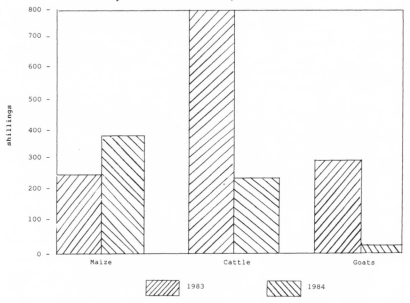

Figure 5A.1. Price changes, 1983–84 (shillings per bag or animal). *Note*: No data for 1984 following September.

wage. But, perversely and malevolently, there was another force at work. Food is a necessity; when it is scarce and therefore expensive, people sacrifice other goods in order to purchase it. As a consequence, the shops, stores, and businesses dotting the wealthy countryside of Meru experienced a massive reduction in demand. In the face of declining business, their owners retrenched. Just as more people went in search of jobs, the owners of businesses began laying off workers.

I interviewed a sample of forty businesses in Meru. I asked them to evaluate their decline in profits. Calling last year's profit level "100," I asked them to place a number on this year's profits. They readily understood the question and, on average, evaluated this year's profits at "23" – a number which suggests a 77 percent decline. I also collected information about employment and wages. Workers are more visible than profits; they are also untaxed. As a consequence, I was able to collect more meaningful data than I was able to do in the case of profits. I found, on average, a 28 percent decline in the wage rate – from an average of Ksh. 400 per month to Ksh. 311 per month. I also found a 36 percent reduction in the labor force. While these reductions took place across all types of enterprises, the declines were most severe in those businesses that sold consumer durables – furniture, radios, or building supplies, for example. Such enterprises had reduced their wage rate by 58 percent and

Table 5A.3. Pediatric admissions: Meru district hospital, 1982–84

	January			February			March			April			May			June		
	1[a]	2[b]	3[c]	1	2	3	1	2	3	1	2	3	1	2	3	1	2	3
1982	—	—	—	—	—	—	—	—	—	—	—	—	—	—	—	—	—	—
1983	220	10	5	276	5	2	460	11	2	121*	2*	2*	—	—	—	—	—	—
1984	263	26	10	334	21	6	264	17	6	—	—	—	—	—	—	—	—	—

	July			August			September			October			November			December		
	1	2	3	1	2	3	1	2	3	1	2	3	1	2	3	1	2	3
1982	317	6	2	274	14	5	208	10	5	184	5	3	162	7	4	155	8	5
1983	—	—	—	—	—	—	119*	2*	2*	219	13	6	215	9	4	228	26	11
1984	—	—	—	94*	23*	56*	10+	6+	30+	—	—	—	—	—	—	—	—	—

[a] 1 = Total admissions to pediatric ward
[b] 2 = Admissions for kwashiorkor, marasmus, or anemia (unaccompanied by malaria)
[c] 3 = Percentage of admissions for nutritional-related diseases ('1' ÷ '2')
* = For two weeks only
+ = One week only
— = Missing data

their work force by 69 percent compared with 1983. The reductions were least great among businesses dealing with clothing, a necessity. In such enterprises the wage rate declined by 14 percent and the labor force by 13 percent.

Because of the drought, the demand for labor *de*creased just when the supply of labor *in*creased. Given the resulting adjustment in the price of labor, a month's average wages would not purchase a bag of grain. The result was malnutrition and disease.

The trend is suggested in data collected from the records of the pediatric ward in the Meru district hospital (Table 5A.3). The rains first failed in March 1983; at the time the crop would have been harvested – around October – the rate of admissions for nutritionally related diseases began to climb. The short rains of October 1983 also failed; the rate of admissions for nutritionally related diseases remained at two to three times those of the previous year's average. The rains failed again in April 1984. When data again became available, in August 1984, the rate of admissions for nutritionally related diseases had grown explosively. Over one-half of the admissions to the pediatric ward in Meru district hospital in August 1984 were for kwashiorkor, marasmus, or anemia (Table 5A.3).[9]

Nationally, the Kenyan bureaucracy had forged a concerted and deliberate strategy for dealing with the drought. Subsequent reports suggest that their efforts were highly successful. While I was in Meru – until the end of September 1984 – their efforts were not. Lest this criticism of the performance of the public bureaucracy be interpreted as advocacy of the private market, let the central lesson of these observations be clear: that famine in agrarian societies results from a collapse of purchasing power. From this case we learn that people in poor, rural societies starve in large part because they have lost the endowments by which to purchase food in the marketplace. In these circumstances the market too provides few defenses against starvation.

Conclusion

This book has provided an interpretation of the contemporary political history of Kenya. It has traced that history from the colonial period to the postindependence era. Beginning with the anticolonial insurrection, it has ended with the presidency of Daniel arap Moi.

The contemporary history of Kenya began with a political rebellion. The result of that rebellion was the capture of power by the prosperous producers of cash crops in the Central Province. In this respect, Kenya came to independence in a way that differed from many of its African counterparts. It came to independence under a government that favored the accumulation rather than the redistribution of wealth.

The distinction is striking. In neighboring Uganda, to illustrate, power was seized by groups from the less-favored, grain-growing regions of the North. Through electoral alliances and military might, these groups used the state to transfer resources from the forested regions of the South, which gained wealth from the production of export crops. In so doing, they created a pattern of politics akin to that prevalent in West Africa, where people in the grain-growing savannah strive to tax those in the coastal forests.[1] In neighboring Tanzania, a coalition of urban consumers in the coastal cities and rural peasants in the semi-arid zones of the interior employed the power of the state to extract resources from the surrounding Highland regions.[2] In both cases, those who seized power committed the government to enhancing the consumption possibilities of the less fortunate by taxing the more favorably endowed.

Kenya differed from its neighbors not only in terms of the regional makeup but also in terms of the class basis of its independence coalition. Many contemporary writers have attempted to document in Kenya the emergence of a nascent bourgeoisie. In so doing, they implicitly contrast the Kenyan case to that in other African countries, where power was captured by a stratum of politicians with but tenuous links to the underlying forces of production.[3] This study has taken a different course.

Conclusion

Embedding the analysis within an ethnographic structure, it has argued that the process of class formation that led to independence in Kenya was more akin to that accompanying the rise of a gentry than that leading to the rise of a bourgeoisie. The process culminated in the Kenyatta era, when the great landed families of Kiambu coalesced about State House. Viewing Kenya's independence coalition from this perspective helps us to understand why public policy in Kenya, unlike public policy in much of Africa, tended to treat export agriculture as a national estate: an endowment to be nurtured rather than consumed.[4]

The tendency toward accumulation did not remain unchallenged, however. As we have seen, powerful forces favored the use of political power to effect economic redistribution. Tapping the grievances spawned by economic inequality and impelled into motion by political ambition, politicians mounted radical challenges to the emerging political order. The ruling elites fought back. By forming alliances with the leaders of opposition parties, they forced the radical movement outside the governing coalition. And by using their power over the instruments of coercion, they quashed and dismembered organized dissent. The conservative commitment in Kenyan politics became institutionalized when the dominant elites ended the process of party competition.

Rivalries among pressure groups and political factions constituted the core of the subsequent era of single-party politics. Not only did the costs rise but also the benefits declined from attempting to organize electoral efforts to implement coherent ideological programs. Under the single-party system, ideological struggles largely ended.

Kenya's exceptionalism has thus been marked by its commitment to economic growth, particularly in export agriculture, and by its destruction of socialist movements, which in other countries have formed governments. The institutional foundations of its agriculture provide a further underpinning to Kenya's conservative commitment. These institutions were put in place to attract capital, particularly from abroad, and to bind it to land and labor in rural Kenya. And these institutions now generate the resources employed in the factional politics that have largely replaced ideological confrontation.

It was within the context of flexible, loosely structured coalitions that Daniel arap Moi was able to isolate his enemies and gather together his friends and thereby succeed to the presidency following the death of Jomo Kenyatta. The question now arises: Do the political forces that underpin the Moi government favor the continuation of Kenyan exceptionalism?

Our analysis has shown that Moi and the members of the Rift Valley elite respond to class-based appeals; it was by accommodating their class interests, after all, that Kenyatta secured their defection from KADU. But

Conclusion

it has also shown that strong regional forces impel Moi toward policies of economic redistribution. Political power has shifted from the Central Province to the West. To secure its regional base, Moi's government must seize economic resources from the centers of export crop production and distribute them to those less favored. Moi thus garbs his regime in populism, accommodating regional demands for acts of redistribution while striving to defend class privileges. Under Moi, Kenya has come more closely to resemble her African neighbors.[5]

Not only has this book analyzed the contemporary political history of Kenya; it has also focused on the agrarian foundations of politics. Ninety percent of Kenya's population resides in the rural areas; agriculture remains Kenya's largest single industry. This proportionality characterizes other developing nations as well. A major purpose of this work, then, has been to ground the analysis of politics upon an understanding of agriculture.

It would be unprofitable to review the topics discussed while pursuing this second theme. More informative is to point to the major lessons learned. One is that it is necessary to imbed the analysis of class formation within the analysis of social structure. In any society, the mechanisms for accumulation vary depending on the institutional endowment; agrarian societies are marked by contrasting institutional forms. While class formation may be a universal process, the process will thus take place in different ways in different societies. A major contribution of this work has been to place the analysis of class formation within an analysis of lineage systems.

A second lesson is that it is necessary to analyze the broader national setting within which agrarian politics takes place. The study of rural societies tends to be intensely micro in its perspective. It often focuses on the impact of such specific features as the ecosystem or the microclimate; sociologically, it often focuses on specific local communities. But as we have seen, whether the interests animating political conflict in agrarian societies result in ideologically motivated clashes or in private struggles among competing particular interests depends at least in part upon the structure of political institutions and the incentives they generate for politicians. The analysis of the politics of rural societies thus must explicitly incorporate the study of national political settings.

Other lessons concerned the impact of market structures upon agrarian political struggles; the origins of laws and regulations in rural societies; the role that economic factors play in the shaping of rural institutions; and the interrelationship between food scarcity and politics. Time and again, political forces in Kenya have taken its agrarian economy as an object of action, shaping its structure and development. Conversely, Kenya's agrarian economy has pervasively shaped its politics. The study of

Conclusion

the interrelation between agriculture and politics has formed the second major theme of this book.

Above all, however, this book has focused on the political economy of development. It has engaged in a sustained dialogue with development economics. It has also sought to explore the relationship between economics and politics by examining the role of institutions.

The new development economics stresses the significance of markets. To secure economic objectives, it holds, the allocation of resources is best left to market forces. And yet we have repeatedly been compelled to draw a basic lesson from the Kenyan experience: that *nonmarket* institutions are organized to promote *economic* objectives. A major source of Kenya's agrarian prosperity, we have found, has been the structure of its agrarian institutions. Bureaucracies and organizations do not necessarily stand in opposition to markets. Rather they are often put in place in an effort to underpin and to unleash market forces. Kenya's capacity to secure the benefits attainable from exchanges in the market has largely been based on its capacity to create organizations.[6]

To assimilate the lessons offered by the Kenyan experience, we have therefore attempted to move beyond market economics to the economics of organization.[7] While approached in many different ways, a common thread in this literature is that people design institutions in order to facilitate the making of transactions allowing higher levels of welfare.[8] Economic organizations are developed in ways that make possible joint gains.[9] When applied to the study of development, this interpretation of the function of institutions becomes a theory of their causes. In an almost Marxian manner, the theory contends that people devise institutions so as to unleash the full productive potential of their economies.[10]

The Kenyan materials do in fact offer much evidence in support of an economic theory of institutions. They suggest that nonmarket forms of contracting are devised when decentralized agreements would fail to secure economically rewarding transactions. And as the economic theory of institutions would suggest, risk and uncertainty played a central role in the creation of institutions.[11] Thus we found bureaucracies and communities being forged in settler agriculture to reduce risks arising from opportunistic behavior in the production and marketing of food crops. And we found economic agents creating institutions in export agriculture to reduce risks of investment arising from uncertainty about the future, about quality, or about the sufficiency of throughput. Above all, risk in capital markets provided a fertile source of institutions; attempts to reduce such risks motivated the provision of legal assurances, as lenders and borrowers sought forms of precommitment that reduced the risks of investing in fixed and specific capital.

At first glance, then, the Kenyan materials thus suggest that progress

Conclusion

could be made in development economics by extending economic reasoning to the study of organizations. But deeper reflection suggests that so limited a revision would not be sufficient. It suggests instead that development economics must also turn to the study of politics. It must become a branch of political economy.

The Kenyan materials demonstrated, for example, that even where institutions were created for economic reasons – that is, to support a higher level of mutually beneficial transactions – a compelling component of redistributive gain also motivated their formation. Whether in food production or export agriculture, large interests took the initiative in creating the institutional foundations for agriculture. That special interests should play so central a role, upon reflection, was not surprising. For while the formation of institutions can move contracting parties toward the Pareto frontier, as the new institutionalists suggest, only large interests can secure a share of the gains sufficient to cover the costs of organizing. It is predictable, then, that even while promoting efficiency, given transaction costs, institutions will be distributionally biased.

There was thus a political element to the creation of institutions. It was distinguished by the central role of distribution; it was also distinguished by the small role played by uncertainty. Uncertainty plays a major role in the economic theory of institutions. But many institutions in Kenya were created not because people were uncertain, but because people knew what they wanted, knew how to get it, and shaped the structure of institutions so as better to secure their claims. Thus, we saw that property rights were created and refined in efforts to privilege the economic claims of those who held power: the white settlers in the Highlands and the elites in the reserves. And we saw that preferences among constitutional forms or concerning the scope and role of the market were closely related to land endowments and positions in commercial agriculture. In environments of uncertainty, institutions may be created that facilitate mutually beneficial exchanges. But in other environments, the Kenyan materials suggest, people see clearly where their interests lie. They invest in the creation of institutions in order to structure economic and political life so as better to defend their positions within them. They invest in institutions so as to vest their interests.

Lastly, the new institutionalism in economics must turn to politics because it is incomplete. As we have seen, institutions created to secure greater productivity create political power as well; they can be employed in distributional struggles. Those in Kenyan agriculture appear to have been transformed into instruments of predation to a lesser degree than those elsewhere in Africa; this fact helps to mark Kenya as an exception. As we have also seen, economic institutions in Central Kenya were less frequently manipulated in the period before Moi's presidency than in the period after. The economic theory of institutions fails to account for such variations. In this sense, it is incomplete. We have indicated what has been left out: the analysis of politics. Those in control of the state may be motivated to employ economic institutions to generate wealth and to protect its accumulation. Or those in charge of the state may be motivated to use its power to seize wealth and engage in redistribution, employing the power of economic institutions to engage in predation. The political base in Kenya's governments has promoted an interest in accumulation that is stronger in Kenya than elsewhere in much of Africa; but, given their differing geographic constituencies, the impetus to redistribution was stronger in Kenya under Moi than under Kenyatta. To create economic institutions is to create power. How it is employed and how the institutions perform depends upon the motivations of politicians.

The neoclassical revival in development economics thus requires fundamental modification. It fails to give sufficient weight to the economic significance of nonmarket institutions. And the attempt to incorporate the analysis of institutions compels a movement away from purely economic reasoning and into the realm of politics. An additional reason for this claim is that, as this study has shown, once in place, institutions influence subsequent actions. They may have been created for economic reasons; or they may have been founded so as to enhance the fortunes of particular economic interests. But, once created, they generate positions of political power and systems of political incentives. They define strategic possibilities and impose constraints. They thereby shape the way in which economic interests are formed and receive political expression.

In keeping with an economic theory of institutions, for example, we have found that the definition of property rights on the Highlands and in the reserves did indeed promote the formation of markets. But we have also found that the impact of institutions ran far deeper than that. For not only did the creation of property rights promote the formation of markets; they also helped to define the structure of interests that sought advantages in the marketplace. The same act that defined property rights on the Highlands, for example, defined as well the role of laborer and landowner.

Put another way, the creation of property rights formed an environment in which the choices of individuals led to the formation of market prices and thus the efficient allocation of resources. But it also prescribed for each actor which variables would form the endowment generating that actor's income; which variables would enter the actor's choice set; and which variables the actor would have to treat as purely exogenous. The definition of property rights thus defined as well the economic structure of the marketplace and the roles of individuals within it.

Institutions also define economic interests in the sense that they create

Conclusion

the conditions that determine which interests receive ideological and organizational expression. Thus, we saw that physical relations to the land defined economic interests in Kenya's agrarian politics; so too did location with respect to the streams of income generated by the commercialization of agriculture. But it was the incentives created by political institutions that shaped the way in which these interests gained effective expression. Responding to the opportunities created in the colonial system, politicians exploited the land issue to forge ethnic rivalries; in the era of national party competition, they transformed former rivals into political allies. In pursuit of the political opportunities offered by competitive parties, politicians created and projected ideological opposition to the economic inequalities in Kenya's rural society; in response to the incentives created by the single-party system, they refrained from doing so. The ideological expression of economic interests and their organizational form thus differed, depending upon the incentives generated for political elites by electoral institutions.

The political significance of institutions was further underlined by the role they play in providing the framework for struggles among competing interests. Many of the agrarian institutions in Kenya may have been created in an effort to render agriculture more productive. But the very institutions that enhanced the productivity of agriculture later became the centers for redistributive struggles between producers and processors and between both groups and the consumers of farm products. Each interest sought to use its institutional base to shape the structure of the industry to its advantage. In league with the surrounding political institutions, economic institutions made it easier for some interests to secure a greater share of the gains to be won from commercial agriculture. And those who helped to create the institutions by which to make agriculture more bountiful – the large economic interests – were victims in the subsequent struggle to divide the gains, losing out to those with more secure bases of institutional power.

Because a central theme of this book has been the agrarian origins of Kenyan politics, time and again, it has been driven to a materialist conception of politics. The political significance of economic factors has intruded into every chapter, be it the relative proportions of land and labor to the politics of the Kikuyu or the failure of the rains to the politics of the Moi succession. It is notable, then, that our analysis has led us from economic materialism to political economy. It has forced us to realize, for example, that institutions shape the relationship between physical factors, such as rainfall, and social outcomes, such as famine; or the relationship between the distribution of opportunities for wealth in Kenya's agrarian economy and the shape of political conflict.

Intriguingly, it has also driven us to view historical change as a dialectic, one structured by the interplay between economic forces and institutions. Even when created to secure mutually beneficial trades, institutions stand partially autonomous from the economy within which they are conceived. They create incentives; and these incentives influence the way in which economic interests are defined and the manner in which they receive organized political expression. When political actors intervene in the economy and seek to restructure economic relations, the policies they choose depend upon the incentives generated by the institutional context within which they are made. Economic forces thus generate institutions and the structure of these institutions in turn shapes the way in which governments transform their economies. Economy and polity thus interact, generating a process of change. But the process of change is path dependent; the course of the path is shaped by the initial institutional endowment. In this way, each society generates its own history.

Viewed from this perspective, there is little reason to expect societies to make choices consistent with the economic optimum. Some may make small departures from the optimum growth path early in their history, and these choices would generate massive departures at later periods. Others, such as Kenya, may make choices which promote economic growth; in so doing, they may institutionalize forces which possess a vested interest in continued growth.

The Kenyan case thus assists us in understanding how politics helps an economy to achieve a distinctive growth path. It illustrates the significance of institutional endowments in shaping that evolution. It thus helps us to comprehend the central role that institutions play in the process of economic development.[12]

Notes

Introduction

1 At nearly 4 percent per annum, the growth rate of its population stands at among the highest in the world.

2 The more recent figures are from IBRD, *World Development Report* (Washington, D.C.: IBRD, 1986); the earlier data are drawn from IBRD, *World Tables* (Washington, D.C.: IBRD, 1980).

3 The World Bank, *World Development Report*. A valuable source of insights into the differences between Kenya and her neighbors is contained in Joel D. Barkan, ed. *Politics and Public Policy in Kenya and Tanzania* (New York: Praeger, 1964) and Michael F. Lofchie, *Policy Makes a Difference: Agricultural Performance in Kenya and Tanzania*, draft manuscript.

4 James C. Scott [in *The Moral Economy of the Peasant* (London and New Haven: Yale University Press, 1976)] plays Baron Haxthausen to Samuel Popkin's Chicherin [in *The Rational Peasant* (Berkeley and Los Angeles: University of California Press, 1979)]. See the discussion in Jerome Blum, *Lord and Peasant in Russia* (Princeton: Princeton University Press, 1961).

5 As, for example, in Joel S. Migdal, *Peasants, Politics and Revolution* (Princeton, N. J.: Princeton University Press, 1974).

6 See, for example, Eric R. Wolf, *Peasant Wars of the Twentieth Century* (New York: Harper Torchbooks, 1968) and Jeffery M. Paige, *Agrarian Revolution* (New York: The Free Press, 1975).

7 Robert Ruark, *Something of Value* (Garden City, N.Y.: Doubleday, 1955).

8 See Robert I. Rotberg and Theodore K. Rabb, *Hunger and History* (Cambridge University Press, 1983); and the essays by Charles Tilly in *The Formation of National States in Western Europe* (Princeton, N.J.: Princeton University Press, 1975).

9 See Deepak Lal, *The Poverty of "Development Economics,"* Hobart Paperback 16 (London: The Institute of Economic Affairs, 1984); Ian M.D. Little, *Economic Development: Trade, Policy and International Relations* (New York: Basic Books, 1982); and the collection in Gerald M. Meier, ed. *Pioneers in Development: Second Series* (Washington, D.C.: The World Bank, 1987). For reviews of the state of development economics, see Paul Streeten, "Development Dichotomies," *World Development* 11, 10 (1983):875–89; Albert Hirschman, "The Rise and Decline of Development Economics," in Albert Hirschman, *Essays in Trespassing* (Cambridge University Press, 1981); and

Dudley Seers, "Birth, Life and Death of Development Economics," in Dudley Seers, *Development and Change* (London: Sage, 1979).

10 Martin Wassell, "Preface," in Lal, *The Poverty*, pp. x-xi.

11 Arnold C. Harberger, "Economic Policy and Economic Growth," in *World Economic Growth*, ed. Arnold C. Harberger (San Francisco: Institute for Contemporary Studies, 1984).

12 Quoted from a paper written by Smith in 1755 in Edward Canan, "Editor's Introduction" to *Adam Smith, An Inquiry into the Nature and Causes of the Wealth of Nations* (London: Methuen, 1950), p. xxxv.

13 Hla Myint, "The Neo-classical Resurgence in Development Economics: Its Strengths and Limitations," in *Pioneers*, ed. Meier.

14 *Ibid.*, pp. 126–7.

15 Alice Amsden, "The State and Taiwan's Economic Development," in *Toward A Political Economy of Development*, ed. Robert H. Bates (Berkeley and Los Angeles: University of California Press, 1988).

16 Peter Katzenstein, *Small States and World Markets* (Ithaca, N.Y.: Cornell University Press, 1985). See also the contributions in Peter B. Evans, Dietrich Rueschemeyer, and Theda Skocpol, eds. *Bringing the State Back In* (Cambridge University Press, 1985).

17 Douglass C. North, *Structure and Change in Economic History* (New York: Norton, 1981); Douglass C. North and Robert Paul Thomas, *The Rise of the Western World* (Cambridge University Press, 1973); and Lance E. Davis and Douglass C. North, *Institutional Change and American Economic Growth* (Cambridge University Press, 1971).

18 See, for example, Yujiro Hayami and Vernon Ruttan, *Agricultural Development: An International Perspective* (Baltimore, Md.: The Johns Hopkins Press, 1978) and David Feeny, "The Development of Property Rights in Land: A Comparative Perspective," in Bates, ed. *Toward A Political Economy.*

19 I regret, but do not retract, the pun.

20 In the words of Lal:

> I have recently found it useful to think of two polar types: the benevolent (platonic guardian) and the self-serving (predatory) state. The objectives of the former are well known as they form the staple of elementary textbook.... For the predatory state the welfare of its subjects... may be at best only a very minor... component of the state's objective function.

Deepak Lal, "Comment," in *Pioneers*, ed. Meier, p. 194.

21 In this sense, I join with Evans and his colleagues in "bringing the state back in" [see Peter Evans, Dietrich Rueschemeyer, and Theda Skocpol, *Bringing the State Back In* (Cambridge University Press, 1985)]. And I do it by making the state partially autonomous. I develop this point more fully in the sections that follow.

22 Evans, Rueschemeyer, and Skocpol, *Bringing the State Back In.*

23 Ronald Coase, "The Problem of Social Cost," *Journal of Law and Economics* 3 (October 1960):1–44.

24 Indeed, when applied to the developing world, the result may be less investment, as the demanders of luxury goods may exhibit a preference for imports from abroad.

25 This analysis bears a close resemblance to that put forward in staple theory. For the classic development, see the works of Harold Innis; an example would be his *The Fur Trade in Canada: An Introduction to Canadian Economic*

History (Toronto: University of Toronto Press, 1930). Useful reviews are offered in Melville H. Watkins, "A Staple Theory of Economic Growth," *The Canadian Journal of Economics and Political Science* 29, 2 (May 1963):141–58, and David McNally, "Staple Theory as Commodity Fetishism: Marx, Innis and Canadian Political Economy," *Studies in Political Economy* 6 (Autumn 1981):35–63. Perhaps the most insightful development of this position remains Robert E. Baldwin, "Patterns of Development in Newly Settled Regions," *Manchester School of Economic and Social Studies*, 24 (May 1956):161–79.

26 Coase, "The Problem;" Oliver E. Williamson, *The Economic Institutions of Capitalism* (New York: The Free Press, 1985); A. A. Alchian and H. Demsetz, "Production, Information Costs, and Economic Organization," *American Economic Review* 62(December 1972): 777–96; and B. Klein, R. C. Crawford, and A. Alchian, "Vertical Integration, Appropriable Rent, and the Competitive Contracting Problem, " *Journal of Law and Economics* 21 (1978):297–326.

27 While substantively different, these "cross-sectional" variations are formally similar to "cross-temporal" variations, as outlined in the language in the text.

Chapter 1

1 Figures from David Throup, personal correspondence. Throup notes that many place the number killed much higher. The ratio of deaths among loyalists to those among the Mau Mau insurgents approximated 1 to 4.

2 Much of the preceding exposition is from Spencer's discussion [John Spencer, *The KAU: The Kenyan African Union* (London: KPI, 1985)]. See the critical review by David Throup, "Moderates, Militants and Mau Mau: African Politics in Kenya, 1944–1952," unpublished. Absolutely invaluable to this and other discussions of Mau Mau are M. P. K. Sorrenson, *Land Reform in Kikuyu Country* (London: Oxford University Press, 1967) and David Throup, *Economic and Social Origins of Mau Mau* (London: James Curry, 1987).

3 Clough and Jackson, Jr., *Mau Mau Syllabus*. Because it became available only while this manuscript was in press, I have been unable to make as full a use as would have been appropriate of Tabitha Kanongo, *Squatters and the Roots of Mau Mau 1905–1963* (London: James Curry, 1987).

4 It is relevant here to note that the Carter Commission determined in 1933 that there were a total of 150,000 squatters and that 110,000 of them were Kikuyu. A survey of squatters in 1947 placed their number at 202,944, more than half of whom were Kikuyu. In that year, more than one-sixth of the Kikuyu population were squatters. See Colony and Protectorate of Kenya, *A Discussion of the Problems of the Squatter* (Nairobi: Government Printer, 1947), pp. 3 and 4.

5 Students of Kenya will realize the significance of these exclusions. Much of the existing work on Mau Mau has focused on the issues of female circumcision, schooling, and constitutional reform. See, for example, the entries in Marshall S. Clough and Kernell A. Jackson, Jr., *Mau Mau Syllabus: Parts I and II* (Stanford: Mimeographed, 1975).

6 This discussion is largely drawn from H. E. Lambert, *Kikuyu Social and Political Institutions* (London: Oxford University Press, 1956); H. E. Lambert, *The Systems of Land Tenure in the Kikuyu Land Unit* (Cape Town:

The University of Cape Town, 1950); M. W. H. Beech, "The Kikuyu System of Land Tenure," *Journal of the African Society* 17 (1917); Apollo Njonjo, "The Africanization of the 'White Highlands': A Study in Agrarian Class Struggles in Kenya, 1950–1974," Ph.D. Dissertation, Princeton University, 1974; M. P. K. Sorrenson, *Land Reform in the Kikuyu Country* (London: Oxford University Press, 1967); J. Middleton, *The Central Tribes of the North-Eastern Bantu* (London: International African Institute, 1953); L. S. B. Leakey, *The Southern Kikuyu Before 1903*, Vols. I-III (London: Academic Press, 1977); Gretha Kershaw, "The Land Is the People: A Study of Kikuyu Social Organization in Historical Perspective," Ph.D. Dissertation, University of Chicago, December 1972; and Godfrey Muriuki, *A History of the Kikuyu, 1500–1900* (Nairobi: Oxford University Press, 1974). A very fine discussion is also contained in David Throup, "The Construction and Destruction of the Kenyatta State," in *The Political Economy of Kenya*, ed. Michael Schatzberg (New York: Praeger, 1987).

7 Jomo Kenyatta, *Facing Mount Kenya: The Traditional Life of the Kikuyu* (London: Secker and Warburg, 1953), p. 76.

8 *Ibid.*, pp. 9–10.

9 *Ibid.*, pp. 13–14. Reinforcing this convention was the custom of alternating generations, in which the name and social personality of an individual was perpetuated by his or her descendants.

10 As with most discussions of the *mbari*, this discussion is of the simple form. Complex and compound forms are analyzed by Greet Kershaw in her forthcoming study of the Kikuyu.

11 Alternatively, the entrepreneurial founder of an *mbari* could act as a patron, enticing "have nots" from the settled portions of Kikuyuland by offering them land and lending them the cattle with which to seek marriage partners.

12 For further commentaries, see Maurice Godelier, *Perspectives on Marxist Anthropology* (Cambridge University Press, 1977) and Claude Meillassoux, *Maidens, Meal and Money* (Cambridge University Press, 1981).

13 Marshall D. Sahlins, "The Segmentary Lineage: An Organization of Predatory Expansion," *American Anthropologist*, 63 (1961):322–45.

14 See E. A. Brett, *Colonization and Underdevelopment in East Africa: The Politics of Economic Change, 1919–1939* (New York: NOK Publishers, 1973); M. F. Hill, *Permanent Way*, Vol. I (Nairobi: East African Railways and Harbours, 1949); M. P. K. Sorrenson, *Origins of European Settlement in Kenya* (Nairobi: Oxford University Press, 1967).

15 The best treatments of settler politics are by Redley and Mosley. See Michael Redley, "The Politics of a Predicament: The White Community in Kenya, 1918–1932," Ph.D. Dissertation, Cambridge University, October 1976, and Paul Mosley, *The Settler Economies: Studies in the Economic History of Kenya and Southern Rhodesia, 1900–1963* (Cambridge University Press, 1983).

16 Mosley,*The Settler Economies*, p. 15.

17 See the data reported in Kenya Colony and Protectorate, *Reports on the Committee on Native Land Tenure in Kikuyu Province* (Nairobi: Government Printer, 1929 and 1930) and *The Kikuyu Lands* (Nairobi: Government Printer, 1945).

18 Rebman M. Wambaa and Kenneth King, "The Political Economy of the Rift Valley: A Squatter Perspective," in *Hadith 5: Economic and Social History*

of *East Africa*, ed. Bethwell A. Ogot (Nairobi: East Africa Literature Bureau, 1976), p. 200.

19 See the data contained in J. H. Martin, "The Problem of the Squatter: Economic Survey of Resident Labour in Kenya," 24 February 1947, which shows the Kikuyu concentrating in Naivasha, Nakuru, and the Aberdares; the Kalenjin in Uasin Gishu; and the Baluhyia in Trans Nzoia.

20 Wambaa and King, "The Political Economy," p. 201.

21 Wambaa and King, "The Political Economy." Frank Furedi, "The Kikuyu Squatters in the Rift Valley: 1918–1929" in *Hadith 5: Economic and Social History of East Africa*, ed. Bethwell A. Ogot (Nairobi: Kenya Literature Bureau, 1976) and "The Social Composition of the Mau Mau Movement in the White Highlands," *Journal of Peasant Studies*, 1, 4 (1974):486–507.

22 As noted most clearly, perhaps, by Van Zwanenberg, many of the tensions that I explore between squatters and settlers occurred in the 1930s as well [see R. M. A. Van Zwanenberg, *Colonial Capitalism and Labour in Kenya 1919–1939* (Nairobi: East African Literature Bureau, 1975)]. That they led to revolt only after the war I attribute to (1) the growing extent of the transformation in settler agriculture; (2) the enhanced capacity of the settlers to act collectively following the war; (3) and the fears arising from the ascendancy of the Labour Party to power in the colonial metropole. The discussion in the text elaborates on all three factors.

23 Some of the best materials on this period are contained in Mosley, *The Settler Economies*; Redley, "The Politics"; John Lonsdale, "The Depression and the Second World War in the Transformation of Kenya," in *Africa and the Second World War*, eds. R. Rathbone and D. Killingray (London: Macmillan, forthcoming); C. C. Wrigley, "Kenya: The Patterns of Economic Life, 1906–1945," in *History of East Africa*, vol. II, ed. V. Harden and E. M. Chilver (Oxford: Clarendon Press, 1965); and Ian Spencer, "Settler Dominance, Agricultural Production and the Second World War in Kenya," *The Journal of African History* 21, 3 (1980):497–514. See also the discussions in Colony and Protectorate of Kenya, *Report of the Board Under the Chairmanship of Sir William Ibbotson* (Nairobi: Government Printer, 1952); Masao Yoshida, *Agricultural Marketing Institutions in East Africa* (Tokyo: Institute of Developing Economies, 1984); and Elspeth Huxley, *No Easy Way* (Nairobi: Kenya Farmers' Association, 1957).

24 My own work and the work of others have interpreted the Maize Marketing Board as a form of production cartel which sets prices against consumers. Certainly, the pooling arrangements prepared during the depression were intended to do this; they were defeated, however, by other economic interests (see Redley, "The Politics," and Mosley, *The Settler Economies*). And the evidence suggests that after the war the Maize Marketing Board operated so as to set prices against consumers. But the data suggest that *during* the war the Board was employed to purchase maize cheaply, by comparison with world market prices (Mosley, *The Settler Economies*, pp. 94–5). During the war, then, price stabilization by the Board enhanced the expected price received by farmers not by raising money prices but rather by reducing price variability.

25 An excellent history of the emergence of these and other institutions in colonial agriculture is contained in Y. P. Ghai and J. P. W. B. McAuslan, *Public Law and Political Change in Kenya* (New York: Oxford University Press, 1970).

26 For addiࢨional examples and analysis, see Oliver Williamson, *The Economic Institutions of Capitalism* (Cambridge, Mass.: Harvard University Press, 1985).

27 Thus Redley states:

> Delegated government authority was the key to the political independence of the white farmers. Local government, crop conferences, advisory boards, and "compulsory cooperation" were the interests by which the owner-occupier as landowner and producer developed the forms of pressure group politics and commercial organization appropriate to the defense of his interests.

Redley, "The Politics," p. 211. Redley is here referring to the early 1930s, though he argues that the same pattern applied in the war years as well.

28 The deployment of public officials to the military during World War II led to the retrenchment of services, including the collection of data on agricultural production and land use. The war years and immediate postwar period are therefore marked by a lack of data, and the argument advanced in this section must therefore remain tentative. It represents a reconstruction of a causal sequence, which on the basis of existing sources cannot be directly observed. One of the best discussions of postwar policy is contained in Throup, *Economic and Social Origins*.

29 See the legal regulations discussed and documented in Ghai and McAuslan, *Public Law and Political Change*. Excellent material on the squatters is contained in Van Zwanenberg, *Colonial Capitalism*. See as well the discussion in David Anderson and David Throup, "Africans and Agricultural Production in Colonial Kenya: The Myth of the War as a Watershed," *Journal of African History* 26 (1985):327–45.

30 See M. McWilliam, "Economic Policy and the Kenya Settlers, 1945–1948" in *Essays in Imperial Government*, eds. Kenneth Robinson and Frederick Madden (Oxford: Basil Blackwell, 1963).

31 R. B. Ogendo, "Kenya Dairy Industry, Part I," *Journal of Eastern African Research and Development*, 2 (1971):161–5. The pace of the transformation is suggested by the dates of the establishment of the creameries. Three had been established by the depression. No more were founded until after the Second World War, with two more being established by 1949 and another in 1951.

32 See, for example, the petitions of farmers seeking to be exempted from the reduction of squatter cattle in file Lab 25/5/4, Kenya National Archives. Note also the minutes of the District Commissioner, Trans Nzoia, to the Executive Council, 17 June 1949:

> The position, roughly, is this. The Sergoit ward wants to be exempted from the Rules and the Soy-Houey's Bridge ward wants the time allowed in the Rules to be extended. In both areas many farmers . . . are feeling the pinch regarding labour. Council will not allow any . . . exemptions and therefore it must . . . face a serious split [Lab 25/5/4].

33 See the discussion in R. S. Odingo, *The Kenya Highlands: Land Used and Agricultural Development* (Nairobi: East African Publishing House, 1971), p. 59. See also Anthony Clayton and Donald C. Savage, *Government and Labour in Kenya, 1958–1963* (London: Cass, 1974). Over the period 1945 to 1959–60, the production of grain increased by 186 percent, sisal by 190 percent, coffee by 284 percent, and milk by 308 percent. See L. H. Brown, *Agricultural Change in Kenya 1945–60* (Stanford: Food Research Institute, 1968), p. 61.

34 See the discussion in Anderson and Throup, "Africans and Agricultural Production."

35 File Lab 25/5/4, Kenya National Archives.

36 *Ibid.*

37 District Commissioner, Naivasha, to Office of the Member for Agriculture and Natural Resources, Nairobi, 26 May 1950, entitled "The Coordination of Policy Regarding Resident Labour," p. 7. Lab 25/5/4, Kenya National Archives.

38 Nakuru District, *Annual Report for 1949*, p. 5.

39 *Ibid.*

40 Rift Valley Province, *Annual Report 1950*, p. 1.

41 The special role of Olenguruone must of course be stressed here, as well as the special conditions that provoked rebellion among its residents. See the discussion in Rosberg and Nottingham, *The Myth* and in Kanongo, *Squatters*. The analysis in the text helps to account for the ability of the political organizers from Olenguruone to gain converts to their cause.

42 When native cattle were disposed of, it was often at a loss. For, as Van Zwanenberg points out, strict quarantine laws prevented the transportation of native cattle from one district to another. When all squatters in a particular district had to dispose of their cattle, then, the price of cattle would plummet. See Van Zwanenberg, *Colonial Capitalism*, pp. 210–74.

43 It should be noted that at the time of colonization population densities were low, particularly in the area newly settled by the Kikuyu. This was a result of recent droughts, famines, and diseases, for both people and cattle. Population levels rapidly built up, however, because of resettlement following the drought and because of high birth rates.

44 See Gavin Kitching, *Class and Economic Change in Kenya* (New Haven, Conn.: Yale University Press, 1980); Michael P. Cowen, "Capital and Household Production: The Case of Wattle in Kenya's Central Province, 1903–1964," Ph.D. Dissertation, University of Cambridge, 1978; Njonjo, "The Africanization of the 'White Highlands' "; and Sorrenson, *Land Reform in the Kikuyu Country.*

45 See, for example, Max Gluckman,*The Judicial Process among the Barotse of Northern Rhodesia* (Manchester: Manchester University Press, 1955).

46 Kershaw, "The Land Is the People," p. 18. Important work on this subject has also been done by Michael Cowen. See, for example, M.P. Cowen and K. Kinyanjui, "Some Problems of Capital and Class in Kenya," Occasional Paper No. 26, Institute for Development Studies, University of Nairobi, 1977; and Michael P. Cowen and Frederick Murage, "Notes on Agricultural Wage Labour in a Kenya Location," in *Development Trends in Kenya*, Proceedings of a Seminar Held in the Centre of African Studies of the University of Edinburgh, 28 and 29 April, 1972, pp. 39–59. See also Kitching, *Class and Economic Change*, and N. Humphrey, "The Relationship of Population to the Land in South Nyeri," in Colony and Protectorate of Kenya, *The Kikuyu Lands* (Nairobi: Government Printer, 1945).

47 See especially the account in R. A. Bullock, *Ndeiya: Kikuyu Frontier* (Waterloo, Ontario: University of Waterloo, 1975).

48 Cowen, "Capital and Household Production." See also Kitching, *Class and Economic Change*, and Sharon Stichter, *Migrant Labour in Kenya: Capitalism and African Response, 1895–1975* (Harlow, Essex, U.K.: Longman, 1982).

49 See the sources synthesized in the review essay, Paul Collier and Deepak Lal, *Poverty and Growth in Kenya*, World Bank Staff Working Paper No. 389, May 1980.

50 Cowen, "Capital and Household Production," p. 74. See also G. C. Mutiso, *Kenya: Politics, Policy and Society* (Nairobi: East African Literature Bureau, 1975), p. 68.

51 In a personal communication with the author, a noted anthropologist who has conducted extensive fieldwork in Kiambu cautions against so stark an interpretation, arguing that participation in land litigation affected land rights only at the margin. Anyone who helped win a case, the anthropologist noted, was not "sent home empty." But in no case known to the anthropologist was a person given ownership of land to which that person did not have other rights as well. And in no case was a person deprived of land for failure to help push a successful land case; rather, the land they were apportioned following litigation was likely to be of a lower quality than that of those who contributed to the costs of the case. Moreover, no one on the winning side was likely to forget that a member of the family who should have helped had refused to pay for their share of the costs of defending the family's inheritance. The costs of nonparticipation were likely to be inflicted in ways other than depriving that person of land. Personal communication, May 10, 1986.

52 Quoted in Sorrenson, *Land Reform*, p. 40. See also Colony and Protectorate of Kenya, *Report on Native Tribunals by Arthur Phillips* (Nairobi: Government Printer, 1946).

53 See, for example, Rosberg and Nottingham, *The Myth of "Mau Mau."*

54 Sorrenson, *Land Reform*, p. 101.

55 See Douglass C. North, *Structure and Change in Economic History* (New York: W. W. Norton, 1981); Williamson, *The Economic Institutions*; David Kreps, "Corporate Culture and Economic Theory," Typescript, Graduate School of Business, Stanford University, August 1984.

56 David Feeny, *The Political Economy of Productivity: Thai Agricultural Development, 1881–1975* (Vancouver: University of British Columbia Press, 1982); Douglass C. North and Robert Paul Thomas, *The Rise of the Western World* (Cambridge University Press, 1973); and Yujiro Hayami and Vernon Ruttan, *Agricultural Development: An International Perspective* (Baltimore, Md.: Johns Hopkins University Press, 1978).

57 Rupert Emerson, *From Empire to Nation: The Rise of Self-Assertion of Asian and African Peoples* (Cambridge, Mass.: Harvard University Press, 1960). See also Karl W. Deutsch, *Nationalism and Social Communication: An Inquiry into the Foundation of Nationality* (Cambridge, Mass.: MIT Press, 1953).

58 Most notably James S. Coleman in *Nigeria: Background to Nationalism* (Berkeley and Los Angeles: University of California Press, 1958).

59 Roseberg and Nottingham, *The Myth of Mau Mau.*

60 See, for example, Barnett and Njama, *Mau Mau from Within*; Van Zwanenberg, *Colonial Capitalism.*

61 James C. Scott, *The Moral Economy of the Peasant* (New Haven, Conn.: Yale University Press, 1976). See also Eric R. Wolf, *Peasant Wars of the Twentieth Century* (New York: Harper Torchbooks, 1973) and Joel S. Migdal, *Peasants, Politics and Revolution* (Princeton, N.J.: Princeton University Press, 1974).

62 An additional difficulty is analyzed by Throup. Throughout the period after World War II, it was the *colonial* government that advocated collective, tribal property and sought to create "traditional" political controls over commercial agriculture. A major source of political frustration on the part of African producers was the economic limitations forced upon them by the government in the name of tradition, including in particular limitations upon their ability to use the market. See Throup, *Economic and Social*; see also Cowen, "Capital and Household Production."

63 See Kitching, *Economic Change*; Cowen, "Capital and Household Production;" Njonjo, "The Africanization of the 'White Highlands' "; and Sorrenson, *Land Reform in the Kikuyu Country.*

64 It happened in the central highlands. But it did not happen in the semi-arid zones. As a result, the demand for individual land rights, which arose among the Kikuyu, did not arise in the semi-arid zones; and later attempts by the government to promote their formation were resisted by people in those areas. See Appendix 1A.

65 Lineage-based theories of rural stratification in Europe are to be found in T. M. Charles-Edwards, "Kinship, Status and the Origins of the Hide," *Past and Present* 56 (August 1972):3–37; Marc Bloch, *Feudal Society*, vol. 2 (Chicago: University of Chicago Press, 1970); and K. J. Lyser, *Rule and Conflict in Early Medieval Society* (London: Edward Arnold, 1979).

See as well the discussion in Jack Goody, *The Development of Family and Marriage in Europe* (Cambridge University Press, 1983), especially Appendix 1 and the works of George Duby cited therein.

66 See Sorrenson, *Land Reform*; Lamb, *Peasant Politics*; and R. J. M. Swynnerton, *A Plan to Intensify the Development of African Agriculture in Kenya* (Nairobi: Government Printer, 1954).

67 I agree with Njonjo, however, that the policy of land registration, which was so central to the program of agricultural development, did provide a barrier against the seizure of land. For the colonial government administered it in a way designed to prevent destabilizing landlessness, and so reined in the aggrandizing tendencies of the rural elites. These elites nonetheless prospered under the government's programs, for they gained ways of intensifying the production of cash crops.

68 David Throup analyzes the way in which state power was used to incorporate landed lineage segments in "The Construction and Destruction of the Kenyatta State." See also the series of articles on the "Royal Family" in *The Sunday Times*, 10, 17, and 24 August 1975 and the materials contained in Thomas Wolf, "Leadership, Resources and Locality-Center Relations in Taita," Ph.D. Dissertation, University of Sussex, 1985.

Appendix 1A

1 For similar kinds of reasoning, see Richard Posner, "A Theory of Primitive Society," *Journal of Law and Economics* 23 (1980):1–53; Joseph E. Stiglitz, "The New Development Economics," *World Development* 14 (1986):257–65; and Hans P. Binswanger and Mark R. Rosenzweig, "Behavioral and Material Determinants of Production Relations in Agriculture," Research Unit, Agriculture and Rural Development Department, World Bank, Report No. ARU 5, 1984. See also James C. Scott, *The Moral Economy of the Peasant* (New Haven, Conn.: Yale University Press, 1976).

2 Marshall D. Sahlins, "The Segmentary Lineage: An Organization of Predatory Expansion," *American Anthropologist*, 63 (1961):322–45.

3 See Gavin Kitching, *Class and Economic Change in Kenya* (New Haven, Conn.: Yale University Press, 1980); Michael P. Cowen, "Capital and Household Production: The Case of Wattle in Kenya's Central Province, 1903–1964," Ph.D. Dissertation, University of Cambridge, 1978; Apollo Njonjo, "The Africanization of the 'White Highlands'; A Study of Agrarian Class Struggles in Kenya, 1950–1974," Ph.D. Dissertation, Princeton University, 1974; and M. P. K. Sorrenson, *Land Reform in the Kikuyu Country* (London: Oxford University Press, 1967). For an example of the criticisms discussed here, see the contributions of Peter Anyang' Nyong'o in *Review of African Political Economy* 20 (1981).

4 As did, of course, many "disinherited" Kikuyu and those groups living in less favored zones.

5 Parker MacDonald Shipton, "Land, Credit and Crop Transactions in Kenya: The Luo Response to Directed Development in Nyanza Province," Ph.D. Dissertation, University of Cambridge, April 1985, p. 30.

See also Margaret Jean Hay, "Economic Change in Luoland: Kowe 1890–1945," Ph.D Dissertation, University of Wisconsin, 1972, and Angelique Haugerud, "Economic Differentiation among Peasant Households: A Comparison of Embu Coffee and Cotton Zones," Institute for Development Studies, University of Nairobi, Working Paper 383, 1981.

6 See Sara S. Berry, "Rural Class Formation in West Africa," in *Agricultural Development in Africa: Issues of Public Policy*, eds. Robert H. Bates and Michael F. Lofchie (New York: Praeger, 1980) and *Fathers Work for Their Sons: Accumulation, Mobility, and Class Formation in an Extended Yoruba Community* (Berkeley and Los Angeles: University of California Press, 1985).

7 Berry, "Rural Class Formation," p. 41.

8 *Ibid.*

9 *Ibid.*, p. 49. It is interesting to note in addition that in the Ivory Coast, where economic policies toward agriculture have resembled those in Kenya more closely than those in Nigeria, lineage systems appear to have evolved in the Kenyan manner, that is "from an extended kinship system toward a [household] system." [Robert M. Hecht, "The Transformation of Lineage Production in Southern Ivory Coast, 1920–1980," *Ethnology* 23 (1984):261].

10 See as well the discussion in Jack Goody, *The Development of Family and Marriage in Europe* (Cambridge University Press, 1983), especially Appendix 1 and the works of George Duby cited therein.

Chapter 2

1 See, for example, Colin Leys, *Underdevelopment in Kenya* (Berkeley and Los Angeles: University of California Press, 1975); Gavin Kitching, *Class and Economic Change in Kenya* (New Haven, Conn.: Yale University Press, 1980); and Nicola Swainson, *The Development of Corporate Capitalism in Kenya, 1918–1978* (Berkeley and Los Angeles: University of California Press, 1979).

2 Examples would include David Goldsworthy, *Tom Mboya: The Man Kenya Wanted to Forget* (New York: Africana Publishing Company, 1982); Guy Arnold, *Kenyatta and the Politics of Kenya* (London: Dent, 1974); and such

autobiographies as Michael Blundell, *So Rough a Wind* (London: Weidenfeld and Nicholson, 1964), and Oginga Odinga, *Not Yet Uhuru* (London: Heineman, 1967). They would also include such studies as Henry Bienen, *Kenya: The Politics of Participation and Control* (Princeton, N. J.: Princeton University Press, 1974); George Bennett and Carl G. Rosberg, *The Kenyatta Election* (Oxford University Press, 1961); and Joseph Kirimi and Philip Ochieng, *The Kenyatta Succession* (Nairobi: Transafrica, 1986).

3 The best account remains Gary Wasserman, *The Politics of Decolonization: Kenya Europeans and the Land Issue 1960–1965* (Cambridge: Cambridge University Press, 1976).

4 See Robert L. Tignor, *The Colonial Transformation of Kenya* (Princeton, N. J.: Princeton University Press, 1976).

5 See the discussion in Y. P. Ghai and J. P. W. B. McAuslan, *Public Law and Political Change in Kenya* (New York: Oxford University Press, 1970).

6 See, for example, the discussion in Gideon S. Were, *A History of the Abaluhya of Western Kenya. 1500–1930* (Nairobi: East African Publishing House, 1967).

7 That the ethnographic theories of administrators promoted tribal consciousness is argued in Robert H. Bates, "Some Conventional Orthodoxies in the Study of Agrarian Change," *World Politics* 36, 2 (January 1984):234–54. For the Kenyan case in particular, see M. P. K. Sorrenson, *Land Reform in the Kikuyu Country* (London: Oxford University Press, 1967), and D. W. Throup, "The Governorship of Sir Philip Mitchell in Kenya, 1944–1952," Ph.D. Dissertation, University of Cambridge, 1983.

8 For the politics of this period, see Wasserman, *The Politics of Decolonization*; Blundell, *So Rough a Wind*; and Apollo Njonjo, "The Africanization of the 'White Highlands': A Study in Agrarian Class Struggles in Kenya, 1950–1974," Ph.D. Dissertation, Princeton University, 1977.

9 See the elections covered in W. J. M. Mackenzie and Kenneth E. Robinson, *Five Elections in Africa* (Oxford: The Clarendon Press, 1960).

10 See the discussion in G. F. Engholm, "African Elections in Kenya, March 1957" in Mackenzie and Robinson, *Five Elections*.

11 See R. J. M. Swynnerton, *A Plan to Intensify the Development of African Agriculture in Kenya* (Nairobi: Government Printer, 1954). See also Judith Heyer, "The Origins of Inequalities in Smallholder Agriculture in Kenya, 1920–1973," *East African Journal of Rural Development* 8 (1975):142–81.

12 Good studies of the coalitional structure of this time would include Edward W. Soja, *The Geography of Modernization in Kenya* (Syracuse, N. Y.: Syracuse University Press, 1968); Wasserman, *The Politics of Decolonization*; Goldsworthy, *Tom Mboya*; Odinga, *Not Yet Uhuru*; and Cherry Gertzel, *The Politics of Independent Kenya* (Nairobi: East African Publishing House, 1970).

13 See the discussion in N. S. Carey Jones, "The Recolonization of the White Highlands of Kenya," *Geographic Journal* 131, (June 1965):186–201.

14 KADU had pressed for a regional government because it wanted to place political constraints on the ownership of land. As its Rift Valley leaders had telegraphed its delegation in London negotiating the structure of the regional constitution: "A unitary form of government could put Mau Mau in control; even now oaths are being taken and guns made.... We do not want such a government forced on us." (*East African Standard*, 12 September 1963).

15 See N. S. Carey Jones, *The Anatomy of Uhuru* (New York: Praeger, 1966); J. D. MacArthur, "The Benefits of Hindsight: Aspects of Experience in the High and Low Density Settlement Schemes in Kenya," *East African Journal of Rural Development* 8, 1–2 (1975):30–56, and "Some Aspects of Credit in the Kenya Settlement Schemes," Makerere University College, Faculty of Agriculture, RDR 39, 21 April 1967; and C.P.R. Nottige and J. R. Goldsack, *Million Acre Settlement Scheme, 1962–1966* (Nairobi: Department of Settlement, 1966). The independent role of the bureaucracy and its impact upon Kenyan development is stressed in John Lonsdale and Bruce Berman, "Coping with Contradictions: The Development of the Colonial State in Kenya," *Journal of African History* 20 (1979):487–505.

16 The introduction of these plans into political negotiations and capital markets is discussed in Wasserman, *The Politics of Decolonization*, pp. 109ff. For an excellent discussion, see as well John W. Harbeson, *Nation Building in Kenya: The Role of Land Reform* (Evanston, Ill.: Northwestern University Press, 1973).

17 *East African Standard*, 20 July 1963; 12 September 1963.

18 *East African Standard*, 2 March 1962.

19 *East African Standard*, 7 May 1962.

20 *East African Standard*, 2 August 1962.

21 *East African Standard*, 3 October 1962.

22 *East African Standard*, 2 October 1962.

23 This correspondence is perhaps best captured by the way in which some leaders in Kenya, as had politicians in the American Plains states in the nineteenth century, actively recruited settlers, thereby building grateful electoral constituencies. Interview, District Officer II, Kitale, 6 July 1984; *East African Standard*, 29 August 1963.

24 *East African Standard*, 18 March 1963.

25 *East African Standard*, 1 June 1963 and 27 December 1963.

26 For details, see Jay Edward Hakes, "The Parliamentary Party of the Kenyan African National Union: Cleavage and Cohesion in the Ruling Party of a New Nation," Ph.D Dissertation, Duke University, 1976.

27 For more details of this "campaign," see Goldsworthy, *Tom Mboya*. See also Wasserman, *The Politics of Decolonization;* Blundell, *So Rough a Wind;* and Njonjo, "The Africanization of the 'White Highlands.' "

28 Carey Jones, "The Recolonization," p. 195.

29 He cites in support of this contention the *Annual Report* of the Department of Settlement, 1963/64; see Hans Ruthenberg, *African Agricultural Production Development Policy in Kenya, 1952–1965* (New York: Springer-Verlag, 1966), p. 66. The use of the large farms to purchase peace is stressed by Colin Leys in *Underdevelopment in Kenya: The Political Economy of Neocolonialism* (Berkeley and Los Angeles: University of California Press, 1975). The independent role of the bureaucracy is stressed by Lonsdale and Berman in "Coping with the Contradictions."

30 Important to this explanation is the behavior of the KADU voters. For unless they would abide by the merger, their leaders could not consent to it, for fear of losing out at the polls.

It may have been the case that the KADU leaders did in fact face greater electoral risks as a result of having defected. But they were compensated for these risks by being appointed to boards of government corporations and senior posts in government.

In addition, the government took measures to reduce the risks they faced. It strikingly reined in Kikuyu demands for land in the Rift Valley, using the armed forces to sweep the Rift Valley clear of militant partisans of the Kikuyu cause. It also assented to Bildad Kaggia's request to leave Naivasha and return to Murang'a; while a KANU official in Naivasha, he had vocally and visibly promoted the demands of the Kikuyu against the Kalenjin. In these ways, the government sought to placate the demands of KADU's constituents.

Lastly, of course, the government reduced the risks by increasing the costs of political competition. As will be argued in the next section, the merger of KANU and KADU represented the first step toward a de facto one-party state.

31 Judith Heyer, "The Origins of Inequalities in Smallholder Agriculture in Kenya, 1920–1973," *East African Journal of Rural Development* 8 (1975):169.

32 *Ibid.*, p. 173.

33 For greater detail, see Parker MacDonald Shipton, "Land, Credit and Crop Transitions in Kenya: The Luo Response to Directed Development in Nyanza Province," Ph.D Dissertation, University of Cambridge, April 1985.

34 See the commentary in Carey Jones, "The Recolonization," p. 193.

35 See also the discussion of the impact of ecological factors upon the structure of property rights contained in Appendix 1A.

36 See the analysis in Z. W. Kmietowicz and P. Weblet, "Statistical Analysis of Income Distribution in the Central Province of Kenya," University of Leeds, School of Economic Studies, Discussion Paper No. 17, 11 April 1975.

37 See the introductory comments in Swynnerton, *A Plan.* As Lamb states, the development schemes were seen "as part of . . . [a] policy of 'rewards and punishments' " [Geoff Lamb, *Peasant Politics: Conflict and Development in Murang'a* (New York: St. Martin's, 1974)]. See also D. Mukaru Ng'anga, "Mau Mau Loyalists and Politics in Murang'a, 1952–1979" in William R. Ochieng and Karim K. Janmohhamed, "Some Perspectives on Mau Mau," *Kenya Historical Review*, 5, 2 (1977).

38 See Goldsworthy, *Tom Mboya* and Odinga, *Not Yet Uhuru.*

39 See the commentary by the United States Ambassador to Kenya, William Attwood, *The Reds and the Blacks* (New York: Harper & Row, 1967).

40 These figures were calculated in June 1964. They are reported in the best discussion of the politics of this period: Gertzel, *The Politics*, pp. 125ff. David Throup (in a personal communication) indicates that the radicals claim that they were in fact much stronger than these figures suggest. Some, such as Kaggia, felt they possessed a majority; they certainly had many sympathizers. Subsidized loans from government agencies, appointments as junior ministers, and appointments to parastatal agencies and government corporations kept many sympathizers in line, however, thus weakening the radical movement.

41 Gertzel, *The Politics*, p. 39.

42 Ruthenberg, *African Agricultural*, p. 107.

43 See, for example, the data in Ronald R. Stockton, "Development and Discontent: A Study of Social Mobilization in the Nyeri District of Kenya," draft manuscript.

44 See, for example, the speeches made in Murang'a against Kaggia, and especially the famous one made by President Kenyatta on 10 April 1965, as reported by Geoff Lamb, *Peasant Politics*, pp. 36–7.

45 See the accounts in Ng'anga, "Mau Mau, Loyalists and Politics in Murang'a." The best overall accounts of the demise of the KPU are contained in Geoff Lamb, *Peasant Politics* and Robert Buijtenhuijs, *Mau Mau Thirty Years After* (The Hague: Mouton, 1970). See also Susan Dorothy Mueller, "Political Parties in Kenya: Patterns of Opposition and Dissent, 1949–1964," Ph.D. Dissertation, Princeton University, 1972.

46 A probing analysis of the legal and procedural barriers placed in the way of opposition parties is contained in C. P. W. Hornsby, "The Member of Parliament in Kenya, 1969–1983," Ph.D Dissertation, Oxford University, 1985. It is to be noted, moreover, that former members of KPU were officially banned from subsequently running for office under the KANU party label, and that other known radicals were denied the chance to run as well.

47 Adam Przeworski, among others, has made a similar argument, contending that the need to generate electoral majorities reshaped the expression of the interests of the working classes in advanced industrial democracies. See Adam Przeworski, *Capitalism and Social Democracy* (Cambridge University Press, 1985).

48 The best analysis of the emergence of single-party systems in Africa is Ruth Berins Collier, *Regimes in Tropical Africa* (Berkeley and Los Angeles: University of California Press, 1982).

Chapter 3

1 It will quickly be noted that the arguments put forward are not systematically tested. I have become convinced, after many struggles, that limitations with the data mean that the arguments cannot be tested statistically. I have had to content myself with rendering them credible through anecdotal elaboration.

2 The initial portions of this chapter can be seen as a contribution to a literature that would include Arthur L. Stinchcombe, "Agricultural Enterprise and Rural Class Relations," *American Journal of Sociology* 67 (September 1961):165–76; Eric R. Wolf and Sidney W. Mintz, "Haciendas and Plantations in Middle America and the Antilles," *Social and Economic Studies* 6 (September 1957):380–412; and Jeffery M. Paige, *Agrarian Revolution: Social Movements and Export Agriculture in the Underdeveloped World* (New York: The Free Press, 1975). See as well David J. Glover, "Contract Farming and Smallholder Grower Schemes in Less-developed Countries," *World Development*, 12, 11–12 (1984):1143–57; Margaret Beattie Bogue, "The Lake and the Fruit: The Making of Three Farm-type Areas," *Agricultural History* 59, 4 (October 1985):493–522; John Umbeck, *A Theory of Property Rights* (Ames, Iowa: Iowa State University Press, 1986); and Lee J. Alston and Robert Higgs, "Contractual Mix in Southern Agriculture Since the Civil War," *Journal of Economic History*, 42, 2 (June 1982):327–53. See as well A. F. Robertson's superb study, *The Dynamics of Productive Relationships* (Cambridge University Press, 1987).

Two pieces which have inspired me to apply this literature to Kenya are Philip Raikes, "The Development of a Middle Peasantry in Kenya," Center for Development Research, Project Papers A 87.3, October 1978, and Tim Aldington, "Pricing and Competition in Agricultural Markets in Kenya," Interministerial Study Team on Costs, Prices, and Market Structures, typescript, 1977. Both take an industrial organization approach to the study of agriculture in Kenya. See as well Barbara Grosh, "Agricultural Parastatals Since Independence: How Have They Performed?", Institute for Development Studies, University of Nairobi, Working Paper No. 435, January 1986.

For relevant theoretical contributions, see Oliver E. Williamson, *The Economic Institutions of Capitalism* (New York: The Free Press, 1985); George A. Akerloff, "The Market for 'Lemons': Qualitative Uncertainty and the Market Mechanism," *Quarterly Journal of Economics* 84 (August 1970):488–500; Samuel L. Popkin, "Public Choice and Rural Development," in *Public Choice and Rural Development*, ed. Clifford Russell and Norman Nicholson (Washington, D.C.: Resources for the Future, 1981); Ammar Siamwalla, "An Economic Theory of Patron–Client Relations," paper prepared for the Thai–European Seminar on Social Change in Contemporary China, April 1980; and Douglass C. North, *Structure and Change in Economic History* (New York: Norton, 1981).

3 Kenneth Arrow, "Limited Knowledge and Economic Analysis," *American Economics Review* 64, 1 (March 1974): 1–16.

4 As noted above, because of the political power of the European colonists, it was important to secure their cooperation in the process of decolonization; the colonial government also feared that without the prospect of a profitable sale, the settlers would run down their farms, and Kenya would enter independence with wasted economic assets. The government therefore purchased the settlers' land at 1959 prices – prices which were formed prior to the realization that the end of white hegemony was near.

5 Hans Ruthenberg, *African Agricultural Production Development Policy in Kenya, 1952–1965* (New York: Springer-Verlag, 1966), p. 82. The discussion that follows is based as well on materials cited in the notes to the previous chapter.

6 For further evidence of popular resistance to the seizure of land because of debt, see the materials in Parker MacDonald Shipton, "Land, Credit and Crop Transactions in Kenya: The Luo Response to Directed Development in Nyanza Province," Ph.D. Dissertation, University of Cambridge, April 1985. Adding to the sensitivity of the issue was that resettlement was taking place at the same time as the rise of the socialist challenge. The government feared that the repossession of land would lead to a fusion of the two radical traditions: the one nationalist and the other socialist.

7 See Eric Clayton, *Agrarian Development in Peasant Economies* (London: Pergamon, 1964).

8 Preface to Edith H. Whetham, *Co-operatives, Land Reform and Land Settlement* (London: The Plunkett Foundation for Co-operative Studies, 1967), p. i.

9 The adoption of such policies is thus not just because of "dirigiste dogmas" or ideological preferences, as some critics would have it. See Deepak Lal, *The Poverty of "Development Economics,"* Hobart Paperback 16 (London: The Institute of Economic Affairs, 1984). See as well A. F. Robertson, *People and the State: An Anthropology of Planned Development* (Cambridge University Press, 1984).

An interesting analogy is presented by the preservation of collective institutions in agrarian France in the eighteenth century. Root argues that the monarchy kept collective controls in place to preserve the capacity of village communities to extract taxes. The institutions provided assurances to foreign lenders, from whom the monarch sought loans so as better to prosecute its wars. See Hilton L. Root, *Peasant and King in Burgundy: Agrarian Foundations of French Agriculture* (Berkeley and Los Angeles: University of California Press, 1987).

Another interesting analogy is provided by the analysis of interdependent or tied markets in the literature on rural India, wherein imperfect credit markets are held to generate "compulsory" labor contracts. For reviews of this literature, see Kaushik Basu, *The Less Developed Economy: A Critique of Contemporary Theory* (Oxford: Blackwell, 1984), and Pranab K. Bardhan, "Interlocking Factor Markets and Agrarian Development: A Review of Literature," *Oxford Economic Papers* 32 (1980): 82–98.

10 See the discussion in Michael Schluter, *Constraints on Kenya's Food and Beverage Exports*, Research Report 44 (Washington, D.C.: International Food Policy Research Institute, April 1984).

11 An interesting discussion of this line of reasoning is contained in Yujiro Hayami, "Community, Market and the State," Elmhirst Memorial Lecture, Twentieth International Conference of Agricultural Economists, Buenos Aires, August 1988.

Technically, the analysis of capital markets could be subsumed under the analysis of information costs; for the inability to acquire information about the future causes the failure of capital markets. The two discussions have been presented separately, however.

12 See the analysis in Akerloff, "The Market." As pointed out by Neil Beck in a personal communication, the Akerloff model is a one-period model. With repeated play, however, reputations for quality could form, and the dilemma would be resolved. That the formation of reputations is unable to resolve the problem in the coffee markets underscores the impact of scale on the costs of information. It is notable how far this analysis has pushed the understanding of the problem of quality beyond that achieved through conventional neoclassical analysis. See, for example, P. T. Bauer and B. S. Yamey, "The Economics of Marketing Reform," *Journal of Political Economy* 62 (1954): 210–35.

The discussion of the coffee industry in Kenya will largely be drawn from the following sources: P. G. McMaster and N. R. Solly, *Coffee and Its Economics in Kenya* (Nairobi: Coffee Board of Kenya, n.d.); Allan Rufus Waters, "Changes and Evolution in the Structure of the Kenyan Coffee Industry," *African Affairs* (April 1982); K. G. Williams and D. Kabagambe, "The Impact of the Coffee Boom in Meru District, Kenya," Kenya Research Project, Working Paper No. 2, Institute of Planning Studies, University of Nottingham, August 1982; J. K. Maitha, *Coffee in the Kenyan Economy* (Nairobi: East African Literature Bureau, 1974); M. J. Westlake and L. D. Smith, "A Critique of Kenya's Present Coffee Policy," Staff Working Paper 70, Institute for Development Studies, University of Nairobi, May 1970; Kenya Planters Cooperative Union, *KPCU: 40 Years Association with World Famous Kenya Coffee* (Nairobi: KPCU, 1970); M. J. Westlake, "Taxation and Control of the Kenya Coffee Industry," Discussion Paper No. 185, Institute for Development Studies, University of Nairobi, November 1973; *Kenya Coffee*, various issues; I. R. Wallace, "The Development of the Meru Coffee Industry in Kenya," *East African Journal of Rural Development* 3, 2 (1970): 1–45; Kenya Planters Co-operative Union, Directors' Report and Accounts, various years; T. M. Sagwe, "Marketing Notes: Kenya Coffee

Notes to p. 77

Marketing Policy," *Kenya Coffee* 43, 513 (December 1978):373–4; Ministry of Agriculture, Crop Production Division, *An Outline of Coffee Processing* (Nairobi: Ministry of Agriculture, 1972); International Coffee Organization, *Coffee in Kenya* (London: International Coffee Organization, January 1978); Ministry of Agriculture, Crop Production Division, *An Outline of Coffee Management* (Nairobi: Ministry of Agriculture, 1971); Coffee Board of Kenya, *Annual Reports and Accounts*, various years; R. Clark and D. G. R. Belshaw, "East African Coffee Policies," in *Agricultural Planning in East Africa*, ed. G. H. Helleiner (Nairobi: East African Publishing House, 1963); G. D. Guyer, "East Africa and Three International Commodity Agreements: The Lessons of Experience," *Economic Development and Cultural Change* 21, 3 (1973).

13 A ratoon is a year's growth of cane from a sugar plant.

14 Mumias Sugar Company, Standard Cane Farming Contract.

15 References used here for tea in Kenya include M. C. McWilliam, "The Kenya Tea Industry," *East African Economics Review* 6, 1 (July 1959):32–48; Dan M. Etherington, *An Economic Analysis of Smallholder Tea Production in Kenya* (Nairobi: East African Literature Bureau, 1973); The Tea Board of Kenya, *Tea in Kenya* (Nairobi: Tea Board of Kenya, n.d.); Colony and Protectorate of Kenya, *Report of the Working Party Set up to Consider the Establishment of an Authority to Promote the Development of Cash Crops for Smallholders and of the Working Party to Consider the Financial Implications of the Proposed Authority* (Nairobi: Government Printer, 1960); N. H. Stern, *An Appraisal of Tea Production on Small Holdings in Kenya* (Paris: Development Centre of the Organization for Co-operation and Development, 1972); D. Sullivan, "Smallholder Tea Project in Kenya: A Review of the Kenya Tea Development Authority," World Bank, Employment and Rural Development Division, Agriculture Rural Development Background Paper, September 1974; Hans Blume, *Organizational Aspects of Agro-Industrial Development Agencies* (Munchen: Weltforum Verlag, 1971); Mogens Buch-Hansen, "Agro-Industrial Production and Socio-economic Development: A Case Study of KTDA Smallholder Tea Production in Buret, Western Kenya," Working Paper No. 11, Institute of Geography, Socio-economic Analysis and Computer Science, Roskilde University Center, 1986, and "Contract Farming and the Peasantry: Case Studies from Kenya," Research Report No. 18, Institute of Geography, Socio-economic Analysis and Computer Science, Roskilde University Center, 1981; Geoffrey Lamb and Linda Muller, "Control, Accountability and Incentives in a Successful Development Institution: The Kenya Tea Development Authority," World Bank Staff Working Paper No. 550 (Washington, D.C.: The World Bank, 1982); Jeffrey S. Steves,"Class Analysis and Rural Africa: The Kenya Tea Development Authority," *The Journal of Modern African Studies* 16, 1 (March 1978):123–33; M. Moynagh, "Smallholder Tea in East Africa: A Brief History," *East Africa Journal of Research and Development* 9, 1 & 2 (1976):37–56; and Waino Emil Arvo, Jr., "A Geography of the Tea Industry in Kenya," Program of Eastern African Studies, Maxwell Graduate School of Citizenship and Public Affairs, Occasional Paper No. 38, 1968.

16 It is clear, however, that this process of regulation has gone further in some industries than in others. Both the tea and the sugar industries have organized in a system of outgrowers, wherein peasant producers supply a central pro-

171

cessing unit. But the investors in tea have adopted a second payment system to secure quality output; the sugar industry has not, and has instead created and enforced legal obligations to employ prescribed dosages of farm inputs. Smallholder tea producers are free to make decisions regarding hubandry practices over which sugar producers possess little discretion. The greater latitude of choice on the part of producers in the tea industry represents a fundamental difference in the degree of the regimentation of the productive life of the two kinds of farmers. It appears to originate in the differences in the scale economies of the two industries. While there may be gains from increasing quality in both sugar and tea, the costs of losses in quantity may be greater for sugar, given the greater scale of the sugar factories and the resultant rise in unit costs resulting from declines in production. At the margin, then, "requisitioning" may be preferable to "enticing" as the economic costs of the fall-off in quality may be less costly than those resulting from declines in the quantity of production.

For analyses of the Kenyan sugar industry, see P. Anyon'g Nyongo, "The Development of a Middle Peasantry in Nyanza," Institute for Development Studies, Working Paper No. 380, February 1981; I. C. A. Obero, "The Western Kenya Sugar Industry, with Specific Reference to Nyanza and Western Province," M. A. Thesis, Department of Geography, University of Nairobi, January 1980; John K. Mulaa, "The Politics of a Changing Society, Mumias," M. A. Thesis, University of Nairobi, 1980; J. E. O. Odada, "Capital Labour Substitution, Returns to Scale and Farm Size in the Kenyan Sugar Industry," Ph.D. Dissertation, University of Nairobi, 1982; J. A. Smith, "The Development of Large-scale Integrated Sugar Schemes in Western Kenya," Working Paper No. 345, Institute for Development Studies, University of Nairobi, August 1978; Mogens Buch-Hansen, "Agro-Industrial Production and Socio-Economic Development: Case Studies of Sugar Production in Muhoroni and Mumias, Western Kenya," Working Paper No. 15, Institute of Geography, Socio-Economic Analysis and Computer Science, Roskilde University Center, 1981; Albert Hampton Barclay, "The Mumias Sugar Project," Ph.D. Dissertation, Columbia University, 1977; Republic of Kenya, "Report of the Inter-ministerial Committee on Sugar Industry," typescript, July 1982; Raphael Kaplinsky, *Sugar Processing: The Development of Third-World Technology* (London: Intermediate Technology Publications, 1984); United States Department of Agriculture, Foreign Agricultural Service, *Report on World Sugar Supply and Demand, 1980 and 1985* (Washington, D.C.: Government Printer, 1977); Interviews, Mumias Outgrowers Company, 15 August 1984; Area Manager, Mumias, 14 August 1984; World Bank, Regional Offices, 18 July 1984; 14, 15, 16 September 1984; Ministry of Agriculture, 18 July 1984.

17 This system offers to the investors the additional advantage of transferring to others many of the costs of securing quality in production. For details of these regulations, see The Coffee Act, Chapter 333, Laws of Kenya; The Pyrethrum Act, Chapter 440, Laws of Kenya; The Tea Act, Chapter 343, Laws of Kenya; The Cotton Seed and Lint Marketing Act, Chapter 335, Laws of Kenya; and so forth.

18 See the analysis in International Labor Organization, *Employments, Incomes and Equality* (Geneva: International Labor Organization, 1972), and Raphael Kaplinsky, ed., *Readings on the Multinational Corporation in Kenya* (New York: Oxford University Press, 1978).

19 C. C. Wrigley, "Kenya: Patterns of Economic Life, 1906–1945," in *History*

of East Africa, vol. II, eds. V. Harden and E. M. Chilver (Oxford: Clarendon Press, 1965). See also Masao Yoshida, Agricultural Marketing Intervention in East Africa: A Study in the Colonial Origins of Marketing Policies, 1900–1965 (Tokyo: Institute of Developing Economics, 1984).

20 See, for example, Mogens Buch-Hansen and Henrick Secher Marcussen, "Contract Farming and the Peasantry: Cases from Western Kenya," Review of African Political Economy 23 (June 1983):9–36. See also the materials contained in the files of the Provincial Cooperative Offices, Western Province.

21 The impact of these factors upon the scale of farms is noted by McMaster and Sully:

> Large acreages of coffee should be avoided, and it is now considered that the ideal coffee farm should be equal parts coffee and grazing. Estates of above 200 acres of coffee seldom give an average yield in proportion to their size. For example, it should be possible to average 7 cwts. per acre, and the smaller estates often do achieve this, but how seldom does one hear of 300-acre farms averaging 100 tons a year! Coffee must have the personal touch of the owner or manager in that every block may have to be treated differently when pruning – ney, even every tree, and if the estate is too large this is impossible. (McMaster and Solly, Coffee, p. 4.)

22 Similar comments could be made for dairy and beef cattle, especially given the problems of disease among the exotic cattle imported for their superior milk production and the problems of milk storage. The economies of scale in the beef industry resulted in large-scale ranches, owned by companies and managed by hired farm managers; those in the dairy industry resulted in a far greater percentage of smaller, owner-operated farms.

An alternative argument would be that the pattern of land use generates a distribution of political power that stabilizes that pattern (and thus the structure of rural class relations). Wheat farming in Kenya offers evidence of such a dynamic, as politically influential wheat producers put an end to the effort of the Ministry of Agriculture to promote wheat farming by small-scale producers (interviews, May 1983).

An approach that emphasizes the use of power to reproduce social forms in Kenyan agriculture must deal, however, with the evidence of the widespread subdivision of large farms, a process that began with the resettlement program but continues. The spread of the production of commodities that can most profitably be produced on small farms appears to have made it profitable to reorganize patterns of landholding. Members of the landed elite appear willing to sell out to small farmers who can afford to pay more for the land than the sellers can earn from using it. This is not to deny that a highly visible portion of the Kenyan elite prefer to act as "lords of manors" and so hold on to inefficiently large farms; that some hold on to them to secure loans from banks and credit programs; or that some retain ownership of large estates, the better to endow their progeny. Nor is it to deny the socially unjust pattern of land distribution in Kenya. It is merely to argue that in the long run, economic forces appear to restructure social forms.

23 If the berries are not of a uniform ripeness, they will ferment at different rates when being processed, with harmful effects on the quality of factory output.

24 It should be noted that in other countries wheat is produced on small-scale farms. Where it is produced in this manner, it is often under irrigation, and the management of water as an input requires precisely the kinds of monitoring and timely intervention that impose diseconomies of scale.

25 Historically in Kenya scale economies in processing dictated the size of production units as well. Tea and sugar, for example, were produced on large estates. The factors we analyze help to explain this change in form.

Before the introduction of the kinds of institutions discussed in this chapter, all contracting was private contracting and vertical integration was the sole form of economic organization available. But, with the legal regulation of inputs and the creation of the right to compel sales to particular factories, those seeking to promote commercial production need not finance only those who can produce enough to lower the unit costs of large-scale processing plants. Loans for production can be separated from loans for processing. In addition, transport costs have declined, enabling a large number of small production units to feed a large-scale, centralized processing facility. Production can therefore take place on small, independent units, even while processing takes place in large-scale factories. The result of the changes in the legal framework and transport costs has been a change in the form of economic organization in Kenyan agriculture. A useful review is provided in Nicholas William Minot, "Contract Farming and Its Impact on Small Farmers in Less Developed Countries," typescript, Michigan State University, 1985.

26 Steves, "Class Analysis and Rural Africa." The Tea Authority confronted extremely powerful scale economies in transport because it funded the construction of the roads employed for the collection of tea.

The argument made here emphasizes the disparity between the rhetoric and performance of the Authority so as to emphasize the significance of transport costs. When the difference between the size distribution in tea and in the production of other crops is noted, however, one must conclude that the Authority has in fact adhered to its small-farmer mandate, even while adjusting its program in the ways described in the text.

27 A premise of this strategy is that the dairies would earn greater revenues from charging a steady price to consumers throughout the year than they would from charging two prices – one covering their low, wet season costs and another their higher, dry season costs – even though the "steady" price might be equivalent to the average of the latter two. It is difficult to imagine a demand curve that would behave this way; but the presumption that the demand for milk behaved in such a way appears to underlie the dairies' pricing strategy. For further references to the dairy industry, see note 31 below.

28 References for pyrethrum include Cabinet Memorandum, "The Crisis in the Pyrethrum Industry," 1982; United States Department of Agriculture, Foreign Agricultural Service, "Kenya: Pyrethrum," May 4, 1982; Marketing Development Project, Ministry of Agriculture, "Background Marketing Briefs for the Agricultural Price Review," various years; Margaret Sire Ongonga, "An Evaluation of Public Enterprise: The Pyrethrum Board of Kenya," M. A. Thesis, Department of Economics, University of Nairobi, 1979; and Colony and Protectorate of Kenya, *Report: Commission of Inquiry into Certain Matters Concerning the Pyrethrum Industry* (Nairobi: Government Printer, 1960).

29 The power is conferred in the Pyrethrum Act, Chapter 440, Laws of Kenya.

30 See the discussion in F. M. Scherer, *Industrial Market Structure and Economic Performance* (Chicago: Rand McNally, 1970). See also George Stigler, "Monopoly and Oligopoly by Merger," *American Economic Review* (May

1950):23–34, and Sam Peltzman, "Toward a More General Theory of Regulation," *The Journal of Law and Economics* 19 (1976):211–40.

31 References for the dairy industry include Philip Raikes, *Livestock and Development Policy in East Africa* (Uppsala: Scandinavian Institute of African Studies, 1961); H. Klemm, "Some Aspects of Milk Marketing in Kenya," Discussion Paper No. 21, Institute for Development Studies, University of Nairobi, January 1966; R. B. Ogendo, "Kenya Dairy Industry, Part I," *Journal of Eastern African Research and Development* 1, 2 (1971):161–5, and "Kenya Dairy Industry, Part II: Location and Structure of the Industry," *Journal of Eastern African Research and Development* 2, 1 (1972):41–67; Peter Hopcraft and George Ruigu, "Dairy Marketing and Prices in Kenya," Working Paper 26, Institute for Development Studies, University of Nairobi, March 1976; Peter N. Hopcraft, "An Evaluation of the Kenya Dairy Production Program," Occasional Paper No. 20, Institute for Development Studies, University of Nairobi, 1976; Colony and Protectorate of Kenya, *Report of the Commission of Inquiry into the Dairy Industry, 1956* (Nairobi: Government Printer, 1956); J. B. Wyckoff and K. W. Gitu, "Market Performance of Kenya's Commercial Dairy Industry," Nairobi, typescript, May 1, 1984; S. G. Moghoh and C. F. W. Buteyor, "Central Policy Issues in the Development of the Marketing System for Milk in Kenya," A Paper Prepared for the Development Policy Division, Ministry of Livestock Development, Nairobi, Typescript, January 12, 1984; Susan Maina, "Evaluation of the Performance of the Marketing Boards: The Small Farm Milk Marketing System in Kenya," Ph.D. Dissertation, Cornell University, 1981; George Munium Ruigu, "An Economic Analysis of the Kenya Milk Subsystem," Ph.D. Dissertation, Michigan State University, 1978; Masao Yoshida, *Agricultural Marketing Intervention in East Africa* (Tokyo: Institute of Developing Economies, 1984); M. F. Hill, *Cream Country: The Story of Kenya Cooperative Creameries Ltd.* (Nairobi: Kenya Cooperative Creameries, 1956).

32 More recently, sales to the school milk program have formed one of the most lucrative portions of the milk market. The Kenya Cooperative Creameries has successfully blocked efforts by the cooperatives to secure direct access to that portion of the market as well.

33 See the debates in the Republic of Kenya, National Assembly, House of Representative, *Official Report*, vol. X, Part II (Fourth Session), 22 November 1966.

34 Mancur Olson, *The Logic of Collective Action* (Cambridge, Mass.: Harvard University Press, 1965); George Stigler, "The Theory of Economic Regulation," *Bell Journal of Economics and Management Sciences* 2, (1971):3–21; and Peltzman, "Toward a More General Theory of Regulation."

35 Interviews, 14 and 18 July 1984; *The Weekly Review*, 12 April 1985.

36 Interviews, Cooperative Bank of Kenya, 23 July 1984. Site visit, Malaba Malikisi, November 1982. Department of Cooperatives, Development Planning Division, "A Survey of Cotton Industry in Nyanza Province," June 1973.

37 Barbara Grosh, "Performance of Agricultural Public Enterprises in Kenya: Lessons from the First Two Decades of Independence," University of California, Berkeley, typescript, November 1986.

38 B. Klein, R. A. Crawford, and A. Alchian, "Vertical Integration, Appropriable

Rents, and Competitive Contracting Processes" *Journal of Law and Economics* 21, 2 (October 1978):297–326.

39 See, for example, John K. Mulaa, "The Politics of a Changing Society: Mumias," M.S. Thesis, University of Nairobi, 1980. See the comments concerning President Moi's direct personal concern with the fate of the pyrethrum industry contained in Telex, Nairobi to Washington, AGR 536, May 1983.

40 These inferences were drawn from informal but lengthy interviews with local politicians in Western Kenya and Meru. For further discussions of the controlling impact of local party structures, see Joel D. Barkan, "Bring Home the Pork: Legislative Behavior, Rural Development and Political Change in East Africa," in *Legislatures and Development*, ed. Joel Smith and Lloyd Musolf (Durham: Duke University Press, 1978); Joel D. Barkan, "Comment: Further Reassessment of 'Conventional Wisdom': Political Knowledge and Voting Behavior in Rural Kenya," *American Political Science Review* 70 (June 1976):452–55; Joel D. Barkan and John J. Okumu, "Political Linkage in Kenya: Citizens, Local Elites and Legislators," in *Political Parties and Linkage*, ed. Kay Lawson (New Haven, Conn.: Yale University Press, 1980); Dirk Berg-Schlosser, "Models and Meaning of Political Participation in Kenya," *Comparative Politics* (July 1982):397–415; Alwyn R. Rouyer, "Recruitment and Political Change in Kenya," *The Journal of Developing Areas* 9 (July 1975):539–62; and C.P.W. Hornsby, "The Member of Parliament in Kenya 1969–1983," Ph.D. Dissertation, St. Anthony's College, 1985.

41 There is a large and fascinating literature on this phenomenon, which is known in Kenya as *harambee*. Much of it is ably reviewed in Frank Holmquist, "Class Structure, Peasant Participation, and Rural Self Help," in *Politics and Public Policy in Kenya and Tanzania*, ed. Joel D. Barkan (New York: Praeger, 1984).

42 Interviews, 14 and 18 July 1984. See also the draft consultancy report, "A Comparative Study of Management Practices in Selected Kenyan Cooperatives," 16 October 1981.

An obvious corollary of this analysis is that national political officials enhance the security of their political careers by securing offices in the local KANU party organizations that clear candidates for elected office. That they do so is documented in Hornsby, "The Member," and Rouyer, "Political Recruitment." Note also the following story about the defeat of a challenger:

> Marima (Narok North) described his clearance process as an ordeal, since his opponent Tipis was also both Narok Branch KANU Chairman and National Treasurer. "It is the Treasurer of the party who issues the complimentary forms to accept the deposit," Marima said, and as a result of stonewalling by Tipis over the deposit, "I was on the line for three days unsuccessfully" ... suggesting that Tipis was simply using his position to safeguard his own future (Hornsby, "The Member," pp. 85–86).

43 *Daily Nation*, 11 May and 6 June 1983.
44 Interviews, August 1985.
45 Republic of Kenya, "Report of the Inter-ministerial Committee," p. 5.
46 Meru Central Cooperative Union, "Minutes of the Special General Meeting Held in Kamunde Hall on 1 July 1980." Interviews, Meru District, 30 August 1984, 29 August 1984, and 4 September 1984.
47 Grosh, "Performance of Agricultural Public Enterprises."
48 Evidence of their inability to do so is contained in the work of Grosh and others, which suggests that while producer prices in Kenya may in the short

run be set against farmers, in most crops they lie below the border price equivalents for but short periods of time; they rapidly adjust to the level justified by market forces. *Ibid.* See especially Cathy L. Jabara, "Agricultural Pricing Policy in Kenya," Discussion Paper, Harvard Institute for International Development, August 1984. See also the preliminary results of the research on pricing conducted by the World Bank under the direction of Uma Lele; the discussion of the dynamics of maize pricing in the chapter that follows; and Jenifer Grace Sharpley, "Intersectoral Capital Flows and Economic Development," Ph.D. Dissertation, Northwestern University, 1976.

49 This analysis reminds us once again of the significance of incomplete capital markets. For had other economic actors owned shares in the processing firm, they then would have possessed little incentive to squeeze the quasi-rents from it. There is a complex and important relationship between the structure of capital markets and the pattern of political conflict, which clearly warrants deeper investigation.

50 See L. Msemakweli and W. M. Manji, "Price Elasticity of Cotton Supply in Kenya," *Eastern Africa Journal of Rural Development* 14, 1 and 2 (1981):163–75.

51 This analysis is, of course, consistent with the analysis of institutions in terms of transaction costs, which stresses that those institutions are more likely to form for which the costs of bargaining or enforcement are least.

52 This account poses a meaningful puzzle. I have assumed the actors are rational; but, in stage two, the large investors who organized the institutions in stage one lose out. One possibility is that they are not as rational as I assumed. Another is that they are myopic. A third is that they adjust in ways I have not documented. They may, for example, adjust by charging higher prices for their capital. Insofar as they do adjust in this way, Kenya would experience losses; the stage two predation of investment would harm the growth of Kenyan agriculture.

It is worth reiterating that the incompleteness of capital markets in the Third World may help to account for the predation of large-scale investments. If the predators owned shares in the prey, there would be fewer reasons to behave in ways that reduced the latter's profitability.

53 V. O. Key, *Southern Politics* (New York: Knopf, 1950).

54 For an argument which parallels our own, see Henry Bienen, *Kenya: The Politics of Participation and Control* (Princeton, N. J.: Princeton University Press 1974), and Jennifer Anne Widner, "Order and Economic Distribution: The Politics of State Formation in a Plural Society," Ph.D. Dissertation, Yale University, 1987.

The argument can be cast more formally. Say there are two candidates, A and B, who stand for different platforms. Say that the voters evaluate the two differently and that $U_A - U_B = K$.

Under a competitive party system, the expected value of A is determined by the subjective probability of A's party winning the election, say Q_A. If the party wins, then A's platform becomes government policy. The expected value of a vote for A is thus $EV_A = Q_A K$.

Under the single-party, multiple-candidate system, the expected value of A is the subjective probability of A winning the election (say P_A) discounted by the size of parliament. For A becomes but one Member of Parliament among many. For a parliament of size N, then: $EV_A = 1/NP_A K$.

One implication is that under the latter system, given the size of Parliament (i.e., that N is large), candidates will emphasize things other than "platforms" to win elections. Another is that unless $P_A > NQ_A$, the expected value of voting is less under the single-party, multiple-candidate system than under the competitive party system. A prediction of this model, then, is that with the move to a single-party system, voter turnout should decline. The decline of voter turnout in Kenya from 83.6 percent of those registered in 1969 to 45.5 percent in 1983 supports our analysis of the incentives prevailing under the two systems. See Hornsby, "The Member."

Chapter 4

1 See Republic of Kenya, *Statistical Abstract 1980* (Nairobi: Ministry of Finance, 1981); D. J. Casley and T. J. Merchant, "Smallholder Marketing in Kenya" (Nairobi: Central Bureau of Statistics, 1979); L. D. Smith, "Smallholder Marketing and Consumption Patterns" (Nairobi: UNDP/FAO, September 1978); Guenter Schmidt, "Maize and Beans in Kenya," Occasional Paper No.31, Institute for Development Studies, University of Nairobi, 1979; and M. M. Shah, "Food Demand Projections, Incorporating Urbanization and Income Distribution" (Nairobi: UNDP/FAO,1978).

2 For a discussion, see Jennifer Anne Widner's chapter on "Rift Valley Populism" in her "Order and Economic Distribution: the Politics of State Formation in a Plural Society," Ph.D. Dissertation, Yale University, 1987.

3 We have already discussed the destruction of the KPU. See as well materials pertaining to the assassination of J. M. Kariuki: *The Sunday Times* [London], 10, 17, and 24 August 1975, and Widner, "Order and Economic Distribution."

4 The best account of this period remains Joseph Karimi and Philip Ochieng, *The Kenyatta Succession* (Nairobi: Transafrica, 1980).

5 Studies of drought and food shortages in Kenya include David J. Campbell, "Coping with Drought in Kenya Masailand," Institute for Development Studies, University of Nairobi, Working Paper No. 337, June 1978, and "Responses to Drought in Masailand," Institute for Development Studies, University of Nairobi, Discussion Paper No. 267, August 1979; P. M. Mbithi and B. Wisner, "Drought and Famine in Kenya," *Journal of East African Research and Development* 3, 2 (1973):113–43, and "Drought in Eastern Kenya: Comparative Observations of Nutritional Status and Farmer Activity at 17 Sites," Institute for Development Studies, University of Nairobi, Discussion Paper No. 167, 1974; Ben Wisner, "Man-Made Famine in Eastern Kenya: The Interrelationship of Environment and Development," Institute of Development Studies, University of Sussex, Discussion Paper No. 96, July 1976; Peter N. Hopcraft and Priscella Reining, "Arid Lands – Economic, Social and Ecological Monitoring," Institute for Development Studies, University of Nairobi, Occasional Paper No. 22, 1972; James L. Newman, ed., *Drought, Famine and Population Movements in Africa* (Syracuse, N.Y.: Maxwell School of Citizenship and Public Affairs, Syracuse University, 1975); David Dalby and R. J. Harrison Church, *Drought in Africa* (London: School of Oriental and African Studies, University of London, 1974); and Thomas Herlehey, "Historical Dimensions of the Food Crisis in Africa: Surviving Famines along the Kenya Coast, 1880–1980," Boston University, African Studies Working Papers, New Series, No. 87, 1984. The dates are culled from these sources.

6 For a description of these techniques, see the materials collected and reported by Mbithi, noted above.

7 See, for example, the data contained in the World Bank, *Kenya: Population and Development*, vols. I and II (Washington, D.C.: The World Bank, 1960).

8 They have succeeded, however, in managing water supplies by other means, as through the construction of catchment basins, irrigation systems, and systems of flood control. For reasons that are becoming increasingly understood, populations in Africa have resisted adopting such techniques to a greater extent than has been the case elsewhere.

9 See references in note 5.

10 The Maize Board has gone by a variety of names, the most recent of which is the National Cereals and Produce Board.

11 In this and other tables all estimates have been corrected for first-order, autoregressive lags by using the Cochrane-Orcutt procedure. The short length of the data series prevented more sophisticated corrections of autoregressive errors.

The data are drawn from the period 1960–61 to 1983–84. Several variables lacked data for all of these years, thus reducing even further the length of the series.

Data on purchases, sales, imports, exports, stocks, and producer prices were collected from Kenya National Assembly, *Report of the Select Committee on the Maize Industry* (Nairobi: Government Printer, 1973); Republic of Kenya, *Grain Marketing Study: Interim Report*, vol. I (Githongo and Associates and Bookers International, July 1983); and Olof Hesselmark and Guenter Lorenzl, "Structure and Problems of the Maize Marketing System in Kenya," *Zeitschrift fur Auslandische Landwirtschaft* 15, 2 (1976):161–79. The data on consumer prices comes from Republic of Kenya, Central Bureau of Statistics, *Statistical Abstract*, various years. The data on rainfall pertains to the number of millimeters of rainfall April to August in Kitale, as published in Michael Schluter, *Constraints on Kenya's Food and Beverage Exports*, Research Report 44, International Food Policy Research Institute, April 1984. I was not able to correct the producer price series for inclusion or exclusion of the costs of grain bags or transport. The rainfall series is particularly short. So too is the consumer price series, because of the introduction of new consumption weights in the early 1970s.

12 The average rainfall in Kitale April through August is 650 mm; there are 11.1 bags of maize per metric ton.

13 See the data in the World Bank, *Kenya: Growth and Structural Change*, vol. I (Washington, D.C.: IBRD, 1984), p. 200.

14 This and much of the following discussion are drawn from Guenter Schmidt, "Maize and Beans in Kenya: The Interaction and Effectiveness of the Informal and Formal Marketing Systems," Institute for Development Studies, University of Nairobi, Occasional Paper No. 31, 1979; D. J. Casley and T. M. Merchant, "Smallholder Marketing in Kenya," Project Working Document, UNDP/FAO Project 1979: and Henry Kimurei Maritim, "Maize Marketing in Kenya: An Assessment of Interregional Commodity Flow Patterns," Ph.D. Dissertation, Technical University of Berlin, 1982.

15 Casley and Merchant, "Smallholder Marketing," p. 3.9.

16 Central Bureau of Statistics, *Integrated Rural Survey 1974–75* (Nairobi: Ministry of Finance and Planning, March 1977), p. 62.

17 Casley and Merchant, "Smallholder Marketing," p. 3.6.

18 J. D. Acland, *East African Crops* (London: Longman, 1971), p. 125. Note that in this discussion we do not take into account variation in the moisture needs of different maize varieties – something that a fuller discussion would require.

19 Ministry of Agriculture, *Farm Management Handbook of Kenya*, vol. II (Nairobi: Ministry of Agriculture, 1984), pp. 149ff.

20 Interview notes, Kenya, 1982–84.

21 KNFU, *Annual Report*, 1974–75, p. 9.

22 KNFU, *Annual Report*, 1975–76. p. 9.

23 *Ibid.*

24 *Daily Nation*, 10 January 1977.

25 *The Standard*, 30 March 1977.

26 *The Standard*, 4 April 1977.

27 *Daily Nation*, 26 March 1977.

28 *Daily Nation*, 2 September 1977.

29 *Ibid.*

30 *The Standard*, 15 March 1978.

31 *Sunday Nation*, 9 April 1978.

32 *The Standard*, 30 July 1978.

33 *The Standard*, 18 July 1978.

34 Internal government review of The Maize Crisis of 1979–80, typescript.

35 Internal Memorandum, NCPB, May 1979.

36 *Ibid.*

37 General Manager, NCPB, to P.S., Ministry of Agriculture, 6 November 1979.

38 *The Standard*, 2 July 1980.

39 Unga is a form of maize meal. From *Daily Nation*, 8 February 1980.

40 *The Standard*, 27 February 1980.

41 *Daily Nation*, 9 September 1980.

42 Republic of Kenya, *Report of the Maize Commission of Inquiry* (Nairobi: Government Printer, 1966); Kenya National Assembly, *Report of The Select Committee on the Maize Industry* (Nairobi: Government Printer, 1973).

43 Kenya, National Assembly, *Report*, p. 16.

44 This analysis can be construed as an attack upon the Board. It would be only if the Board made policy. But the Board is constrained by the policy choices of others: the Cabinet, which sets producer prices and chooses the timing of exports, and the Ministry of Finance, which sets the retail price of maize.

It should be noted that the Board contains its own best critics; skilled personnel in the Board helped to outline the perverse dynamics summarized in this chapter. And as demonstrated during the droughts of the 1980s, the Board is capable of moving vast amounts of grain and thereby preventing famine. These positive aspects of the Board must be stressed; but they do not alter the picture portrayed in this chapter.

I have made many efforts to develop and to test models of the arguments made in this chapter. Almost all fell afoul of limitations in the data. The absence of monthly data reduced the number of observations; it also prevented estimation of the impact of midyear changes in prices or weather conditions. Market price series are not available for the same span of years as official price series. And so forth.

It is notable, however, that one researcher performed a spectral analysis of Kenyan production data and detected a 2.8-year production cycle in maize. Such a cycle would be consistent with the productivity of the adjustments in producer incentives induced by the operation of the Board. See Tichaendepi R. Masaya, "Spectral Analysis of Coffee, Maize, and Wheat Production in Kenya," IDS Working Paper No. 218, May 1985.

It is also notable that in the year following the drought of 1983–84, the Board again faced major problems of glut. Imports to deal with the famine and increased production resulting from higher producer prices led to massive surpluses of grain. See, for example, *Daily Nation*, 4 October 1986 and 9 January 1987.

45 *The Standard*, 9 February 1980.

46 *Sunday Standard*, 30 November 1980.

47 *Daily Nation*, 12 March 1980.

48 Interview, 17 August 1983.

49 See, for example, *Daily Nation*, 1 July 1980.

50 Interviews, NCPB, 18 August 1983. Evidence in fact suggests that the Minister of Agriculture canceled one set of tenders that threatened to impose losses on the Board (see "Notes on the Background Leading to the Present Maize Crisis," p. 9). Certainly, however, the history of the grain trade in Kenya provided ample ground for giving credence to the rumors. As noted in the government's investigation of the 1979–80 maize crisis, "The [Board's] auditors gave a report indicating that much larger losses were made on exports [in 1975–76] than [were] justified by world market conditions. There was no invitation to tender and there was no instruction given on price. The only reference found was that certain cargoes should be given to specified persons in letters from the Ministry of Agriculture" (*Ibid.*, p. 1). For an account of similar conduct in earlier years, see Republic of Kenya, *Report of the Maize Commission of Inquiry* (Nairobi: Government Printer, 1966).

51 See, for example, the Parliamentary debates reported in *The Standard*, 19 March 1980.

52 See, for example, the speech of James Osogo, *The Standard*, 12 March 1980.

53 The "tribal" nature of these charges brought a rare Parliamentary statement from Njenga Karume, the organizer of GEMA. See *The Standard*, 19 March 1980.

Chapter 5

1 As historians of Western Europe stress, the police in early modern Europe, to preserve order, maintained control over urban food supplies; "to police" connoted "to feed." See especially Steven L. Kaplan, *Bread, Politics and Political Economy in the Reign of Louis XV*, 2 vols. (The Hague: Martin Nijhoff, 1976).

2 See the files of the food committees in Trans Nzoia, Kakamega, and Nandi. See, as well, the Minutes of the Food Review Committee Held in the D.O.I.'s Office, 1 July 1984, Kakamega. See also interviews 13, 14, 15 August 1984.

3 For an interesting discussion of the details of such a transfer, see Permanent Secretary, Ministry of Agriculture, to Treasury, Nairobi, "Strategic Transfer Files of the Maize – Costs," 31 August 1979, Strategic Transfer Files of the NCPB. Also, interview, United States Agricultural Attaché, 9 and 10 July 1984.

4 See, for example, the directive: Finance Manager NCPB to Area Manager, Kakamega, 13 May 1981. Files of the NCPB, Kakamega.

5 See, for example, the interchange between the Permanent Secretary, Administration in the Office of the President and the Managing Director, NCPB, which runs from February to April 1980, concerning the illicit transport of grain. These are included in the Strategic Transfer Files of the NCPB.

6 For statistical materials on the two districts, see Ministry of Finance and Planning, *District Development Plans, 1984–88* (Nairobi: Ministry of Finance and Planning, 1984). For historical discussions, see Gideon S. Were, *A History of the Abaluhya of Western Kenya, c. 1500–1930* (Nairobi: East African Publishing House, 1967); H. Fearn, *An African Economy* (Oxford: Oxford University Press, 1961); G. Wagner, *The Bantu of North Kavirondo*, ed. L. P. Mair (Oxford: Oxford University Press, 1956); Jan J. de Wolf, *Differentiation and Integration in Western Kenya: A Study of Religious Innovation and Social Change among the Bakusu* (The Hague: Mouton, 1977); and John Lonsdale, "Maize and Migrants, Church and Chief: The Nyanza Province c. 1890 to 1960 and the African Foundations of White Settlement in Kenya," unpublished manuscript, Cambridge University.

7 See the material in Republic of Kenya, Ministry of Finance and Planning, *Bungoma District Development Plan 1979–80* (Nairobi: Ministry of Finance and Planning, January 1980), pp. 70ff and the companion volume for Kakamega. Interviews, District and Provincial Cooperative Offices, Kakamega, 7–10 July 1983.

8 Interview, Cooperative Bank of Kenya, 23 August 1983.

9 AFC stands for the Agricultural Finance Company, the government's rural credit organization that funds small-scale farmers through the Cooperative Bank of Kenya and the cooperative movement. Provincial Cooperative Officer to District Cooperative Officer, 3rd June 1980, re: Produce Marketing and Storage Meeting Held... on 2 July 1980.

10 Area Manager, Western Province to District Commissioner, Kakamega, 2 September 1980. Files of the NCPB, Kakamega.

11 Operation Manager, NCPB, Report on Maize Purchases 15 October 1981. Files of the NCPB, Nairobi. See also the discussion in Chairman, Bungoma District Co-operative Union to Managing Director NCPB, 25 August 1981, in which he complains at length about the Board's campaign against his organization. Files of the Provincial Co-operative Officer, Kakamega.

12 See Gary Wasserman, *Politics of Decolonization* (Cambridge University Press, 1976).

13 Interesting materials are contained in John Carlsen, *Economic and Social Transformation in Rural Kenya* (Uppsala: Scandinavian Institute of African Studies, 1980), and Richard Henkel, *Central Places in Western Kenya* (Keidelberg: Selbstverlag des Geographischen Instituts der Universitat, 1979).

14 For histories of the Kenya Farmers' Association, see E. Huxley, *No Easy Way: A History of the Kenya Farmers' Association and Unga Ltd.* (Nairobi: The KFA: 1957); Michael Redley, "The Politics of a Predicament: The White Community in Kenya, 1918–1932," Ph.D. Dissertation, Cambridge University, October 1976; Paul Mosley, *The Settler Economies: Studies in the Economic History of Kenya and Southern Rhodesia, 1900–1963* (Cambridge University Press, 1983); and Masao Yoshida, *Agricultural Marketing in East Africa* (Tokyo: Institute of Developing Economies, 1984).

15 Interview, former Managing Director, NCPB, 23 August 1983.

16 Finance Director, KFA to Managing Director, NCPB, 26 July 1980. From files of the KFA, Nakuru.

17 Managing Director, NCPB to Finance Director, KFA, 17 September 1980.
18 Managing Director, KFA to Acting Managing Director, NCPB, 24 September 1980. From files of the KFA, Nakuru.
19 Interview, Financial Accountant, KFA, 16 August 1983.
20 See FAO/FIAC, *Fertilizer Marketing in Kenya* (Rome: FAO, 1983); Lewis Berger International, *Fertilizer Marketing and Distribution in Kenya: A Case Study* (Nairobi: Lewis Berger International, April 1983); and Paul Mosley, "The Politics of Economic Liberalization: USAID and the World Bank, 1980–84," University of Bath, Program in Political Economy, Working Paper 1284, 1985.
21 For brief introductions, see the works of A. T. Matson, such as "Reflections on the Growth of Political Consciousness in Nandi," in *Politics and Nationalism in Kenya*, ed. Bethwell A. Ogot (Nairobi: East African Publishing House, 1972). See also G. W. Huntingford, *The Nandi* (Nairobi: Government Printer, 1944).
22 See John C. de Wilde, ed., *Experiences with Agricultural Development in Tropical Africa*, 2 vols. (Baltimore, Md.: The Johns Hopkins University Press, 1967).
23 Files of the Area Manager, NCPB, Kakamega.
24 D. C. Baringo to Area Manager, Nakuru, Maize and Produce Board, 3 December 1979. From files of the KFA, Nakuru.
25 Area Manager, Maize and Produce Board, to D. C. Baringo, 24 December 1979. Files of the KFA, Nakuru.
26 Managing Director, NCPB to Deputy Cereals and Produce Executive, KFA, 6, 13, 20 October 1980. At the time, the KFA was still in charge of grain purchasing in the Rift Valley.
27 W. A. Kikwai to Area Manager, Nakuru, 9 December 1982. Files of the NCPB, Nakuru.
28 From the files of the District Agricultural Officer, Nandi.
29 Area Manager, Western Province to All Depot Managers, 31 August 1982. Files of the NCPB, Kakamega.
30 Operation Manager to Managing Director, 1982–83 Buying Centers, 15 June 1983. Files of NCPB, Nakuru.
31 *Ibid.*
32 *Ibid.*
33 The best account of this period is Joseph Karimi and Philip Ochieng, *The Kenyatta Succession* (Nairobi: Transafrica, 1980). There is every reason to believe that the writing of this book was promoted by Charles Njonjo.
34 See Circular Ref. CS/1530/vol. vi/44 of 29 January 1982. This requirement was relaxed in May 1984.
35 See, for example, interview notes of conversations in Meru, 27 August 1984, and the Appendix to this chapter.
36 See, for example, the literature reviewed in Robert H. Bates, "Lessons from History," *World Politics* 40 (1988):499–516.

Appendix 5A

1 Ministry of Agriculture and Livestock Development, Submission for Food Situation Report, Meru District, July 1980.
2 Minutes of Famine Relief Committee Meeting Held on 20 July 1984 at the

City Council Hall, Meru. Igembe's estimates were submitted later in the week, its District Officer failing to make the meeting. From Files of the NCPB, Meru.

3 It should be noted that a medical team in Embu was studying nutrition at the time of the drought. They compared their list of malnourished people with that compiled by the chiefs and found that not a single one of their cases failed to make the list of the chiefs.

4 Minutes of Famine Relief Committee held on 20 July 1984.

5 Interview, 27 August 1984.

6 Production Manager to Acting General Manager, Meru Central Farmers' Cooperative Ltd., 16 July 1984.

7 Production Manager to Acting General Manager, 17 August 1984.

8 The results of this investigation substantiate the analysis put forward in Amartya Sen, *Poverty and Famine: An Essay on Entitlement and Deprivation* (Oxford: Clarendon, 1981). See as well the analysis of famine in E. Anthony Wrigley and Roger Schofield, *The Population History of England, 1541–1871: A Reconstruction* (Cambridge, Mass.: Harvard University Press, 1981).

9 See also the reports of subsequent outbreaks of cholera in Meru in *The Daily Nation*, 17 December 1984.

Conclusion

1 See, for example, John Dunn, *West African States: Failure and Promise* (Cambridge University Press, 1978).

2 See Andrew Coulson, *Tanzania: A Political Economy* (Oxford: Clarendon Press, 1982).

3 See the review in Irving Leonard Markovitz, *Power and Class in Africa* (Englewood Cliffs, N. J.: Prentice-Hall, 1978). See also John Iliffe, *The Emergence of African Capitalism* (Minneapolis: University of Minnesota Press, 1983).

4 For a contrast, see the materials synthesized in Robert H. Bates, *Markets and States in Tropical Agriculture* (Berkeley and Los Angeles: University of California Press, 1981).

5 Suggestive are Moi's attacks on the coffee industry. Through the registrar of cooperatives, he purged the wealthy coffee cooperatives of influential residents of the Central Province. And his government has sponsored legislation that would restructure the coffee industry in ways that would render its governing institutions more subservient to the central government. See, for example, the report in F. O. *Licht's International Coffee Report* 2 (December 1987):123.

6 Hla Myint, "The Neo-classical Resurgence in Development Economics: Its Strengths and Limitations," in *Pioneers in Development: Second Series* (Washington, D.C.: The World Bank, 1987).

7 See the very useful review paper, Gary Miller and Terry Moe, "The Positive Theory of Hierarchies," Paper presented to the 1983 Meeting of the American Political Science Association, Chicago, 1983.

8 See Oliver E. Williamson, *The Economic Institutions of Capitalism* (New York: The Free Press, 1985).

9 See the path-breaking work of Yujiro Hayami and Vernon W. Ruttan, *Agricultural Development: An International Perspective* (Baltimore, Md: The

Johns Hopkins Press, 1985). See also such works as Richard Posner, *The Economic Analysis of Law* (Boston: Little, Brown, 1986), and *The Economic Structure of Tort Law* (Cambridge, Mass.: Harvard University Press, 1987).

10 See G. A. Cohen, *Karl Marx's Theory of History: A Defense* (Princeton, N. J.: Princeton University Press, 1978), and Jon Elster, *Making Sense of Marx* (Cambridge University Press, 1985).

11 See Williamson, *Economic Institutions*. See also David M. Krepps, "Corporate Culture and Economic Theory," Typescript, Graduate School of Business, Stanford University, August 1984.

A corollary of this analysis, it should be noted, is that private firms may prefer regulated industries. The forms of economic organization found in Kenya and other developing societies may be preferred by private investors, particularly when markets for risk do not exist to the degree that they do in economies that are more developed.

These considerations would help to explain why efforts at privatization in the developing world have been so unsuccessful thus far; there is little demand for it even in the private sector. This failure is something which the devotees of the miracle of the market would find difficult to explain.

12 It will be noted that my approach thus differs from that of Mancur Olson in *The Rise and Decline of Nations* (New Haven: Yale University Press, 1982). According to Olson, as societies age, interest groups form, leading to lower rates of economic growth. By my formulation, a society's growth path is in part determined by its initial conditions, including its institutional endowment. The incentives created by those institutions shape the kinds of interest groups that form. And not all interest groups will be concerned with redistribution; indeed, some will be concerned with preventing it and protecting the process of accumulation and investment. As a consequence, while I agree with Olson that a society's trajectory of change is shaped by its interest groups, I would argue that a rich variety of growth paths are possible.

Index

Abaluhya tribe: in Kenya African Democratic Union, 53, 55; Kikuyu land claims effects on, 52; land claims of, 52, 61–2; population statistics on (1969), 51t
Aberdare Forest, land elevation of, 54f
Aberdare Mountains, Mau Mau refuge in, 12
accumulation of property, 147, 148
Acland on maize rainfall requirements, 105
AFC (Agricultural Finance Company), 127
age grade councils, 14, 16
agrarian politics: conflicts in, 2; natural forces affecting, 2–3; neoclassical reasoning and, 3–5; theories of, 2
Agricultural Finance Company (AFC), 127
Agricultural Production and Settlement Board, 24
Akerloff model, 170n12
Alchian, Armen, on institutions, 9
alliances: Abaluhya with Nandi, 55; elite class of natives with British government, 39; in Kenya African Democratic Union, 53, 55; in Kenya African National Union, 53, 55–6; Luo with Kikuyu, 52, 55, in radical movement defeat, 148; settlers and Kenya African National Union, 47; in transition to independence, 52–3
altitude, see elevation of land
Amsden, Alice, on institutions and economic growth, 4
anemia in Meru famine, 145t, 146
Arrow, Kenneth, on transfer of capital, 73–4
Asian businessmen, maize crises and, 113
assassination: of Chief Waruhiu, 12; as Mau Mau specialty, 31–2

assets: distribution of, in family, 41–2; see also land; property rights; wealth
athomi (those who can read), 30–1

bananas, land elevation suitable for, 54
banks: cooperatives' deposits in, 137; credit program of, for maize purchases, 126; maize buying centers and, 117; resettlement program capital from, 74
Baringo District: maize buying centers in, 117t, 132–3; as Moi home region, 133
beans, production of, in Meru District, 141t
Beck, Neil, on Akerloff model, 170n12
beef, price increase in, 106
Berry, Sara, on agricultural diversification and social relationships, 43–4
Boran tribe, geographic distribution of, 50f
bourgeoisie class in tribes, 38, 39, 147–8
bread basket of Kenya, Trans Nzoia as, 128
bridewealth, 14–16
British colonial government: administration structure established by, 47–8; electoral system organized by, 48–9; political parties legalized by, 52; withdrawal of, 46–7, 48–9
British military: land purchases by demobilized officers, 23–4; provisions for, from Kenya farms, 21
Buane, squatter migration to, 19
Bungoma District: food crises in, 123–8; food supply committees in, 125–6, 127; maize buying centers in, 117t; maize production in, 125; population of, 125
Bungoma tribe, market output of (1969), 56t
bureaucracy: deficiencies of, in World War II, 21; educated natives in, 31; in

187

Index

Index

distribution/redistribution: versus accumulation, 147, 148; conflict about, 152–3; institution formation and, 151; Moi policies on, 149; *see also* income distribution; inequality/equality, economic districts: Baringo, 117t, 132–3; Bungoma, 117t, 123–8; Busia, 117t, 132; Elgeyo, 48, 117t; Fort Hall, 12; Kamba, 48; Kericho, 117t; Kikuyu, 48; Laikipia, 17, 117t; Loitokitok, 117t; Marakwet, 48, 117t; Murang'a, 56t, 65, 69; Naivasha, 26–7, 51; Nanyuki, 17; Narok, 117t; Nyandarua, 51, 117t; Nyeri, 12, 17, 94; Pokot, 117t; Thika, 17; *see also following districts*: Kakamega; Kiambu; Meru; Nakuru; Nandi; Trans Nzoia

district councils, labor contract policies of, 26–7

Dorobo tribe, geographic distribution of, 50f

droughts: definition of, 95; duration of, 95–6; famine and, institutional links in, 97–106; famine and, noninstitutional links in, 96–7; farm technology and, 96; geographic spread of, 96; grain prices and, 110–11; livestock problems in, 96; magnitude of, 95–6; versus Maize Board purchases, 98, 99t, 103; versus Maize Board sales, 99, 99t, 103; versus Maize Board stocks, 98, 98t, 103; major, dates of, 95; in Meru District, 139–46; pastoralism versus settled agriculture and, 97; pastoralists change of location in, 96; population factors and, 96–7; seriousness of, 96; vulnerability to, 96–7

Eastern Province: agricultural assets of, 63–4; crop switching in, 89; maize production in, 104t

ecology versus crop value, 43

economic efficiency: institutions effect on, 35; versus property rights, 7–9

economic interests: institutional preferences in, 53–6; partisan alliances and, 49–53

economic organizations, 150

economic status of Kikuyu, 14–17

economies of scale: in cattle raising, 173n22; in coffee industry, 79–80; in cotton industry, 78; in crop processing, 77, 79–82; in crop processing but not in production, 80; in dairy industry, 81, 83–4, 173n22; effects of, 78–82; in farm size, 79; in farm zoning, 58–9; market power from, 83–5; in production versus processing, 85; risks of, investments and, 89–90; social effects of, 80; in sugar industry, 78–80; in tea processing, 79–80, 81; transportation and, 80–1; in wheat production, 79

education: labor market and, 30–1; lack of, in influential residents, 87; land disputes and, 30–1; Mau Mau support correlated with, 65

efficiency, economic: institutions effect on, 35; versus property rights, 7–9

egalitarianism versus inequality in Kikuyu, 17

Egerton College, squatter migration near, 19

Egerton School of Agriculture, 24, 25

egg production on reserves, 28

Elburgon: dairy industry of, 26; Mau Mau activity in, 27

Eldoret: maize mills at, 105; maize moisture standard changes and, 108; maize transport from, 113

elections, 48–9; of African representatives to Legislature, 46; interest-group politics in, 90–1, 148; Kenya Farmers' Association in, 131; material interests shaped by, 50; procedure for, 86–7; restrictions in, 48–9; in single-party system, 86–7, 92

Elementaita, worker migration through, 19

elevation of land: as advantage in land claims, 49; versus crop suitability, 43, 53, 54f; farm plans and, 75; pyrethrum production and, 82–3; versus rainfall, 43, 53, 105, 105t, 141

Elgeyo District, 48; maize buying centers in, 117t

Elgeyo tribe: administrative district of, 48; geographic distribution of, 50f; Kikuyu land claims effects on, 52; market output of (1969), 56t

elite class (gentry), 38–9, 148; as British allies, 39; Kalenjin, land purchase by, 63; land ownership of, 173n22; political parties formed by, 47; property rights of, 151

Embu tribe: geographic distribution of, 50f; market output of, 56t, 64

Emerson, Rupert, on nationalism and rebellion, 35

employment, *see* labor

endowments: economic interests and, 53; of Kikuyu, 14–17, 55; land claims and, 49, 51; market power from, 82–3; political preferences determined by, 56; property rights and, 152; *see also* elevation of land; land; rainfall

Index

purchases by Maize Board, *see* Maize Board purchases

pyrethrum: growers of, as political constituency, 87; as high value crop, 49; land elevation suitable for, 53, 54f; processing of, 83; production of, 26, 82–3

quality control of products, 76–8

quasi-rents in agricultural processing, 86, 88–9

race: in dispute between large- and small-dairy farmers, 84–5; land rights and, 20–1, 36

radicalism: defeat of, 148; in Parliament, 63–70, 68f; *see also* militants

railway system: Coase Theorem and, 6–7; land development along, 18; maize transport by, 113, 124, 133

rainfall: as advantage in land claims, 49; versus crop suitability, 43; versus elevation, 43, 53, 105, 105t, 141; insufficient, *see* droughts; versus Maize Board purchases, 98, 99t, 103; versus Maize Board sales, 99, 99t, 103; versus Maize Board stocks, 98, 98t, 103; for maize production, 105–6; in Meru District, 140; in Nandi District, 132; raw milk supplies related to, 81; *see also* long rains; short rains

ranches, *see* farms

redistribution, *see* distribution/redistribution

Redley, Michael, on settler farming during World War II, 23

regional assemblies: dismantling of, 63; Rift Valley, 59, 60; Western, 60

Regional Boundaries Commission, 62

regionalism, international politics and, 67

religious beliefs of Kikuyu, 15

reserves: administrative structure of, 47–8; agricultural opportunities in, postwar, 28; class divisions in, 30–1; economic change in, postwar, 27–9; educated persons in, 30–1; establishment of, 19; family law changes in, 29–30; geographical location of, 12; labor market in, 30; land distribution in, 31; land right disputes in, postwar, 27–31; movement to White Highlands from, 19–20; population pressures in, 27–8, 58; property rights in, 151, 152

resettlement after independence: armed conflict in, 60; bureaucracy role in, 57–9; capital for, 58, 74–5; conflict resolution in, 60–3; economies of scale considerations in, 58; farm plans for, 75;

high-density schemes for, 59; institutions for, 59; Kenya African National Union radical faction on, 67–8; land claim procedure and, 49; land conflicts and, 46–7; land prices in, 58; large farm protection during, 129–30; low-density schemes for, 59; maize surpluses and, 125; regional influence in, 59; violence and, 57–63; zoning in, 58–9

Resident Labour Ordinance of 1937, 25–7

revolution: in rise of nationalism, 35; *see also* Mau Mau rebellion

Rift Valley Province: agricultural school in, 24; buying centers in, 116, 123; colonists settlement in, 18–19; escarpment of, pyrethrum growers of, 87; Kenya African Democratic Union domination of, 57; Kenya Farmers' Association influence in, 131; land claim conflicts in, 52, 61–2; large-scale dairy farmers in, 85; maize production in, 103, 104t; Mau Mau rebellion in, 11–12; Moi supporters from, 148–9; squatter unrest in, 27

Rift Valley Regional Assembly, 59, 60; Moi activities in, 93; Nandi leadership of, 132

risks: in capital markets, 73–6; in institution formation, 150; investments and, 89–90; of Kenya African Democratic Union defectors, 166–7n30; in maize production contract, 22–3; management of, kinship in, 41–4; of uneconomical crop processing, 78

Rongai: dairy industry of, 26; squatter migration to, 20

Rosberg, Carl, on nationalism and rebellion, 35

rust infestation of wheat, 79

Ruthenberg, Hans: on capital for resettlement program, 74; on Trans Nzoia zoning, 63

Ruttan, Vernon, on institutions, 4, 35

Sahlins, Marshall, predatory lineage system model of, 17, 38, 41–4

sales by Maize Board, *see* Maize Board, sales of

Samburu tribe, geographic distribution of, 50f

Samia tribe, geographic distribution of, 50f

scale economies, *see* economies of scale

semi-arid zones: drought vulnerability of, 97; land rights in, 163n63; Luo tribe claims in, 55; of Meru District, 140; population movement into, 97

Index

Serem, maize buying centers at, 133
settlement plan: after independence, *see* resettlement after independence; after World War II, 24
settlers: administrative problems caused by, 47; agricultural management by, in World War II, 21–3; collective action by, 21; conflict of, with squatters, 23–7, 159n22; cooperation of, during decolonization, 169n4; electoral system organization as protection for, 48–9; farm products sale by, 20; farms of, 19; KANU alliance with, 47; labor recruitment by, 19–20; land acquisition by, after World War II, 23–4; mixed farming by, in Trans Nzoia, 128–9; property rights of, 151; recruitment of, 18–19; reputation of, in agricultural control, 22–3; war contributions from, 21; *see also* colonialism; White Highlands
Shikuku, Martin, as Moi supporter, 137
Shipton, Parker MacDonald, on ecological zone versus attitudes toward sharing, 43
short rains: failure of, 95; season of, 106
Siaya tribe, market output of (1969), 56t
single-party system, *see* politics (single-party)
Siret Tea Estate, violence threats at, 60
sisal production, 26; economies of scale in, 58; land elevation suitable for, 54f; in Trans Nzoia, 128
Sluiter, Greet, on land ownership in reserves, 31, 32t, 33t
Smith, Adam, on government intervention in markets, 3
social stratification, kinship relationships and, 41–4
social values of tribes, 14–17
socialism, opposition to, 148
socialist nations, Odinga support from, 66
Solai, violence threats at, in resettlement, 60
Somali tribe, geographic distribution of, 50f
sorghum in Meru District, 140
Sorrenson, M. P. K.: on class conflict theory, 37; on Mau Mau as civil war, 33
South Imenti region, food needs of, 141
Soviet Union influence on domestic politics, 66
Spencer, John, on Mau Mau rebellion geography, 12
squatters in White Highlands: conflict of, with settlers, 159n22; dairy industry effects on, 25–7; farms of, 19–20, 23, 28; as labor pool, 19–21, 30; land ownership denied to, 19–20; limitations on,

23–6; movement from reserves, 19–20; numbers of, 157n4; opposition to, in postwar period, 23–5; railway construction and, 18–19; removal of, 39
staple theory, 156–7n25
Steves, on large-farm bias, 81
Stigler, George, on lobbying, 85
storage, *see* food storage; Maize Board stocks; maize storage
"Strategic Areas Purchasing Account," 130
stratification, social, kinship relationships and, 41–4
subsistence crisis, *see* food crises
Subukia, maize buying centers at, 133
Sudan rebellion, Kenyan support of, 67
sugar: growers of, as political constituency, 86–7; quality of, 76; ratio of producers to processors in, 85
Sugar Authority, 111
sugar processing: bankruptcy in, 86; economies of scale in, 77, 78–80
sugar production, 125; inappropriate equipment ordered for, 88; land elevation suitable for, 54f; on poor quality land, 64; specifications for, 77
Swahili-speaking tribes, geographic distribution of, 50f

Taita tribe, market output of (1969), 56t
Tanzania, economic policies of, 147
tea: as high value crop, 49; marketing of, in standardized lots, 77; monopoly of, 77; processing of, 79–80, 81; ratio of producers to processors in, 85; split payments for, 76–7; transportation costs of, 81
Tea Authority, 174n26
tea production, 125; in Central and Eastern provinces, 64; economies of scale in, 81; inherent difficulties in, 79; land elevation suitable for, 53, 54f; in Meru District, 140; prosperity created by, 84; on reserves, 28, 44; specifications for, 77
temperature: effects of, on crop choice, 49, 53; pyrethrum production and, 82–3
Teso tribe, geographic distribution of, 50f
Tharaka region, food needs of, 141
Thika District, land alienation in, 17
Thomas, Robert Paul, on institutional changes, 35
"thought experiment," 9–10
Throup, David: on Mau Mau rebellion deaths, 157n1; on radicalism, 167n40
ticks, cattle disease and, 25

Index

Tigania region, food needs of, 141
Timau region, food needs of, 141
timber production on reserves, 28
Tinderet, Kikuyu settlements in, 51
tobacco production in Meru District, 140
topography, complexity of, 9–10
Trans Nzoia District: Abaluhya land
claims in, 52; as bread basket of Kenya,
128; farm zoning in, 62–3; food crises
in, 123–5, 128–31; land claims in, during resettlement, 61–2; maize buying
centers in, 116, 117, 117t, 118; maize
production in, 103, 109, 128; maize
storage in, 128; mixed farming in,
128–9
transaction costs, Coase Theorem and,
7–8
transportation (dairy products), 24, 84
transportation (general): access to, as advantage in land claims, 49; Coase Theorem and, 6–7; economies of scale and,
80–1
transportation (maize): costs of, 134–5;
during food crises, 113; Maize Board
authority over, 98; political patronage
in, 134; to strategic areas, 124
Treasury, maize surplus problem of,
108
tribal councils: function of, 14, 16; land
disputes and, 29, 31
tribe(s): Abaluhya, 51t, 52, 53, 55, 61–2;
Boran, 50f; bourgeoisie class in, 38, 39,
147–8; Bungoma, 56t; Busia, 56t;
coastal, 51t; Dorobo, 50f; Elgeyo, 48,
50f, 52, 56t; Embu, 50f, 56t, 64; Galla,
50f; geographic distribution of, 49, 50f;
Kakamega, 56t; Kamba, 48, 50f, 51t; in
Kenya African Democratic Union, 52–3,
55; in Kenya African National Union,
52–3, 55; Kericho, 56t, 64; Kilifi, 56t;
Kipsigis, 50f, 52, 56t; Kirinyaga, 56t;
Kisii, 51t, 56t; Kitui, 56t; Koro-
koro, 50f; Kwale, 56t; land claims of,
institutional origins of, 47–9; Luhya,
50f; Machakos, 56t; Marakwet, 48,
50f, 56t; market output of, 56t; Masai,
50f, 53, 94; Meru, 50f, 56t, 64;
Njemps, 50f, 52; Nyandarua, 56t;
Nyanza, 56t; Nyeri, 56t, 64; Pokot,
50f, 64; reserves of, see reserves; Samburu, 50f; Samia, 50f; Siaya, 56t; social
values of, 14–17; Somali, 50f; Swahili-
speaking, 50f; Taita, 56t; Teso, 50f;
Tugen, 50f, 52, 60; Turkana, 50f; see
also ethnic groups; following tribes: Kalenjin speaking; Kikuyu; Luo; Nandi
truck transport of maize, 113, 124–5

tsetse fly in Luo lands, 55
Tugen tribe: geographic distribution of,
50f; Kikuyu land claims effects on, 52;
violence threats of, in resettlement,
60
Turkana tribe, geographic distribution of,
50f

Uasin Gishu District: maize buying centers
in, 117t; maize planting reduction in,
109
Uganda, economic policies of, 147
uncertainty: in capital market, 74; in creation of institutions, 150
unga, see maize
United States: assistance programs of,
130; influence of, on domestic politics,
66
urban markets, 43, 64; for agricultural
products from reserves, 28; for dairy
products, 24, 83–4; easy access to, land
claims and, 49; maize forms sold in,
104, 105t

Van Zwanenberg on cattle prices, 161n42
vegetable production: land elevation suitable for, 54f; on reserves, 28
vice presidency, of Kenya African National Union, 66
Victoria, Lake (Nyanza Victoria), rain
shadow of, 105
violence: in Mau Mau rebellion, 11–12,
31–2; postindependence land settlement
and, 57–63; of settlers versus natives,
theories of, 36–7

wages, famine effects on, 144, 146
Wambaa, Rebman, on labor recruitment
by settlers, 19–20
Waruhiu, Senior Chief, assassination of,
12
water supply management, 179n8
wattle production: land elevation suitable
for, 54f; in reserves, 30
wealth: as advantage in land claims, 49,
51; economic interests and, 53
Western Province: buying centers in, 123;
crop switching in, 89; maize consumption in, 104; maize production in, 104t;
maize surplus marketing in, 107–8; patronage in, 134; Trans Nzoia District
land claims conflict and, 61–2; see also
specific districts
Western Regional Assembly, 60
wheat: prices of, 106, 110; production of,
30, 79, 128, 141t; rust infestation of,
79

Index

White Highlands (preindependence designation): African property rights taken in, 19; ethnic groups in, 49, 50f; farm organization in, 20; livestock grazing in, 20; movement to, from reserves, 35; native movement into, 19–20; race relations in, 36; squatters in, 18–27, 39; tribal land claims in, 53, 55–6; see also Highlands (postindependence designation)

Williamson, Oliver, on institutions in economic development, 9

women in Kikuyu society, 14–16

wood products, 28, 30; in Meru District, 140, 143

World Bank: maize buying center and, 117; resettlement program capital from, 74

world systems theory, 5

World War II: economic changes caused by, 23–5; farming practices changed by, 23–7; institutional development in, 21–3; Kenya Farmers' Association in, 129; lack of agricultural data during, 160n28; land purchases after, by demobilized officers, 23–4

Yoruba people, agricultural diversification of, 43–4

Z-plots in Trans Nzoia District, 62–3

Zaire rebellion, Kenyan support of, 67

zoning policy: African property rights taken in, 19; for resettlement of Trans Nzoia farms, 62–3